Managing High Technology and Innovation

Nino S. Levy

Prentice Hall, Upper Saddle River, New Jersey 07458

Senior Editor: David Shafer
Assistant Editor: Lisamarie Brassini
Editor-in-Chief: Natalie Anderson
Editorial Assistant: Christopher Stogdill
Marketing Manager: Tami Wederbrand
Production Editor: Judith Leale
Managing Editor: Dee Josephson
Manufacturing Buyer: Diane Peirano
Manufacturing Supervisor: Arnold Vila
Manufacturing Manager: Vincent Scelta
Cover Design: Bruce Kenselaar

Library of Congress Cataloging-in-Publication Data
Levy, Nino S.
    Managing high technology and innovation / Nino S. Levy.
        p.   cm.
    Includes bibliographical references and index.
    ISBN 0-02-370462-4
    1. High technology industries—Management.   2. Technological innovations.   I. Title.
    HD62.37.L48   1998
    620'.0068—dc21   97-37465
                                                                                        CIP

Prentice-Hall International (UK) Limited,London
Prentice-Hall of Australia Pty. Limited, Sydney
Prentice-Hall Canada Inc., Toronto
Prentice-Hall Hispanoamericana, S.A., Mexico
Prentice-Hall of India Private Limited, New Delhi
Prentice-Hall of Japan, Inc., Tokyo
Pearson Education Asia Pte. Ltd., Singapore
Editora Prentice-Hall do Brasil, Ltda., Rio de Janeiro

Printed in the United States of America

10 9 8 7 6 5 4

Brief Contents

Contents

v

Preface

As the millennium approaches, we are living one of the most exciting adventures in the history of humankind: the technology revolution No other socioeconomic development has changed so much for so many and in so short a time as the outburst of technology at the end of the twentieth century The impact of this revolution is truly astounding in all aspects of our life health, education, administration, communication, transportation, business, recreation, and others

The main revolutionary forces are the constantly increasing large and small innovative companies, some of which are famous today but were totally unknown just a decade ago These, together with some older and well-established pioneers of high technology, are contributing more to the economy of their respective countries and to the global economy than any other industrial sector Accordingly, no other industrial sector rewards success more generously than the high-technology sector

The fast pace of growth in the technology sector has created a strong demand for competent and well-educated managers specifically trained to lead in the complex and challenging technology-based business world Courses in management of technology are being introduced in a growing number of universities and business schools Some leading institutions have created departments specifically dedicated to this relatively new discipline

A most important characteristic of the technology revolution is its global facet Success in technology depends today, more than ever, on the broad international perspective of its managers Innovation, talent, and entrepreneurship know no boundaries Highly respected European universities become centers of research for leading U S companies Mergers, acquisitions, and joint ventures between and among U S , European, Japanese, and Chinese firms strengthen through synergy the competitive muscle of their partners Even small countries, like Israel or Singapore, play an important role in boosting innovation in some niches like information technology At the beginning of the twenty-first century, only well-prepared managers, who bother to learn and understand multinational cultural particularities, will be able to lead their firms successfully into the "global village "

This book differs from and complements other texts in the same field It focuses on the major issues a manager in a high-technology enterprise is most likely to face in real life Although the theory presented reflects some of the latest thinking in specific areas, it also reflects practical experience and lessons learned from applying the theory in the real business environment of today's high-technology firm The author, a teacher of management of technology at the Graduate School of Business Aministration, Tel-Aviv University, has held various executive positions in the high-technology industry Methods, approaches, and techniques recommended throughout this book have been tested and shown to bring noteworthy results

Another difference between this book and other texts is the global rather than national perspective on the subjects treated As the leading powerhouse of technology, the United States provides the largest share of examples and cases presented However, where appropriate, examples of other experiences are given Special attention is devoted to the global high-technology market and to factors affecting success in international joint ventures The author's widespread international contacts have allowed him to discuss various relevant issues with some of the most competent professionals in the field and bring their points of view on important subjects As an example, the subject of mergers and acquisitions in the high-technology industry as presented here reflects the strategy and experience of Bernard Schwartz, until recently CEO of Loral and a world-recognized authority in high-technology acquisitions Interviews and conversations with leading executives of U S , European, Israeli, and Asian high-technology companies helped the author focus on those theories that have been found to be effective in the field

I wish to express my gratitude to the many wonderful people who contributed to the making of this book In the early stages, the following people read the manuscript and provided useful comments and advice Professor B Ronen, University of Tel Aviv, A Loewenstein, of Dimotech, Professor I Bar-David, Technion, Israel Institute of Technology, and Professor G Salvendy, Purdue University, West Lafayette Bernard Schwartz, already mentioned above, provided the material for an entire chapter David Shafer, my editor at Prentice Hall, presented me with worthy comments together with some constructive criticism from his reviewers that helped improve the text in many aspects His assistant, Christopher Stogdill did an efficient job in preparing the production package I was lucky to have Judith Leale as my production editor She assisted me in all possible ways to keep the production schedule, removing obstacles gracefully and professionally I am much indebted to two special people without whose help this book would not be seeing daylight First, my special thanks goes to my dear friend Col (res.) Frank Philips of the U S Marines, who translated many awkward expressions from the first manuscript into genuine American English Finally, I owe much to my wife for her constant support, for typing the manuscript, for trying to improve my grammar, but above all, for the many weekends sacrificed during the long journey preceding the publication of this book

Nino S. Levy

About the Author

Dr Nino S Levy is an internationally recognized expert in the management of high-technology enterprises He teaches courses in management of technology (MOT) at the Leon Recanati Graduate School of Business Administration, Tel Aviv University His academic work draws from his vast practical experience as a researcher, project leader, and manager in the high-technology industrial sector

Dr Levy has held a variety of executive positions during his professional career While managing director of ELTA, Electronics Industries, a leading Israeli high-technology company, he introduced methods for reducing and controlling innovation risks, for smoothing the transfer from research and development to production, and for shortening times to market Under his leadership, annual sales grew from $70 million to $200 million in eight years During that same time, net profits grew from $4 million to an average of $17 million Compared with the performance statistics of U.S. companies in the same field, ELTA ranked high in the top 10 percent Coming from a country with limited internal markets, Dr Levy has always looked at the world as a global opportunity He lived in Europe for six years while president of EAT, European Advanced Technologies, and helped promote the company's business from an annual average of $50 million to $300 million.

Dr Levy has been honored with a number of prestigious awards, including the Israeli Defense Award, for original research contribution to the Israeli defense, the Kaplan Prize, and the National Export Award He holds a Ph D from the University of Southern California, Los Angeles, and is a member of Sigma-Xi and Alpha Pi Mu

CHAPTER

Introduction

1

TOWARD THE HIGH-TECHNOLOGY CENTURY

At the eve of the twenty-first century, the world is marching ever faster toward what may be called the *high-technology revolution* This revolution promises to bring radical changes in most of our business activities Its strong impact will be much more dramatic than that of the industrial revolution at the turn of the twentieth century High technology is about to enter most aspects of our daily life, rapidly changing the way we learn, educate, and entertain ourselves The way we work, communicate, and do business is going to shift rapidly in the direction indicated by already existing technologies Home computing, massive use of the Internet, the application of fiber optics, satellite, cellular, and other means for multimedia communications, and the progress made in deciphering DNA are just a few of the leading indicators for the future impact of the high-technology revolution

The beat with which the industrial revolution marched through Europe, the United States, Japan, and a few other countries was modest by comparison Many countries in Asia and South America and even parts of Europe were left out of the process of industrialization In contrast, the pace of change now is breathtaking, global, and overwhelming It imposes on people, companies, and society the need to adapt and move forward in much shorter time spans than were required a few decades ago The pressure to reengineer corporations is by no means unique to high technology, but in no other industry is it so pronounced The dynamic change of technology, the ever decreasing product life cycles, global competition, and many other factors demand a truly professional approach toward managing for success in this environment

Managing high technology is today an extremely challenging and lucrative profession No other branch of industry rewards success more generously than does this field Innovative people like Bill Gates and companies like Intel, to mention just two famous examples, have made their fortunes in less than a decade Before 1995, the name Netscape was hardly known in the business community In August 1995,

1

Netscape, which makes software for browsing the Internet, made its initial public offering, with shares at $28 By January 1996, the price of shares had quadrupled. The company was then valued by the market in excess of $1 billion, making its entrepreneurs and managers instant multimillionaires Note that General Electric needed about half a century to cross the billion dollar bar

These cases are not unique Many other high-technology companies can tell similar success stories Naturally, some of these are on a more modest scale, but all share many characteristics One such example is Xylan, which makes a local area network (LAN) switch that greatly increases the amount of data available to each computer connected in the network Unlike Netscape, Xylan is not a software but a hardware company It was founded in 1994 to address a market that grew from $330 million in 1994 to $1.2 billion in 1995 The company sold $14 million worth of switches in 1995 and expected to more than double this figure in 1996 With such a strong market demand, the company is almost assured to perform well Whether it develops as a world player will depend on its ability to manage its fast growth

Along with the importance and the undeniable contribution of many successful start-up companies, the high-technology revolution is much the making of a great number of mature and well established high-technology companies Motorola, Hewlett-Packard, Texas Instruments, and many others in the United States, GEC-Marconi, Phillips, Alcatel, and similar firms in Europe, and companies in Japan and Korea are all bringing us closer to the *high-technology century*

DOING BUSINESS IN THE GLOBAL VILLAGE

One of the major trends impacting the way companies do business as they near the twenty-first century is the process of market globalization A number of powerful factors are driving this trend· a series of international agreements on free trade, the liberalization of the economies in countries formerly surrounded by physical or ideological walls, and the outburst of technology Technology has helped to shrink the cost of international transport and communications It allows remotely located people to work jointly on complex problems sharing a common database Finally, it is helping to bring together people, companies, and capital and to create a single market for goods and commercial services That is what is known as *"the global village"*

The globalization of the economy creates ample opportunities and challenges as well as threats to companies, especially to high-technology firms, where often the trade involves intellectual property Many high-technology companies can no longer insulate themselves within protected national borders On the other hand, globalization makes it possible for once obscure firms, such as Creative Labs from the small country of Singapore, to become a major player in the multimedia market worldwide

Today, leading high-technology industries are looking for talent, innovation, and entrepreneurship all around the world Intel, Motorola, IBM, and others are conducting research and development (R&D) in Israel, a small country that has become a mini-powerhouse for innovation. Companies like Hewlett-Packard have created joint ventures and are tapping the availability of competent software programmers as far away as India. In an effort to lure the very best computer scientists, Microsoft went to Cambridge University in the United Kingdom, and opened a world class research center there in 1997.

Most high-technology managers today share the view that high technology is becoming a global business This trend strongly emphasizes the need for competent management with a good global view and international perspective Understanding how high-technology companies operate in various countries and to know their strengths and weaknesses has become imperative for a firm to stay competitive and successful in the global village

THE NEED FOR THIS BOOK

In the last decades of this century, dramatic changes have revolutionized the process of manufacturing products as well as marketing them worldwide The economic life cycle of products has been constantly decreasing More and more items are sold on the basis of innovation rather than on pure price competition Moreover, new, more sophisticated products are often cheaper than their predecessors and offer the buyer better performance and a better price

These phenomena are particularly evident in the high-technology industry (See definitions in the last section of this chapter) Without referring to a formal definition of high technology, we can generally concur that products with embedded electronic control, logic, or intelligence fall within this category Also, products made of new materials with substantially improved characteristics resulting from new technologies are considered high-technology products

Examples of such products are most of the electronic equipment—computers, communications, radar, and medical electronics devices, biotechnological products, software products, and a multitude of by-products from space and satellite technologies. The aerospace industry in general, the emerging genetic engineering industry, and many more traditional industries, such as the chemical, pharmaceutical, automobile, and machine manufacturing industries, are becoming high-technology industries in order to survive and remain competitive New, better equipment often replaces existing equipment, long before the end of its originally projected operational life Updating is driven by technological obsolescence rather than age attrition The most striking example of this is the way companies and individuals replace still functioning computers with new, much more powerful and more productive versions

The common denominator for all high-technology production is the considerable amount of research and development (R&D) invested in the inception phases of the product Innovative concepts and innovative technologies and materials all play an important role in establishing a company's competitive edge against similar products in the marketplace

The drive for better products and shorter development cycles, however, is imposing a different approach toward efficient and effective management for high-technology companies. Innovation by definition implies risk Breaking new ground, introducing new concepts and technologies, often results in costly surprises, delays, and sometimes economic disaster These uncertainties, together with a number of other factors, make the management of high technology particularly difficult and demanding Therefore, a manager must have a thorough understanding of the differences between classical management techniques and those necessary in high technology to manage risk and motivate inventors effectively

Throughout this book, we focus on the specific factors that make the management of high technology and innovation a somewhat different and often more challenging task than managing other firms Naturally, there is a certain degree of overlap between general management approaches and high-technology management, and the methods and techniques proposed in this text may also be applicable in general Although a number of books and articles already treat some of the relevant topics, others need specific attention This book presents a coherent and comprehensive view of the entire industrial process, from product inception through the research and development cycles, industrialization, and marketing and product support All approaches described in this text have been successfully tested and applied in a real-life, high-technology business environment

The challenges and pitfalls of managing high-technology industries and institutions at all levels—top, middle, and floor management—are such that the authors of a recent book, *Management of R&D Organizations* (Jain and Triandis, 1990), chose to subtitle it "Managing the Unmanageable " There are numerous indicators that this field lacks a comprehensive body of managerial knowledge Even though more and more universities are offering courses on these and related subjects, most of the managerial positions in the high-technology industry are still taken by insiders These people have normally grown from the grass roots of the organization They have learned from practical experience how to lead successfully the people for whom they are responsible They have developed the feeling and practical understanding of what made the organization successful, but they often lack the formal education that could make them much better team players and much more effective managers

This characteristic holds true up to the very top of the pyramid Cases in which successful chief executive officers (CEO) in high-technology companies come from outside the organization are extremely rare Most CEOs in small, medium, and large companies come from an engineering background One typical example is the president of Intel, Andrew Grove, who leads one of the world's most successful companies In the introduction to his book, Grove (1983) describes himself as "an engineer by training and a manager of a high-technology company by profession" (p xii).

Some high-technology managers have complemented their engineering education with courses in management and economics, but such courses specifically for management of high-tech and innovation have only recently begun to appear in leading universities No wonder some time has to pass before the impact of the process is sufficiently felt in the industry

The need for trained personnel at all managerial levels in the specific field of high technology and innovation has become urgent In the last decade, no industrial sector has grown faster than the high-technology sector This is true in the United States, Europe, Japan, and some of the fast developing countries A recent European study made by the German Institute I S I in Karlsruhe reported that two-thirds of new jobs created in Germany between 1984 and 1991 were in the high-technology sector. In 1991, the trade balance of Germany showed a surplus of 23 billion deutsche marks (DM), whereas the trade balance of the high-technology sector alone showed a surplus of DM 87 billion Clearly, without the high-technology contribution, the overall trade balance of Germany would have been negative

Growing needs for competent professional management in the high-technology industrial sector and the acknowledged complexity of managing these companies require enhanced skills of high-technology managers Fortunately, from a learning perspective, we can take advantage today of the recent body of experience accumulated by firms that have successfully adapted their management approach to the challenge and compare them to those that failed to do so This practical experience, together with a growing number of publications that examine the relevant topics from different points of view, allows us in the present to compare and contrast management approaches to determine what really works in this environment It is now possible to focus on those factors that prepare a company and an organization more adequately to handle rapid technological changes and to stay competitive in the emerging business environment

FOR WHOM IS THIS BOOK INTENDED?

This book is an effort to fulfill the need for a comprehensive text, specifically adapted for students with interest in technology and management, or for graduate students in industrial engineering and industrial management The text complements classical courses in industrial management and helps to prepare the student who seeks to become a competent manager in a high-technology company.

For master of business administration (MBA) students interested in a career in the rapidly growing high-technology business sector, this book offers much that is not usually covered by the classic MBA curriculum From it, the students will get a good general view of the entire high-technology product life cycle. They will find material illuminating such important business aspects as marketing high-technology products in global markets, organizing strong product support, and understanding high-technology particularities in organizational behavior and personnel management

Finally, the book is intended for the large community of engineers and scientists currently engaged in the high-technology industry and moving from technical and research and development assignments into positions of managerial, marketing, or business responsibility Practitioners such as project managers, group leaders, department heads and chief executive officers will probably find situations described in this book that are familiar or similar to the ones they have experienced in their own companies The text will give them an opportunity to examine and understand their specific problems objectively in the light of the theory and experience it describes.

One particular feature of this book is that the author has applied in real life the theory it describes During a long period and in a large variety of practical cases, the author had the opportunity to observe what happens when the principles and approaches described in this book are actually applied Therefore, this material represents a synthesis of theory and practical experience that has been successfully tested in a true, high-technology business environment

HOW TO USE THIS BOOK

The essence of business in the high-technology industry sector consists of designing, developing, manufacturing, marketing, and supporting innovative products The chapters of the book follow the sequence a high-technology product goes through during its life cycle—that is, innovation, research and development, manufacturing, marketing, sales, and after-sales product support and service This order is different from the organization of most other management of technology texts, which usually devote chapters to concepts and definitions, such as innovation, entrepreneurship, new ventures and products, corporate research, technology forecasting, and so on In this text, we focus on giving the student or the practicing manager a comprehensive view of the modern high-technology enterprise The emphasis is on critical management decisions, as seen by real-life managers in the high-technology industry Concepts and definitions are introduced as means to support and clarify the major business issues but not as a goal in themselves The reader who wants to learn more about such concepts and definitions is referred, at the end of each chapter, to some of the best literature available covering these issues in depth

Chapters 3 to 10 follow the sequence as described This organization allows a reader who faces a marketing problem to refer quickly to chapter 7, whereas another reader interested only in ideas to shorten research and development cycles can quickly narrow the search to chapter 4 Chapters 2 and 11 are more general Chapter 2 examines the most important factors for the success of a high-technology company, whereas chapter 11 focuses on some of the most frequent causes for the decline and failure of companies that were successful at one time All chapters focus on principles and procedures important to the development of management skills in the high-technology environment Finally, in chapter 12, a real-life high-technology company case is presented for analysis and discussion Following is a short description of the material treated in each of the chapters

Chapter 2 describes and analyzes the factors most critical for successful management of high-technology companies Some factors that have received little attention in the literature so far are treated in detail First, the impact of market uncertainties as well as technology and supply uncertainties are examined Then, the special character of highly qualified personnel and the typical behavior of very creative people are analyzed Problems associated with growing from a start-up organization to a multiproduct, diversified company are discussed next Finally, appropriate management approaches are proposed for handling professionally the complexity of activities in a high-technology company

Chapter 3 is devoted to methods for creating a favorable environment for inventors and innovators First, we explain the paradox of the need to stimulate innovation in companies in which innovation is the major business. Factors suppressing creativity are exposed and examined Then, we analyze effective means to encourage and motivate innovation in company personnel. Finally, a number of practical, real-life methods for creating a culture of innovation and entrepreneurship in a high-technology company are described in some detail The material covered in this chapter should be of particular interest to managers of fast-growing, high-technology start-up companies to help them avoid stagnation and possible decline

In chapter 4, methods for minimizing the research and development (R&D) cycle are described and analyzed Factors influencing the duration of the R&D cycle are examined, and methods for identifying and reducing the negative effect of bottlenecks in R&D organizations are introduced Formal procedures for early identification of risk areas are outlined and effective risk-reduction techniques are proposed Application of these methods and techniques can help a company lead the market by introducing new innovative products without accepting levels of uncertainty and financial risk that are too high The last part of the chapter shows that the inventory policies that work well for mass-production companies are inadequate for the R&D environment An analytical model leading to a rational purchasing policy for such organizations is presented

Chapter 5 discusses another critical factor for success in high technology the smooth transition of an innovative product from the laboratory (R&D phase) to the factory (manufacturing phase) Some common pitfalls are identified and methods to avoid them are suggested The notion of *concurrent engineering*, which has been gaining acceptance both in Europe and the United States in recent years, is shown to hold significant potential for the high-technology industry Task force teams, continuous innovation, and total quality management (TQM), which contributed much to the success of the Japanese industry in the 1980s, are now changing the management style in a growing number of Western companies. Modern production organization techniques, such as JIT (just in time) and OPT (optimized production technology), which have proven their effectiveness in large-scale manufacturing organizations, are shown to be applicable as well in high-technology organizations, but only after being adapted to the significantly different industrial environment In general, the readers are encouraged to avoid blind emulation of Japanese success formulations or any other "miracle" procedures without first adapting them to their specific company environment

Chapter 6 deals with the complex, multiproduct high-technology organization Because resources are always limited, the competition between the different products at a given work station for obtaining service often results in waiting lines Those waiting lines significantly lengthen the research and development and manufacturing cycles This queuing phenomenon is the major cause of frequent delays and cost overruns typical in many multiproduct high-technology companies To help resolve this important problem, still poorly understood by many, the notion of "queuing penalty" is introduced Methods for reducing this penalty to an acceptable minimum are proposed and analyzed

Chapters 7 and 8 are devoted to different aspects of marketing high technology Chapter 7 deals with one of the most critical success factors: winning the war of competition in the high-technology markets As in any war, one must have a winning strategy to prevail A methodology for establishing such a company strategy is described Having reliable and timely intelligence is as important for a high-technology company as for any army. Methods for collecting perfectly legal industrial and market intelligence are outlined. With the right strategy and with good intelligence, the company must develop appropriate tactics adapted to any specific competitive situation Such tactics require a clear definition of objectives, concentration of effort and resources, good timing, and total dedication Situations typical in the competition for large, high-technology projects are discussed and contrasted with those where the battle is fought for market share

Chapter 8 is devoted to methods and approaches that can prepare a high-technology company to operate successfully in the global village The important question of how best to organize for a long-term international presence is analyzed Questions such as how to establish an effective network of representatives and local agents are treated, and some of the characteristics of agents are discussed The approach necessary to succeed in a foreign industrialized country is compared with the strategy appropriate for less-developed nations Finally, at the end of the chapter, the latest thinking about "competing on value" and looking at the customer as an asset are brought together

Mergers and acquisitions have played and can play an important role in the development and the growth of a high-technology company. More than any other business, high technology generates opportunities for growth through acquisitions because of the large amount of start-ups created in this sector Mergers and acquisitions are not unique to this sector, but the approaches appropriate for successful acquisitions in high technology differ significantly from those most often applied in general business. Chapter 9 is devoted to the real-world experience of one of the most successful masters of high-technology acquisitions: Bernard Schwartz, a founder and, until recently, chairman of Loral Under his leadership, Loral grew from a small defense electronics company into a $10 billion business Most of this growth was achieved through successful acquisitions in only five years, between 1990 and 1995. One can hardly find a more competent tutor than Schwartz for learning the art of growing in high technology by acquisitions Hence, most of this chapter is his direct contribution in the form of conversations, an interview, and revisions by him of the draft text

In chapter 10, the product support factor is discussed Customers of any product should feel confident about the availability of after-sale support, but with the new, innovative products, the importance attached to this factor is very high, especially when customers need help to obtain maximum results with the new product

Often, in the business of high technology, new start-up companies achieve a striking success in a short time, only to decline and fade away a few years later To perpetuate success, companies must reorganize and adapt their management structure to the challenges imposed by their initial success This often painful but necessary reengineering process is described in chapter 11 This chapter summarizes and adds some final remarks on the business of beating the competition more often than not, and points out how to recover when a competitor's product proves more successful than your own in the marketplace To put in a nutshell the most important lessons learned during more than 25 years of applied high-technology management, the author concludes the chapter with "The Ten Commandments," which come strongly recommended to every high-technology manager wishing to achieve better than average results

Finally, chapter 12 introduces a real case of a leading U.S computer firm that found itself at the crossroads during the first half of 1996 This becomes a case study for analysis and for comparing the approaches taken by the management of the company with the methods proposed in this book

If a student, the reader will probably be instructed in how to read this book The best way is to read the text in its entirety, as there is a natural relation between the subjects discussed in the different chapters However, it is written so that the reader can get a good insight on the topic treated in each chapter without having to read the previous or the following one

For the busy practitioner whose time is totally absorbed by the daily challenges of managing a high-technology organization, we strongly recommend that you read at least chapters 2 and 11 in addition to the specific chapter of interest We hope that managers who have read the book will return to specific topics of interest when they need to solve a concrete problem and thus benefit from the experience of others who have treated similar problems with success

---

USEFUL DEFINITIONS

Technology

Technology can be defined as the assembly of hardware and software means and tools used by human beings to achieve socioeconomic goals From dawn of civilization, man has used technology. The plow, the wheel, and the chariot are just a few examples of first-generation technologies Use of technology is one important discriminator between mankind and other animals With the advent of ever newer technologies, the gap between these two categories has constantly grown over the centuries In the 1994 edition of the *ZCI Publishing Concise Encyclopedia* (1st ed , S V. "Technology History of Technology" Text 33, p. 1) one can read

> Technology refers to the ways in which people use discoveries to satisfy needs and desires and to alter the environment to improve their lives From the very beginning of human life on earth, people have had to work to obtain food, clothing, and shelter Throughout human history, men and women have invented tools, machines, materials, and techniques to make their work easier They also discovered power sources such as water power and electricity to increase their work rate Technology, therefore, involves the use of tools, machines, techniques, and sources of power to make work easier and more productive It is the human activity that changes the material world to satisfy human needs As such, technology comprises the vast body of knowledge and devices by which humans have progressively mastered their natural environment over the centuries

Until less than two centuries ago there was an almost complete separation between science and technology Scientists were usually interested only in advancing the state of knowledge Technology, on the other hand, was carried on primarily by craftspeople Today science and technology are closely related Referring to this relatively new phenomenon, the *ZCI Publishing Concise Encyclopedia* (1st ed , S V "Technology: History of Technology" Text 33, p 3) says:

> Many modern technologies such as nuclear power and space flight depend on science and the applications of scientific knowledge and principles Each advance in pure science creates new opportunities for the development of new designs and ways of making things to be used in

daily life, and in turn, technology provides science with new and more accurate instruments for its investigations and research. .It was not until the 19th century that technology truly was based on science and inventors began to build on the work of scientists For example, Thomas Edison built on the early experiments of Faraday and Henry in his invention of the first practical system of electrical lighting So too, Edison carried on his investigations until he found the carbon filament for the electric light bulb in a research laboratory he started in Menlo Park, New Jersey This was the first true modern technological research

It is precisely this union of science and technology that gave birth to a relatively new concept the notion of *high technology* or high tech

High Technology

High technology, also known by its popular abbreviation high tech, refers to a branch of technology based on exploitation of science and applied research for the development of innovative products This branch of technology laid the groundwork for the development of the fastest growing segment in industry today the high-technology industry In the *Encyclopedia Britannica* one can find the following definition for *high technology*

> high technology n: scientific technology involving the production or use of advanced or sophisticated devices especially in the fields of electronics and computers *

This definition, although recent, seems quite outdated Today high technology encompasses a much wider spectrum of industrial and business activities, including biotechnology, aerospace, communications, software, and others

Innovation

Most people have a reasonably good understanding of the idea of innovation Nevertheless, we can usefully review this concept and examine its definition, particularly in its relation to the history of technology Looking again in the *Encyclopedia Britannica* we read the following

> The word innovation raises a problem of great importance in the history of technology Strictly, an innovation is something entirely new, but there is no such thing as an unprecedented technological innovation because it is impossible for an inventor to work in a vacuum and, however ingenious his invention, it must arise out of his own previous experience The task of distinguishing an element of novelty in an invention remains a problem of patent law down to the present day, but the problem is made relatively easy by the possession of full documentary records covering previous inventions in many countries For the millennium of the Middle Ages, however, few such records exist, and it is frequently difficult to explain how particular innovations were introduced to western Europe The problem is especially perplexing because it is known that many inventions of the period had been developed independently and previously in other civilizations, and it is sometimes difficult if not impossible to know whether something is spontaneous innovation or an invention that had been transmitted by some as yet undiscovered route from those who had originated it in other societies *

---

* Reprinted with permission from "The History of Technology," *Britannica CD 97*, © 1997 by Encyclopaedia Britannica, Inc

The above quotation evokes the distinction between spontaneous innovation and transmitted innovation The issue is important because it generates a conflict of interpretations about the transmission of technology In this respect, the *Encyclopedia Britannica* clarifies as follows

> On the one hand there is the theory of the diffusionists, according to which all innovation has moved westward from the long-established civilizations of the ancient world, with Egypt and Mesopotamia as the two favorite candidates for the ultimate source of the process On the other hand is the theory of spontaneous innovation, according to which the primary determinant of technological innovation is social need Scholarship is as yet unable to solve the problem so far as technological advances of the Middle Ages are concerned because much information is missing. But it does seem likely that at least some of the key inventions of the period—the windmill and gunpowder are good examples—were developed spontaneously It is quite certain, however, that others, such as silk working, were transmitted to the West, and, however original the contribution of Western civilization to technological innovation, there can be no doubt at all that in its early centuries at least it looked to the East for ideas and inspiration *

Today, with the advent of modern communications, innovative ideas can travel with the speed of light from one research center to another, located continents and oceans away Obviously, time for technology advances to diffuse from one country to another has shortened enormously Nevertheless, popular wisdom is here to remind us that need is the mother of all inventions, hence, emerging needs are sure to inspire new, original and spontaneous inventions

References and Further Reading

Afuah, Allan N , and Nik Bahram (1993) *The Hypercube of Innovation* Boston, MA: Sloan School of Management

> The authors provide definitions and discuss basic concepts of innovation Innovation has frequently been categorized as either radical, incremental, architectural, modular, or niche, based on its effects on the competence, other products, and investment decisions of the innovating entity Often, however, an innovation is considered quite differently by different groups One that is considered architectural by the innovator/manufacturer may turn out to be radical to customers, incremental to suppliers of components and equipment, and something else to suppliers of critical complementary innovations These various faces of one innovation at different stages of the innovation value-adding chain are what the authors call the *hypercube of innovation* For many high-technology products, a technology strategy that neglects these various faces of an innovation and dwells only on the effects of the innovation at the innovator/manufacturer level, can have harmful effects. This is especially so for innovations whose success depends on feedback coming from lessons learned at customers premises

Grove, Andrew S (1983) *High Output Management* New York: Random House

> The book, written by the president of Intel, one of the world-class high-technology companies, gives his view on managing in the high-technology environment Grove focuses on

---

* Reprinted with permission from "The History of Technology," *Britannica CD 97*, © 1997 by Encyclopaedia Britannica, Inc

three basic ideas The first is an output-oriented approach to management The second idea is that the work of a business is something pursued not by individuals but by teams The third idea is that a team will perform well only if peak performance is elicited from the individuals in it The book has the special merit of reflecting the real-life experience of one of the most successful leaders in the high-technology industry

Jain, R K , and H C Triandis. (1990) *Management of R&D Organizations Managing the Unmanageable* New York: John Wiley & Sons

The book is a well documented text on important topics in the management of research and development (R&D) It defines research and development organizations and research categories It incorporates results from research in behavioral sciences on topics such as how to resolve conflicts, how to change attitudes, how to motivate subordinates, and how to design the best R&D work environment

Utterback, James M. (1994) *Mastering the Dynamics of Innovation How Companies Can Seize Opportunities in the Face of Technological Change* Cambridge, MA: Harvard Business School Press

To answer the question in the subtitle of the book, the author draws on the history of innovation Using examples ranging from the birth of typewriters to the emergence of personal computers, gas lamps to fluorescent lighting, George Eastman's amateur photography to electronic imaging, he develops a practical model for how innovation enters an industry, how mainstream firms typically respond, and how—over time—new and old players wrestle for dominance. Utterback asserts that existing organizations must consistently abandon past success and embrace innovation—even when it undermines their traditional strengths He sets forth a strategy to do so, and identifies the responsibilities of managers to lead and focus that effort

von Hippel, Eric (1988) *The Sources of Innovation* New York: Oxford University Press

In his book, von Hippel challenges conventional common sense which holds that innovation is carried out by manufacturers who perceive a need for new products and then develop and market them This view has had a far-reaching impact on innovation-related research as well as activities ranging from the ways firms organize their research and development (R&D) to the ways governments measure innovation According to his study, von Hippel challenges this assumption by demonstrating that innovation occurs in different places in different industries He presents a series of examples showing that innovation users and material suppliers are the typical sources of innovation in some professional fields

CHAPTER

The Critical Factors for Success

2

In the highly competitive business environment at the turning of the century, management of high technology poses a particular challenge To manage a high-technology, innovative organization successfully, one needs not only to master the basic managerial knowledge and skills necessary to run any type of organization but also to acquire and thoroughly understand a body of specific knowledge about factors that play a key role in this industry These factors are critical and make management of high technology more demanding and challenging than management of most other industrial sectors (Pinto and Slevin, 1989) However, the rewards for success in this area largely compensate for the extra effort required to obtain the necessary knowledge Few industrial sectors can show a better rate of growth than high technology Few offer more generous recompense for the additional effort one invests to become an educated, professional manager.

We begin with the concept of *innovation*. Clearly, innovation is in the soul of high technology Innovation distinguishes it from the more traditional industries and makes its products attractive (Roberts, 1987, Thomson and Maybey, 1994) We define and distinguish between *technology-driven innovation* and *market-driven innovation* This prepares for discussion of the *innovation uncertainty factor* and other innovation-related critical factors

The second factor of particular significance in the high-technology industry is the *human factor* Extremely important in the management of any organization, this factor becomes critical in high technology for two reasons First, high-technology companies, unlike the more traditional industries, are based on innovation Innovation depends entirely on individuals Second, in high-technology organizations, the proportion of engineers, scientists, mathematicians, and other professionals is much larger than in low-technology industries This concentration of highly qualified employees requires a different management approach from the one appropriate in the more traditional industries To motivate these specialists to make their best contribution to the company, managers must adapt to the needs, aspirations, and special characteristics of the high-technology company's personnel

In traditional industries, success may depend on such factors as availability of natural resources (petrochemical industry) or machines and capital investment (automotive industry) In contrast, success in high technology depends mainly, if not solely, on human resources No other industry relies so much on the human factor as the high-technology industry Talent, imagination, and entrepreneurship are the spirit and essence of this sector

The third critical factor that must be adapted specifically to high-technology needs and requirements is the *organization factor* Most companies need to change and adapt their organizations over time, but the pace in the high-technology sector requires a much faster and more dynamic matching of the organizational structure to the changing needs of a company as it grows from a start-up to a mature, diversified firm In addition, changes in technology and production processes also require organizational change and restructuring

The fourth critical factor in the high-technology industry is the *management competence factor*. A certain degree of professionalism is required to manage any type of organization successfully In the high-technology area, however, managers at all levels have to be better educated and more competent to perform their task than other managers because of the extreme complexity of balancing the factors just discussed

Next, the *know-how factor*, which is a prerequisite for business success in the high-technology sector, needs to be complemented by and distinguished from the *know-why factor* Much as one differentiates between efficiency and effectiveness, one should distinguish between know-how and know-why *Know-how* is important to develop an innovative product *Know-why*, however, implies insight and understanding of future trends and is essential for exploiting the market success of the product

In this chapter, we define, discuss, and analyze these five critical factors In certain cases, subsequent chapters complete the discussion and propose solutions to important problems, such as creating a favorable environment for inventors In others, we use the notions analyzed in this chapter and explain how these critical factors affect the management of a high-technology company

INNOVATION

Innovation plays a key role in the high-technology industry For general definitions of innovation, see Martin (1994), Bray (1995), and others Throughout this text, we deal with the impact of innovation on a large variety of aspects that are critical in a high-technology organization Some of these roles are positive, others are negative For example, the bigger the innovative jump a company makes with its products, the better will be its competitive position in the marketplace On the other hand, big innovative jumps often carry risks that are difficult to manage, as discussed in subsequent sections Before we start these discussions, we need to distinguish between *technology-driven innovation* and *market-driven innovation*

Technology-Driven Innovation

An innovation is said to be technology driven if the basic stimulus for its implementation comes from the availability of a new technology or a combination of new technologies The very fact that a new technology may allow the development of products that were difficult or even impossible to create in the past is by itself a strong motivation to develop such products

There are many successful examples of technology-driven innovation Companies like Motorola in the United States, Ericson in Europe, and others developed the mobile cellular telephone business, using advances made in technologies such as electronic switching, signal processing, and microelectronics Thus, they created a huge market for which there had been no prior demand Once established, such companies usually generate significant profit from the market success of their innovation This was the case, years ago, with the first generations of transistor radios, cassette recorders, camcorders, compact discs, and so on

Generous market rewards continued to drive competent companies to use new technologies to create innovative products and services In the not-too-distant future, Motorola, Loral, TRW, and others will launch their constellations of communication satellites that will cover every spot on earth with reliable, high-quality, fixed, or mobile communications

Unfortunately, not all technology-driven innovations are economic successes In addition to all other risk factors, discussed in following sections, there is a peculiar danger associated with technology-driven innovation Acting on the temptation to develop a product just because technology has made such development feasible often results in market disappointments. To illustrate, examine the well-publicized case of interactive TV (Case 2 1)

The most important lesson from this case material is that anyone planning to engage in technology-driven innovation should first make sure that his or her potential customers' culture, attitude, and habits are ready to accept the new product Of course, all other technical and cost problems have to be resolved as well, as pointed out by Harmon and colleagues (1995) in the *International Herald Tribune* The article, entitled "Where Is Interactive TV? Not in Your Living Room," states that "a huge gap lies between what it costs and what people will pay" (p 14)

Still, it is possible that through the creative contribution of some genius or by taking some new, innovative form, interactive TV may yet materialize However, this example shows clearly that special caution is due when one deals with technology-driven innovation

Market-Driven Innovation

An innovation is said to be market driven if the basic stimulus for its implementation comes from well-perceived market needs or, better, from an established market demand Innovation in this case usually consists of creating a new product to replace an existing one, or a new generation of products, with better, more attractive price-performance ratios In other cases, well-defined customer demand stimulates the develop-

---

CASE 2.1

An Example of Technology-Driven Innovation:
Interactive TV

At the beginning of the 1990s, the development of fast digital communications, of video and data mass storage, and of some associated hardware and software technologies created expectations for a new, multibillion-dollar market—namely, the business of interactive television (ITV) Indeed, there is no basic technical difficulty today in dialing a movie on request Television studios and large and small companies rushed to take part in riding the wave For example, Disney acquired ABC, Westinghouse took over CBS, and just before the end of 1995, NBC and Microsoft teamed up to launch a 24-hour news service via cable and the Internet

To the disappointment of many, the promise that lured such companies into ITV has failed, so far, to materialize The reasons reported include higher than expected cost, regulatory obstacles, and most important, the basic question of who needs interactive TV? This last question arises from a cultural problem Is ITV adding real value to entertainment or is it diluting the emotional experience created by a good, classic movie or TV play? In this excerpt from an article published in *Newsweek*, Levy analyzes the problem and hints at a possible solution

> Can a computer game make you cry? That was the provocative question posed by an upstart software house in its first ad campaign, more than a decade ago Though the company (Electronic Arts) was ultimately successful, the promise implicit in the marketing campaign has yet to be fulfilled Interactive programs may be a multibillion-dollar industry, but by and large they don't reach our imaginations—or our hearts—as much as mildly compelling genre movie does, or even an afternoon soap Computer games divert, addict, sometimes even teach But they don't make you cry
>
> While interactive content can be addictive for engaging in virtual massacres (Doom) or intricate puzzle solving (Myst), no one has figured out yet how to hit the cultural jackpot, the equivalent of Forrest Gump Interactive or even Beverly Hills CD-ROM It goes like this: Interactive entertainment is just like film in its early days. And then along came Eisenstein, who created a grammar that allowed movies to mature. All we need is a genius—a digital messiah—who will do the same for interactive Since the word "genius" in Hollywood is synonymous with one person, this theory can be dubbed Waiting for Spielberg
>
> It's not going to be that easy The problem lies with the essential nature of interactive entertainment For centuries people have been entertained by listening to stories—some psychologists even think our brains are hard-wired to appreciate narrative. But interactive eschews narrative. "We're all about engaging the player, saying that he or she has as much to contribute as anything else," explains Tom Zito, head of Digital Pictures "That's nothing that Hollywood wants to hear " No wonder—it's like asking Homer to pause during the Odyssey to ask the audience what they think Ulysses should find upon his

home-coming How can you believe in a character when his or her fate is contingent on your ability to shoot down a lot of hostile aliens?

Another difference is that "interactivity dilutes your point of view," says Michael Backes, a screenwriter\videogame exec who understands both cultures. Backes cites the Tyrannosaurus rex sequence in *Jurassic Park* Spielberg carefully orchestrates every shot for maximum terror, controlling where the viewer looks at every instant But in an interactive, virtual-reality-type environment, he or she probably wouldn't be looking at the dinosaur at all—just running.

. Instead of competing directly with movielike experiences, where character and plot are king, the most successful games treat the environment itself as the star. "The idea is to make an interesting world," says Mike Backes "You can't just plunge the person into the third act of *King Lear* "

Will this be enough? For the short term, there's still plenty of mileage left in simulations that place people in challenging roles. But I see interactive worlds really taking off when people can network them together Then people can compensate for the lack of strong fictional characters by acting out their own personae in multiplayer environments The advance guard of this movement right now is the on-line Multi-User Dungeon (MUDs), virtual communities of game players whose deeply personal interactions can have profound effects on the participants (They have even been known to make people cry) Significantly, the MUD phenomenon is deeply entrenched in the realm of the technoid—far, far off Hollywood's radar screen

Does this mean we can count the studios out? Not exactly Guess who showed up last week at the Electronic Entertainment Expo? Spielberg It turns out that His Stevenhood has invested in a game company and has already begun shooting footage for his first made-for-computer production Whether or not the program breaks new ground, it does represent a wake-up call from Hollywood to Silicon Valley: "He's heee-re "

ment of original products that fulfill specific requirements in a totally new and innovative way

There are plenty of examples of the first type The development of new, faster microprocessors; large storage capacity hard disks, and RAM memory chips are only a few examples from the fast-moving computer industry Practically all second, third, and subsequent generations of a high-technology product fall within this category.

In the second category, one finds some unique high-technology systems specifically developed to meet a customer's requirement Some military high-technology systems are ordered according to such specifications. Medical electronic systems such as computerized axial tomography (CAT) and magnetic resonance imaging (MRI) scanners are another example of systems first developed to meet a well-defined medical need Often, the system creates a new market that was nonexistent prior to its success, but as long as the innovation is specifically ordered by a well-defined customer, it is still considered to be market driven (see Case 2 2)

CASE 2.2

An Example of Market-Driven Innovation: The Internet

An excellent illustration of the power of market demand to stimulate innovation is the recent and continuing rush of companies to conquer a place in the new "eldorado"—the World Wide Web (W W W) In *Business Week* (October 23, 1995), Cortese and Hof wrote

> Aug. 9, 1995, is a date investors are not likely to forget That is the day Netscape Communications Corp , a maker of Internet software, went public Netscape's stock, offered at $28 a share, soared to nearly $75 before ending its first trading day at a less stratospheric $58, making multimillionaires of its founders and insiders

Naturally, such remarkable success received worldwide media attention and captured the imagination of scores of entrepreneurs and innovators The market demand for a variety of software packages for the Internet in 1995 was indeed remarkable, as reported in the same article, "Sales of software for the World Wide Web are expected to swell from $260 million this year to $4 billion in 1996, according to Hambrecht & Quist Inc "

By 1997, scores of new companies were created in the drive to satisfy this tremendous market appetite for programs designed to make better use of the Web Companies like InfoSeek and Yahoo quickly offered improved solutions for browsing the Web Hotmail, RocketMail, and others came up with attractive e-mail services Firewall and others designed special software to increase security on the Internet Many of these newly created companies became an almost instant commercial success Others, less fortunate or less expeditious, died in the fierce competition for the same market niche.

Two major lessons should be learned from this example One: Companies engaged in market-driven innovation are most often in competition, sometimes fierce competition, with others, all addressing the same well-identified market needs Two The time between the initial identification of the need by the pioneers in a field and the moment "the crowds" invade it has shortened in high technology to less than one year These observations emphasize the quick response required in high technology, as we discuss in chapters 4 and 5

At this point, we are ready to begin examining how to handle the impact of innovation on the factors critical to management of high technology As we shall see from the discussions in the following sections, innovation, whether driven by technology or the marketplace, always represents an opportunity and a risk Usually, the greater the opportunity, the higher will be the risk. With technology-driven innovation, one should be especially careful to avoid investing in products that customers don't really need In market-driven innovation, on the other hand, the major challenge is to stay ahead of the competition

THE INNOVATION UNCERTAINTY FACTOR

Innovation and uncertainty go hand in hand The development of a new and innovative product necessarily implies that at least some of the steps in the process are being done for the first time Hence, the spectrum of associated uncertainties is much larger than in traditional industries The *innovation uncertainty factor* is made up of three types of uncertainty: market, technology, and supply. The way the market accepts an innovative product is hard to predict Hence, one has to account for the *market uncertainty* associated with innovation Another set of uncertainties induced by innovation are the *technological uncertainties* Using new, innovative technologies inevitably requires acceptance of a certain amount of risk This risk should be managed and minimized accordingly Finally, innovation is also associated with certain *supply uncertainties*, resulting from the need to use single and sometimes unique sources of supply for critical parts. Such parts and suppliers, if unreliable, may jeopardize the entire business cycle We begin with market uncertainties, examining them in more detail than in the previous section and exploring practical ways to reduce their effect

Market Uncertainties due to Innovation

An innovative product may be accepted by the marketplace with varying degrees of success Crockford (1986), in his discussion on "marketing risk," writes "The launching of any new product involves the risk that, however well the market has been researched, customers may reject it The proportion of new products which survive to gain a significant market share is quite small Even if it becomes established, there is always the possibility that a change in needs, attitudes, taste and fashion may render it obsolete" (p 18)

Before we examine the market uncertainties that apply in both market- and technology-driven innovative products, we should make another distinction high-technology products designated for a large customer base as opposed to those specified for a specific single customer or for a small number of customers with similar needs For simplicity, we call products in the first category *commercial* high-technology products and those in the second *institutional* high technology products Examples of commercial high technology are most of the software industry products, personal computers, biotechnology products, and others In institutional high technology, one finds innovative systems required and specified by government agencies or large private organizations Examples are modern communication systems, information systems, traffic control systems, and all the military high-technology systems.

In the case of commercial high technology, one often tries to reduce market uncertainty by conducting preliminary market research (Urban, Weinberg, and Hauser, 1994) However, no such research is perfect, and management is always faced with a larger risk concerning acceptance of the product by the market compared to products with a well-established market demand On the other hand, if the innovative product turns out to be a hit, market rewards can fully compensate for the risk, as we saw in the discussion of technology-driven innovation

Market uncertainty exists also in the case of market-driven innovation, including the case of institutional products Even if a high-technology contractor agrees to deliver a system according to a customer's specification, there is always the risk that the customer and the contractor have different interpretations of the specifications A worse case occurs when a long time elapses between the specifications of the system and its delivery, and someone other than the original contact person represents the customer at the moment of delivery This person may have a totally different view of what was meant by some of the specifications Similar problems may exist in other sectors of activity, but in high technology, the problem is aggravated by frequent time overruns, caused by some of the factors discussed later

There is no perfect solution for these types of problems, but a good beginning is to keep the time between inception and the introduction of the product to the market as short as possible This important topic is elaborated at length in chapter 4 At this stage, though, we see clearly that the time between the market research that justified the decision to develop the product and the date of its actual introduction to the market must be kept as short as possible The shorter this time span, the better are the chances that the findings of the market study will still be relevant and accurate The same rule applies to large systems The shorter the delivery time, the higher is the probability that the same people who represented the customer when the system was specified will be around to take delivery Ideally, they will still be in the same positions, thus decreasing the risk that a new person will introduce a different interpretation of the system's requirements.

The case of large systems, particularly those required and specified by government agencies, is of special interest One might think that because the customer is well defined and the requirement is clearly specified, there should be no market uncertainty In reality, many high-technology companies working under government contracts often report such horror stories as working on an innovative system for several years, then having the entire requirement dropped by the customer, leaving the company with no market at all In such circumstances, even if the customer has covered all the costs under the contract, the end result is still a very significant loss for the company, considering that some of its best human resources have been devoted to a dead-end road

An enlightened management should do everything possible to avoid such extreme situations (Cox, 1992) A number of approaches can help achieve that goal

First, investigate the *stability of a requirement* Often the need for a system is strongly dependent on the will of a dominant individual As long as this individual is the key decision maker, there is a strong requirement for the system Once that individual is gone, however, nobody needs the system This kind of "vanishing requirement" has caused troubles for a number of high-technology companies Therefore, if the slightest doubt exists, before committing the company to a road that may lead nowhere, a good and solid needs analysis is always necessary in order to establish the stability of the requirement

Second, avoid as much as possible having most of the company's research and development resources dedicated to a single project For a mature company, reasonably diversified, a good rule of thumb is to have no more than 10 percent of its R&D resources committed to any one effort

Third, if any project engages more than 10 percent of the company's research and development resources, prepare contingency applications for transferring those resources as smoothly as possible to a new, useful direction in the case of a "vanishing requirement" (see Case 2 3)

CASE 2.3

An Example of Market Uncertainty

Some years ago, I had a quite traumatic personal experience with a very important, large research and development project involving more than one-third of the company's best R&D staff I knew this was in strong violation of the second principle mentioned earlier I knew the requirement was sensitive to the personalities who had defined the system and that if they changed their position, the requirement might vanish On the other hand, this was a unique opportunity to make a major technological leap and advance the state of the art in three strategic business areas for the company A successful completion of the R&D phase of the project would have given the company more than $500 million in business backlog, which, compared to roughly $200 million in annual sales, was also very attractive Therefore, despite the risk, we fought fiercely against strong competition to win the contracts for this challenging project

The research and development phase of the project was planned for five years After four years of successful R&D work, the key decision makers—those who initiated the project—were transferred to other positions Sure enough, the new team had different views and a different set of priorities After they reassessed their priorities, one September day we were informed that for economic reasons, the project was canceled This blow was terrible On that day, hundreds of people in the company—scientists, engineers, technicians, and professional workers—felt as if the ground had opened below their feet

Luckily, we had not violated the third principle Two years before this tragic day in September, we had initiated a strong and conscientious drive to prepare alternative applications for the systems required by the project When the blow came, we were prepared The company was shaken but did not fall A few months later, we had the first customer for one of the contingency systems that had been prepared The company profit dropped that year below our usual average but it remained positive Within a year, most of the R&D work done for the interrupted project found new applications and new customers.

It wasn't easy, though Some managers in the company had viewed such contingency work done in parallel with the project as a nuisance and a distraction from the mainstream effort Also, such work had to be done using internal company funds, which created opposition Most important, I had to be careful, in explaining the need for contingency planning, to avoid creating the feeling that the "boss has lost confidence" in the project This would have had a demoralizing effect on the team working on it After the cancellation of the project, of course, everyone agreed that the small investment made in the contingency work was well justified.

To summarize, the market uncertainty factor is present in almost all high-technology, innovative companies, regardless of whether their innovation is technology or market driven and whether their products are for consumer or institutional use Following the three principles described earlier, the manager of a high-technology company should be able to reduce this risk to an acceptable level

Technological Uncertainties due to Innovation

Anyone dealing in high technology is obviously aware of the uncertainty associated with innovative technologies However, I have been involved in so many situations in which responsible managers miscalculated the risks associated with these uncertainties that I find it essential to write about the most frequent ones

A priori, one should acknowledge the need to take a certain amount of risk in any innovative process The development of a new product that is supposed to perform much better than existing ones is bound to involve some new features that make it capable of beating the competition in the marketplace Such features are usually achieved by a combination of new concepts and ideas, novel product architecture, incorporation of new components and materials, or application of new technological processes. Hence, one should account for the risk (see Copp and Zannella, 1992, Crockford, 1986) and try to avoid multiple risk situations that may amplify the overall uncertainty to unacceptable levels, as illustrated in Case 2 4

CASE 2.4

An Example of Multiple Technological Uncertainties

One of the most frequent situations occurs when the market success of a product is based on a large number of innovations To illustrate, think about a current example. An aerospace company considers the development of a new supersonic transport aircraft (SST) for the beginning of the twenty-first century Learning from the economic problems associated with the Concorde, the first-generation SST that was developed in the 1970s, the company concludes that the new aircraft will become a business success only if some of its important features are significantly improved in comparison with the Concorde

Such features include keeping or improving the speed, increasing passenger comfort to a level comparable to the one available in wide body aircraft, reducing the per seat-mileage cost to a level acceptable to commercial airline companies, and resolving the ecological problems that would limit its landing rights in most of the important world airports

Now, suppose a team of brilliant engineers, headed by a well-known scientist, develops a totally new aerodynamic approach The team claims that they have taken into account all the previously mentioned considerations and that they have appropriate solutions for each of them. Subsequently, a serious feasibility study is made by an independent institution It shows that the concept is indeed feasible, provided that the following events occur

1 A new supercritical wing is successfully designed

2 The new engine under development by one of the best international consortia is successfully finished four years from now for use in the airplane

3 The development of a new and revolutionary composite material reaches the stage of reliable manufacturing that allows its use in the airplane

The new engine is promised to improve thrust by 50 percent and reduce fuel consumption by 20 percent compared to present-day engines By employing the latest technological advances in large turbomachinery aerodynamics, combustion, materials, metallurgy, and vibration control, the new engine will offer unprecedented performance in terms of environmental friendliness (35% less oxides of nitrogen and a 50% decrease in hydrocarbons, carbon monoxide, and smoke compared with current turbofan engines), fuel consumption (20% reduction), reliability, and a very low operating cost for the airlines

To meet the SST requirement, the new engine will need only 10 percent increase in thrust and 15 percent additional weight reduction The leader of the engine consortium has assured our technical team that his group should have no problem introducing these additional improvements after they successfully complete the present design Supporting the engine designer's promises, some basic research is already showing quite encouraging progress on the development of a new alloy for turbine blades If successful, the new material will allow operation at significantly higher temperatures and provide the increase of thrust and the reduction in weight by the amounts requested

A revolutionary new composite material is said to have been successfully demonstrated in one of the leading national laboratories It can decrease the total aircraft weight so significantly that, together with the new aerodynamic concept and the new engines, the total operating cost can be reduced to a level quite acceptable for commercial airline operations

---

In this example, one can easily identify at least six major risk areas the novel aerodynamic concept, the new wing design, the development of a new engine, the availability of a new turbo-blades alloy, the development of a new composite material, and the development of a reliable and cost-effective manufacturing process for this material when it is finally out of laboratory research Even if one assigns a probability of success as high as 80 percent to each of these challenging tasks, taken together, the probability that all risk areas will be successfully resolved is less than 30 percent

The example, being purposely a bit too obvious, clearly suggests that a responsible and experienced management should decline such a project on the basis of multiple risks Even though each part by itself may have a reasonable chance for success, the effort taken as a whole is almost certainly an unacceptable risk

Unfortunately, in many real-world situations, not all multiple risk areas are properly identified from the outset An enthusiastic research team, which by itself is a positive factor, combined with inexperienced management, has often allowed the combination effect of multiple risks to be miscalculated Eagerness to achieve a decisive competitive advantage has led many companies to approve risky programs that become economic disasters

One way of controlling the multiple risk situation is to institute a formal, internal risk analysis group (RAG) or to assign risk control to a competent independent institution. Their assignment should be to quantify the risks as much as possible and to present to management a comprehensive assessment of those risks, together with a concrete proposal outlining the formal steps for their reduction.

Supply Uncertainty due to Innovation

An innovative product will have innovative components Even without multiple risks, the inevitable presence of novel components implies certain supply risk that must be taken into account

A useful contrast is with the supply strategy of traditional industries that manufacture mature products Such companies normally establish long-term agreements with reliable, high-quality, and cost-effective suppliers for the just-in-time delivery of the next batch of components necessary for the manufacturing process All the components are mature, their performance characteristics are well known and repeatedly reproduced The delivery times, the quality, and the price are all without surprise Now, to contrast this with the supply situation of just one critical and innovative component, examine the example in Case 2 5

Cases similar to this have certainly occurred to most people engaged in developing high-technology, innovative products. In a product containing several hundred or several thousand components, avoiding such problems totally is virtually impossible However, a competent product management organization should be fully aware that such problems will eventually arise and be ready to cope with them energetically and without unjustified optimism

If you wish to decrease supply uncertainty as much as possible, consider the following principles:

First, try diligently to avoid having to rely on a single supplier If exceptions are made to the rule, each case should be formally controlled and tracked An individual should be assigned with personal responsibility for checking and following each of the critical suppliers.

Second, if you have a choice between using novel system architecture rather than a critical component to achieve competitive advantage, choose the first method The system architecture depends entirely on your organization, therefore, you have much greater control over it than over an externally produced component

Third, in situations when you must depend on critical components, the moment a supply problem arises, like the one described in Case 2 5, immediately take some contingency steps To illustrate using the example, you should begin redesigning the power supply while you continue negotiating with the supplier for a product that meets the original specifications

---

CASE 2.5

An Example of Supply Uncertainty due to Innovation

Suppose a novel electronic system requires a broad-band, high-power transistor The choice of manufacturers of such a high-performance device is limited Often, the choice is one supplier, which has just announced the availability of this new transistor You buy some samples of the unit, test them in your system, and find that because of their superior performance, you can significantly reduce the number of parts in the circuit and thus reduce the weight and the price of the system

Naturally, you introduce the new transistor into your product The first quantities produced are very successful Then, all of a sudden, a large percentage of the systems fail final tests, or worse, are returned with transistor failures by your customers You immediately alert the supplier of the transistors He promises to fix the problem The new batch of transistors, however, does not arrive on time The manufacturer explains that he has minor problems with his process control, but his team is working hard to correct them You are given another promised date After a few missed delivery dates, you finally receive the new batch of transistors Their performance is all right, but their power consumption has risen

You refuse to redesign your power supply and ask the manufacturer to provide you with the product as specified and with exactly the same characteristics as the first transistors you received The supplier agrees but requests more time, claiming that some irreversible changes have occurred in his process and he needs to try a new method that promises to resolve all problems

Now you learn that key personnel changes have taken place in the supplier company The supervisor of the power transistor division was engaged in a major effort to reduce the manufacturing cost As a result, the people who knew how to produce your critical component left the company Of course, you are tempted to terminate the contract and look for another supplier for your high-power, broadband transistor, but you realize that there are no alternatives Your choices are to wait and hope the original supplier will eventually overcome his problems, or to redesign your equipment and adapt it to the lower-performing transistors readily available in the market

---

THE HUMAN FACTOR

The human factor is of predominant, fundamental importance in all management activities (Dessler, 1993) Clearly, whatever the nature of the business, all basic managerial tasks have to do with managing people In high-technology and innovation companies, however, managers have additional concerns In addition to the general, well-known, and accepted principles of leading, guiding, and motivating people, managers must adapt their leadership approach to the characteristics of the personnel responsible for the vital activities of the organizations

The Special Characteristics of High-Technology Company Personnel

An important characteristic of the high-technology industry is the large proportion of top-level professionals it employs Often they hold advanced degrees in a variety of professional fields Depending on the stage of development of the company—from a start-up to a mature organization (Greiner, 1972)—this proportion may vary, but it always remains high compared with low-technology industry in the same stage of development. In some organizations with particularly high levels of innovative research and development activities, some authors (Jain and Triandis, 1991, Katz, 1988) speak of a "prima donna effect," claiming that it is virtually impossible to manage these egos Whatever the case, one thing is sure There cannot be any significant innovative activity without that special breed of inventors and innovators who generate, promote, and sometimes fight against all obstacles for acceptance of their ideas

It is important to understand the basic behavioral characteristics of inventor-type people and to find ways to accommodate their peculiar sensibilities A manager must distinguish among a number of behavioral characteristics typically found in exceptionally talented people if he or she is to optimize their creative output while limiting the negative effects of their behavior on the organization Controlling prima donnas is difficult, but if you want to run a world class show you had better learn how to manage these most valuable individuals

The most important commonality among all inventors and innovators is creativity This trait has been widely discussed in the literature (Jones, 1993, Katz, 1988) We are not going to examine here ways to measure creativity, how to detect creative people, and other such issues Our interest is in how best to manage such people In the next chapter we discuss and describe in greater detail ways to create an optimum environment for innovators. First, however, we should enumerate some of their additional, important characteristics

Typical Behavior of Highly Creative People

The creativity common to all innovators often allows them to look at a situation from an entirely different perspective from that of most people, and to see novel ways of solving a problem No wonder, therefore, that innovators are often individualists with varying degrees of ability—or disability—in communicating effectively with the rest of the organization

Another characteristic found frequently with innovators is optimism, which at the extreme approaches naivete Inventors tend to overlook many of the practical difficulties associated with the realization of their inventions Almost all their estimates regarding time, cost, and resources necessary to realize their ideas are significantly underestimated Naturally, such behavior is bound to create serious problems and conflicts, especially in more mature organizations with well-established, formal procedures of planning and control.

In close association with excessive optimism, another typical characteristic of inventors is their lack of interest in "small details " Once the problem is solved in principle, all the routine work that has to be done to make an innovation a commercial success is seen by most inventors as being of secondary importance In extreme cases, such an attitude approaches "detail blindness" or an almost complete disregard for what they consider trivial and boring tasks

Innovative people typically share other characteristics (see Coney, 1990, Jain and Triandis, 1991), but *individualism*, *unrealistic optimism*, and *neglect of details* are the major and most frequent causes of problems associated with managing organizations involving inventors and innovators In the next chapter, "Creating a Favorable Environment for Inventors," we discuss some of the solutions for typical problems created by the special behavior of such individuals At this stage we need to stress again that there is no replacement for inventors and innovators In any high-technology, innovative organization, these individuals represent a key element for success Rather than trying to change their behavior—an endeavor doomed to failure—one must take their attitude as given and find effective ways to overcome the ensuing problems Practical solutions will inevitably vary according to the situation and the individuals involved, but if managers are aware of problems and accept as normal some degree of individualistic behavior from exceptionally creative people, they will take an important first step in solving the problem

Recruiting High-Technology Personnel

One of the most important policies that managers of a high-technology company must establish concerns recruitment of new personnel In view of the critical role the human factor plays in high technology, management should strive to get the best people for every job in the company—not only the best engineers, scientists, and technicians but also the best craftsmen, secretaries, and maintenance people This is the most important task of the personnel manager and his department His or her performance should be measured as a function of success in achieving this goal while keeping the company's payroll at a fair market level

Recruiting the best professionals is not a trivial job It becomes particularly challenging in periods of strong competition between companies for talented and/or experienced people in a given professional field Here, an intimate knowledge of the character, inspirations, and behavior of highly creative and ambitious people can help, as illustrated in Case 2 6

This recruitment and retention strategy may not be applicable to all environments and to all cultures, but the principle of adapting the recruitment approach to the character and aspirations of the recruits is universally important A high-technology company cannot afford to compromise on the quality of people it recruits The methods may differ but the end result must be to find a way to provide the company with the best quality of the most important of resources the human resource Because the most critical capability in high-technology industries is knowledge, and because knowledge resides in people, managers cannot expect to achieve a long-term competitive advantage if they compromise the quality of people recruited

---

CASE 2.6

An Example of Recruiting High-Technology Personnel

In the mid-1980s, my company was having serious difficulties recruiting new engineering personnel, in both the hardware and software fields During these years, there was a strong demand from various high-technology companies for such personnel and the competition for good people drove the initial salaries offered much above the limit our company was able and willing to pay As a result, our teams of interviewers frequently returned empty-handed after participating in a number of campus recruitment conventions organized by different universities. We could not get the best candidates, and even the second best were hard to convince We found ourselves short of recruits but unable to raise the salaries we offered

We decided then to try a different approach We knew that there is never a shortage of candidates to serve in elite units in the army, and that people are ready to pay high prices for admittance to exclusive and prestigious clubs, so we gave new instructions to the personnel department We had them prepare a set of ambitious screening criteria, including psychometric tests (Jones, 1993) as prerequisites for employment in our company To the surprise of many, this strategy worked on the recruits much better than the previous "begging" and convincing approach After a few conventions, the difficulty of being accepted by our company was already well publicized by the students themselves The challenge of being selected became so attractive in the eyes of the best candidates that it largely compensated for the initial salary difference that remained in our disadvantage

Finally, even the most careful and serious process of screening candidates is never without error It is therefore important to establish a formal procedure for correcting those errors One such method that proved effective in our company was to review the actual performance of all recruits after a given period of time three, six, nine, or twelve months, depending on the complexity of the job assignment Such reviews are done in many companies Our procedure though, required the compulsory layoff of the bottom 10 percent, after all recruits had been ranked in descending order of demonstrated performance

Following this approach, our company was able to hire some extremely brilliant candidates Today, many of them occupy key technical and managerial positions, contributing greatly to the continued success of the company

---

THE ORGANIZATION FACTOR

Organization is important in the success of any company Most successful companies periodically adapt their organizations to fit the evolving needs dictated by external as well as internal factors This is particularly true for the high-technology, innovative industry, which, in addition to all other factors, has to adapt itself to rapid technology changes The fast pace of change in high technology makes the organization factor critical for the business success of the company

The most important role of an industrial organization is to create a framework that increases the motivation of its personnel to achieve the company's objectives If this is not the case, company performance is inevitably below optimal levels When the organization structure caters to the needs and ambitions of dominant personalities but suppresses the initiative, creativity, and motivation of key personnel, the results may be disastrous and the entire company may be ruined

In high technology, it is important to distinguish between the different phases of development an organization experiences as it grows from a start-up to a diversified, mature company Organization appropriate in one phase normally becomes a burden as the company grows to the next phase. Reporting on an organization development project sponsored by the Harvard Business School, Greiner (1972) maintains that "growing organizations move through five distinguishable phases of development, each of which contains a relatively calm period of growth that ends with a management crisis" (p 40) These phases are (1) creativity, (2) direction, (3) delegation, (4) coordination, (5) collaboration

He argues that "since each phase is strongly influenced by the previous one, a management can anticipate and prepare for the next developmental crisis" (p. 40) The pace of the process depends on the growth rate of the market in which the specific company is acting If the company is in a low-growth market, the process may take many years In such a case, the management team may be in charge for just one phase If, as is the case with most high-technology companies, the firm is in a high-growth sector, it may go through a number of those phases well within the life span of a single management team

If management is enlightened, well educated, and prepared to make necessary organizational changes, both the managers and the company will survive such management crises and continue to grow and prosper If they resist change, either the management or the company with its management may perish in today's highly competitive business environment

In the high-technology industry, the five phases defined by Greiner can be identified without difficulty However, for the sake of coherence with the terminology accepted in the high-technology industry, we distinguish between a *start-up* company, a *single product line* company, and a *multiproduct, mature* company—the three stages a company passes through We examine the impact of the five phases on high-technology companies in their development and in their passage through these three stages

The Start-Up Company

A *start-up high-technology company* is almost always built around an innovative idea, a new invention, or a novel, more efficient approach to building a product or providing a service (Roberts, 1990) At the center of the start-up company is the inventor, or possibly a team of inventors The entire organization is small and composed mostly of "believers" in the idea The people are highly motivated and ready to work long hours, they expect the reward for their efforts to come from the success of the idea in the marketplace

The organizational framework at this stage is simple, informal, and almost nonexistent Usually the inventor leads, but the entire group works in close collaboration with its members, communicating and exchanging information frequently on an informal basis

Feedback and some degree of control come usually from the potential customer's reaction and/or from the venture capitalist, in the general sense of this term, meaning the person or institution that provides the financial support to the start-up company Naturally, this person or institution is most interested to see a return on the investment

In Greiner's (1972) terms, this is the "creativity" phase in the life of the company As long as a start-up company is in this phase, success depends mostly on the creativity and entrepreneurship of the people involved and much less on the organization

Once successful, the start-up company needs to become better organized to manufacture and market its new product or service efficiently The know-how to do this is not necessarily found within the original staff who created the company, so appropriate specialists are normally hired to organize production, to build a marketing organization, to create an accounting system, and to provide support to the customers

As the organization grows (Slater, 1992), communication becomes more formal and the original pioneer spirit of the founders is not automatically shared by the newcomers It is they who play an increasingly important role for the commercial success of the company, and accordingly, demand more and more authority. This shift leads to what Greiner (1972) calls the "leadership crisis," and it almost inevitably precedes the second phase of development of the start-up organization

This leadership crisis has a number of possible solutions In the lucky event that one of the founders happens to have managerial qualities and talent (if not the qualifications), such an individual may grow to become the new business manager and lead the company with all the authority and respect he inspires In any case, the company will have to be reorganized to accommodate its changing needs Even if some outside specialists are appointed to senior positions, the amount of resistance to necessary changes will be significantly reduced if the leader remains "one of ours "

Such a case, unfortunately, is the exception to the rule Generally, only after serious problems have shaken the company would the founders call in a competent and experienced business manager from the outside In this situation, the leadership crisis will be profound, poignant, and painful

In the transitory period between two phases of development of a start-up company, the ability to resolve the organizational problems successfully becomes a critical factor for survival Often, the founders do understand that organizational changes have to be made, but they make them only halfheartedly This foot-dragging only aggravates the situation and makes the process more painful In extreme cases where the resistance is so great that necessary changes are postponed for too long, the company may not survive to enter the next growth stage, that of a *product line high-technology company*

The Product Line High-Technology Company

In becoming a product line company, after having successfully resolved its first organizational problems, the firm develops and introduces to the market a family of products and/or services similar to and mostly derivative of the original innovation These products and services are produced in a well-defined and formal organization Typically the company has a board of directors, a president or a managing director, and directors of marketing, research, manufacturing, quality, human resources, and so on The number of people under each director is already quite significant Communication in the organization is now mostly formal

As long as the company is in the phase of exploiting the market success of the original product and its derivatives in a well-organized and controlled manner, the company grows and generates returns—which make both the owners and the management happy People are rewarded according to their position in the hierarchy The importance of innovation and innovators gradually fades In some extreme cases, the attitude toward innovators becomes negative, as they propose changes that tend to interfere and disrupt the well-organized product line flow. Management wants to concentrate on "what we know best" and rejects initiatives for further diversification and for entering new markets and fields of business

The seeds of the next management crisis are found in the very success of the company conquering a significant share in a specific market A natural tendency to "freeze" the success develops Clearly, if appropriate management steps are not taken to unfreeze the organization, it is in trouble. By the time an innovative and aggressive competitor appears on the market, the company will have no answer and no time to prepare one Therefore, managers must encourage innovation and diversification to decrease dependency on a single product and a single market while the company is still strong and successful In addition, this is the time to decentralize, to delegate authority, and to increase motivation at an organizational level as low as possible.

Adapting the operating structure to the changing needs of the company as it develops and grows successfully may become a critical factor in its continual success or in its decline and eventual failure If the company survives the crisis, it will be ready to enter the third stage, becoming a *multiproduct high-technology company*

The Multiproduct High-Technology Company

By the time a business has become a multiproduct high-technology company, it has diversified its activities It has either developed a number of significantly different product lines or has acquired companies already operating in a different product line or, more important, in different and diversified markets The diversified multiproduct high-technology company enjoys greatly improved business stability compared to the single product line company If one product is jeopardized by competition or if its specific market is hit by recession, the company can rely on other products and other markets for its survival and prosperity

Such a company is usually organized around a number of operating divisions, groups, or strategic business units as well as some staff or corporate functions The operating divisions are normally responsible for research and development, manufacturing, and sales of product lines whereas the staff functions are to maintain coherent corporate strategy, coordination, and control.

As long as a reasonable balance is kept between the need for flexibility and quick response on one hand and the need to coordinate and control on the other, the company will most probably grow and prosper, using efficient allocation of limited resources. It should take full advantage of the large number of opportunities that are made available by information coming from a widely spread marketing organization covering a variety of markets Effective use of this information can increase company stability even further To keep that balance, however, is not an easy task Personalities as well as external factors frequently damage confidence between line and staff From here it is easy to slip into a more centralized and tightly controlled organization or toward separation and disintegration

In the first case, for the management of a relatively large organization to feel that it is in control, it may introduce formal procedures to govern almost every aspect of the operation from "a" to "z", from accounting to procedures for buying coffee and cookies More and more red tape and bureaucratic paperwork become necessary before any important and not-so-important decision is made Although responsibility remains theoretically decentralized, authority is more and more centralized This tightening inevitably leads to a degree of sclerotic rigidity that threatens to paralyze the entire company.

In the second case, each product division has won its "war of independence" from corporate control and drifts more and more toward full separation Thus the segmented corporation becomes more and more vulnerable to the problems and uncertainties associated with a single product line organization

In both these cases, a company striving for survival pays little attention to innovation in its product lines Resources are mostly spent to take care of present and very near future needs Nothing is left to invest for the long term The question is how to avoid either of these undesirable organizational developments

As usual, a good first step for keeping the right balance of authority and responsibility in a multiproduct, diversified high-technology company is increased awareness among managers of the importance of keeping this balance To achieve this state, there must be collaboration and careful development of a team spirit—which cannot grow from the bottom up in the organization Probably the first and most important job of the chief executive is fostering this spirit It must come from management top-down through the entire organization.

Greiner (1972) recommends the transition to what he describes as the fifth, and so far, the final phase of organizational development found now in many big U S companies the phase of *collaboration* This stage is characterized by a more flexible and behavioral approach to management, with these emphases:

- Focus is on solving problems quickly and efficiently through team action Teams are combined across functions for group activity in addressing tasks
- Corporate staff is reduced to a minimum and combined in interdisciplinary teams to advise rather than direct line units.
- A matrix-type structure is frequently used to assemble the right teams for appropriate problems; previous formal systems are simplified
- Conferences of key managers are held frequently to focus on major problem issues Educational programs are used to train managers in both teamwork and conflict resolution
- Real-time information systems are integrated into daily decision making, and experiments in new practices and innovation are encouraged throughout the organization

- Economic rewards are geared more to group and team performance than to achievements of individuals.

- A special framework is introduced for the cultivation of innovation and entrepreneurial initiatives, as elaborated in the next chapter

To summarize, organization plays an important role for the success of a high-technology, innovative company. It becomes more and more critical as the company grows from a start-up to a large, diversified organization. The organizational structure must be adapted to the company's current stage of growth In each phase it should be designed to *increase the motivation* of the key individuals to achieve the short-, medium-, and long-term goals of the company

An organizational structure that has been effective in the past may become detrimental to future growth of the company. This is especially possible if it perpetuates individual positions of power and fails to encourage a smooth transition to new structures that are better adapted to meeting the needs of the fast-changing, high-tech business environment If any change is to create resistance to change, organizational shifts are certainly good candidates as they directly affect the status and position of important individuals However, such changes are a difficult but necessary task for top management of every high-technology company

THE MANAGEMENT COMPETENCE FACTOR

A competent management must be totally aware of the special nature of the high-technology and innovation business and have a good understanding of all its critical factors. Being itself a critical factor for the success of the company, management must cover all aspects of company life, directing all-embracing attention to external and internal factors It must give timely assistance, guidance, and leadership for the continual success of the organization (For additional reading on leadership see Bass, 1985, Bennis, 1992; Blades, 1986; Bogue, 1994, Briner, 1990, Conger, 1993, Hein and Nicholson, 1990, Hitt, 1993)

Our examination has shown how a company's management needs change as it grows from a start-up to a multiproduct, diversified organization The degree of competence required from management also grows as the company does In the start-up organization, relatively little professional management is required because the team is small and highly motivated. At the other extreme, however, the competence and managerial professionalism required to lead a multiproduct, high-tech company successfully is far beyond the skill needed to manage sometimes bigger but less complex organizations Therefore, in this section, we highlight the factors in which managers must have special competence in the framework of a large and complex high-technology company. Many of the principles we discuss also apply to the simpler cases of smaller, less complex organizations

Implications of the human factor on managerial style and behavior deserve special attention As noted earlier one basic distinction of the high-technology company is its large proportion of top-level professionals, some with very inventive minds and many with advanced university degrees Such people tend to be individualists and in extreme cases can be difficult Still, keeping their motivation high is essential. Equally important is keeping their enthusiasm focused on company objectives To reach this goal, the manager must win their respect, confidence, and appreciation He or she can accomplish this by adopting an appropriate management style (see Crosby, 1990, Frankel, 1993, Langdon, 1993, Levinson, 1994, Matsushita, 1991, Slater, 1992) and by developing a true team spirit

The Coach Type of Manager

In looking for appropriate management styles, we might usefully examine similar situations in other fields Two examples come to mind an athletic coach and a symphony conductor A top-level team of football or basketball stars who play for a championship provides a good example of a highly competitive activity involving outstanding players Coaches of such teams are very often former stars They may not be able to score as magically as before, but their experience and ability to assess the weak and strong points of the competing teams allow them to devise strategies and tactics that are accepted and respectfully applied by their teams

A similar emergence of group dynamics occurs when high-technology managers themselves have proven records of achievement in the same or relevant professional fields In the best case, they have grown from strong engineering-scientific backgrounds, have successfully directed research and development, and over the years have acquired some formal as well as informal education in business management, which provide them with the necessary managerial tools Such managers usually have the right combination of solid scientific know-how, good intuition or "gut feeling," and a realistic assessment of the business situation

Coach-type management is by no means unique to high-technology companies, but in no other industrial sector is this type of management more appropriate, given the specific character of high-technology personnel The coach-type manager not only sits in management meetings analyzing and devising the company's strategy and tactics but quite often visits the laboratory, the workshop, or the test field where the most critical action for the company takes place He or she asks pertinent questions, discusses difficulties, offers assistance, and provides guidance and advice. This manager's presence, genuine interest, demonstrated appreciation for achievements, support, and encouragement are usually more motivating and morale boosting for a group of professionals than many material rewards.

Competent managers should know their limits, however In no case should they create the impression that they are taking away the responsibility of others They must remember that they are only "coaches" and that the actual results must come from the "players" in the field The coaches' duty is to make their players stars, not to try to do their jobs.

The other example of a management style is the director of a first-class symphony orchestra, a first-rate ballet company, an opera house, or any similar highly artistic performing body.

The Professional Director Type of Manager

For this example, we compare the high-technology manager to the director of an orchestra that has a number of virtuoso performers The director does not necessarily have to be a virtuoso himself, similarly, the high-technology manager need not have a proven record of high technical achievement He must, however, have a solid professional background and understand thoroughly the nature of the business He must be familiar with the pertinent technoscientific terminology that will allow him to listen and make competent assessments of the status of research and development projects, of changing technology, of moves made by competitors, and so on

To win the respect and appreciation of key personnel, such a manager must bring important values to the organization—for example, outstanding marketing abilities, organizational talent, and a sense for grasping changing situations He should be a good strategist and an inspiring leader

A high-technology, innovative company, striving for excellence and world-class performance, must be managed and guided by people who are respected and trusted by top-level professionals These professionals perform at their best if their achievements are appreciated by someone they themselves respect and appreciate Therefore, if the director-type manager does not come with an impressive record of achievement in the company's professional field, he or she must bring a proven history in some other relevant activity to rouse, if not admiration, at least a sense of reliability and confidence in the competence of his or her judgment

If these principles are not respected, what one finds in real life is a gradual decline of morale and motivation in the company One hears expressions such as "What does he understand anyway?" "Who is he to appreciate what we are doing?" and so on Once this attitude develops, most brilliant "soloists" tend to concentrate their attention on their personal interests to the detriment of the performance of the entire "orchestra"—the company.

A large, high-technology, innovative company is in constant competition for market share and profit with smaller as well as larger innovative competitors. As in a first-rate sport team or a top-rate orchestra, a most important factor in keeping the company at the top is team spirit True team spirit creates a high degree of collaboration among individuals and groups inside the company with the devotion and will to win every important competition for the benefit of the company and the pride of its employees Cultivating this spirit is one of the most important duties of the top management of a diversified, multiproduct, high-technology company—and most of all, of the chief executive officer

Team Spirit

To be successful in creating a true team spirit—a sense of belonging, of pride, of being a member of the organization—top management must take at least the following steps:

1. *Lead by personal example.* This old and well-known rule has proven effective for many people—from successful battlefield commanders to small community leaders A chief executive is the model and example to follow for staff, management, and employees of the entire organization. Employees will have difficulty being proud of belonging to a group whose leader does not inspire trust and who behaves differently from what he preaches

2. *Show respect for fellow managers.* Although a certain degree of competition between the different divisions of the multiproduct organization is healthy and should be encouraged, it has to be kept strictly within the limits of optimizing the overall company results.

Beyond this limit, competition and conflict between the managers at all levels may have disastrous consequences for the company

3. ***Focus on problem solving.***   Often, when a serious problem develops in a company, the first question managers ask is "Who is responsible?" or worse, "Who is to blame?" In a company with highly developed team spirit, managers at all levels should ask what the problem is and how it can be solved most efficiently Once the problem is resolved, an entirely legitimate and necessary next step is to learn all the lessons it can teach, including personal lessons, to avoid repetition of a similar undesirable situation However, the emphasis should be on learning, not on punishing—unless somebody deliberately caused problems to damage the company

4. ***Set high standards of excellence.***   A manager cannot expect to be successful in a high-technology company without setting high and ambitious standards for achievement with respect to all the activities of the company Among the most important are these:

   a *Hire excellent personnel.*   Management should strive to get the best people for every job in the company Setting such high standards of achievement enhances the self-esteem of the employees and contributes to the mutual respect and self-confidence of the team However, one must be careful to require the same standards from every employee in all disciplines, even the nonprofessional workers Everyone should be expected to be among the best of his or her professional field Everyone should enjoy the satisfaction of being appreciated for his or her performance by the entire organization.

   b *Compete against the best*   One cannot expect a long-term success in the high-technology marketplace unless the company's products and services rank among the best In every product's life cycle, at a certain time, a product coming from a competitor is bound to outperform it At the time of its introduction, however, the product should stand among the best-performing, innovative products available In addition to all other advantages, competing against the best is a strong motivating factor for the kind of personnel a first-class high-technology company should have.

   c *Use best process technology*   Even with the best team of highly motivated personnel, your company may fail to achieve world-class performance without adequate investment to keep instrumentation, manufacturing, and process technology up to the standards required to compete successfully Managers of many high-technology companies believe that once a significant investment has been made in equipment and process technology, it should be kept as long as possible to save valuable capital for other needs Indeed, in more traditional industries, once the manufacturing process has been set up and established, often no significant upgrading and modifications are required for the company to stay competitive

   Unfortunately, the high-technology world is much more dynamic Therefore, a competent management should devise a different capital investment strategy Constant advances in instrumentation and process technology require replacement of some equipment long before the end of its operational life Hence, company planning should include investment in regular improvements and updates To minimize the investment, however, one should examine in each case such factors as flexibility and compatibility Keeping the process technology up to date is not only a matter of equipment but also of software, procedures, and people Hence, flexible, easy-to-upgrade solutions are better adapted to the high-tech environment than advanced but rigid solutions

   Competent management should always strive to get the best people and the best equipment to accomplish a job The combination of good people and good equipment is bound to give good results This may not be a total guarantee for success, but it is a step in the right direction d *Demand excellence throughout the company* Managers of many organizations who set high standards of achievement have learned that they can't strive for excellence in some areas and content themselves with mediocre results in others Excellence in performance, in quality, and in service must go together with excellence in working environment, in food served in the company's cafeteria, and in the care the company shows for employees in need

The last point is worth a few additional words In elite combat units, wounded comrades are not left beyond enemy lines, even if their evacuation is complex and sometimes risky From this somewhat extreme example, one can deduce the importance of solidarity in any organization that expects from its members the kind of devotion, loyalty, and team spirit necessary to be a top, world-class player

Striving for excellence in every field of activity of a high-technology organization does not mean wasteful spending on luxury buildings, lavish reception rooms, or anything else that does not contribute to or improve the company's efficiency Resources should always be spent with the right sense of priority First attention should always be given to improving the company's financial health and competitive position If additional resources for improving the company's physical plant are not available at a certain period of time, management can see that the working environment is clean and orderly, show a true interest in employees' needs, and accommodate those the company can afford Such actions can contribute to keeping employee morale high even in the most difficult times

---

THE KNOW-HOW AND THE KNOW-WHY FACTORS

The Know-How Factor

In a high-technology company, the importance of having the most up-to-date know-how in all relevant disciplines is well understood Keeping abreast of the latest developments and advances in a large spectrum of relevant technoscientific fields poses problems even for some of the largest high-technology companies Facing the staggering costs of staying in the front line of technology, many high-technology companies form alliances to share expenses and risks as well as results In the industrialized world, some government institutions provide significant support to companies to keep national industry competitive in this most critical area of technological know-how One example is the funding by the European Community of such advanced research and development programs as "Eureka" and "Prometheus " The governments of the United States, Japan and many other countries follow similar policies

The question is what the management of a high-technology company can do internally, within its own jurisdiction (beyond alliances and participation in government-sponsored R&D programs), to advance state-of-the-art know-how in the company One sure approach is to avoid spending company resources in reinventing the wheel In the age of information and communication, everyone has convenient access to an immense and growing database of scientific and technological know-how In almost any field of science and technology, numerous papers are published monthly in the open literature Much of this material is available today on the Internet

Many young engineers and scientists are adequately trained to conduct competent literature searches before beginning their own research Unfortunately, this is not universally true Some engineers and scientists, especially those from the older generation, find it easier to start their own development work rather than do an exhaustive literature search This omission can result in duplication of work already done by others and a significant waste of valuable company resources To avoid such situations, the management of a high-technology company must require a literature search as an integral component of any company authorized project

To help members of the company's technical staff who have difficulties conducting database searches, a small number of professionals in this field should be recruited to help make the interface between the engineer or scientist and the databases as easy and convenient as possible Investment made to provide such assistance is largely offset by savings from avoiding the "reinvent" waste By enforcing such a policy, R&D work done in the company concentrates only on advancing knowledge and on adding value to work already done by others The know-how thus obtained becomes a synthesis of the latest advances achieved by others and new work done in the company

Another important company policy should be to encourage, develop, and use extensively relations with academic and research institutions. Although there are many difficulties in creating and maintaining a fruitful dialogue between industry and universities, rewards from success are well worth the effort Granted, success depends on the attitudes of both those in industry and in the academy Some universities do better than others in encouraging such relations with industry, but in most cases success depends on individuals To maximize the chances of success, the company should identify and assign the right type of person to this task Those assigned must readily understand the possibilities and the limitations existing in the academic world and be able to work between the needs of industry and the interests of the academy

The Know-Why Factor

The know-how factor is well understood in the high-technology industry but another extremely important factor, the know-why factor, is understood much less The know-why factor can be defined as the assembly of knowledge, experience, and intuition that gives certain individuals the ability to correctly predict future trends and needs in a given professional field, a market, or an activity A company may be very successful in developing a certain state-of-the-art know-how, but if this know-how is outside the prevailing trends of the marketplace, it will fail to keep the company competitive

The process and procedures necessary to obtain and maintain a high level of professional know-how are relatively well established Unfortunately, this is not the case with the know-why factor Although one can apply a number of techniques to detect a trend, forecast technology, or research a market, the usefulness and applicability of the results depend on their interpretation Interpreting all the available data and predicting the future correctly require special talents, and certain individuals are more gifted than others. For a high-tech company, identifying and promoting such individuals to appropriate positions of responsibility is extremely important

Knowing the right direction to take and when to take it is always more important than knowing how to get there Normally, finding a specialist with the appropriate know-how is not too hard Finding one who knows why and when certain things are more important than others is much more difficult Because this trait borders on art, a person's past performance or proven record of success in knowing why is probably the best guideline for a manager in selecting the right individuals for key positions By pointing out the right directions, such individuals can play a key role in determining the long-term success of research and development efforts. This type of prediction, when accurate, significantly increases the probability that a company will maintain its competitive edge in future markets

SUMMARY

This chapter begins with a discussion of innovation After the important roles innovation plays in high technology are explained, a distinction is made between different types of innovation. The particular opportunities and risks associated with technology-driven versus market-driven innovation are illustrated with current examples The major lessons that management of high-technology companies must learn from these examples are emphasized

Five major factors that are critical for the success or failure of a high-tech company are described and discussed. Some of these, like the human factor and the organization factor, are important in any type of business or industry However, in high technology, these factors become critical because of the special character of high-technology personnel and of the quick changes needed in the organizational structure of high-technology companies if a company is to stay competitive

The special character and typical behavior of the high-technology company's personnel are discussed Then, specific organizational issues affecting the high-technology company during the different phases of its growth and development are examined We see that as the company grows from a start-up to a multiproduct, diversified firm, it needs different organizational structures Reorganizing is therefore a vital process, if this process is interrupted or frozen because of management resistance to change, the future of the company may be jeopardized

Other factors, such as the innovation uncertainty factor, the management competence factor, and the know-how, know-why factors, are more specific and critical to the high-technology industry than to traditional industries. Analysis of the innovation uncertainty factor shows that it has three components: market uncertainties, technological uncertainties, and supply uncertainties Methods to cope with these conditions are proposed Cases of technological uncertainties and companies running into multi-technology risk situations are described and illustrated with examples Supply uncertainty is shown to result from the need to use novel and often unique components in a new product

The management competence factor is concerned with the manager's ability One may be a truly professional manager by achievement, by education, or by both Two management styles are described, with the conditions necessary to direct a high-tech organization successfully Enhancing team spirit is discussed, with suggestions to help managers align and motivate personnel around the objectives of the company

Finally, the well-known know-how factor, which is important in the high-technology industry, is compared to the less-known know-why factor Without special management attention to the latter, a company may be very efficient in activities that have little or no impact on its effectiveness in the marketplace

Some of the factors discussed here are so important that they deserve special chapters This is the case with the need and the methods to create a favorable environment for inventors and innovators This subject is treated in detail in chapter 3

For Further Reflection

1. What are the major difficulties with management of high-technology personnel? Why is it different from managing and motivating people in more traditional industry?

2. How does one stimulate a strong team spirit in a large high-technology company? What are the management styles that enhance motivation in a high-technology organization?

3. If a high-technology company is working mostly on large institutional projects, are there any market uncertainties? If yes, what strategies can decrease those uncertainties?

4. Give some examples of a multiple risk situation typical in high technology. What are the methods for decreasing such risk to an acceptable level?

5. Is it better to strive for a competitive advantage by somewhat unique product architecture, or by using the latest components available? Describe the advantages and disadvantages of each approach

6. If you want to establish high standards of excellence in a high-technology company, what are the most critical aspects to be addressed? How?

7. What are some of the effective methods to keep know-how in a high-technology company up to date?

8. What is the know-why factor and how does it relate to the promotion policy in a high-technology company? How can one identify people with a gift for the know-why factor?

9. What are the major risks and opportunities associated with technology-driven innovation? In reference to interactive TV, get an update on the present situation Analyze and explain what has changed since the article quoted in Case 2 1 was written Draw conclusions and make recommendations for management of companies engaged in technology-driven innovation

10. What are the major risks and opportunities associated with market-driven innovation? In reference to Case 2 2, "The Internet," get an update on the present situation Analyze and explain what has changed since the article describing this case was written. Draw conclusions and make recommendations for management of companies engaged in market-driven innovation

References and Further Reading

Afuah, Allan N , and Nik Bahram (1993) *The Hypercube of Innovation* Boston, MA: Sloan School of Management

The authors provide definitions and discuss basic concepts of innovation Innovation has frequently been categorized as either radical, incremental, architectural, modular, or niche, based on its effects on the competence, other products, and investment decisions of the innovating entity Often, however, an innovation is considered quite differently by different groups One that is considered architectural by the innovator/manufacturer may turn out to be radical to customers, incremental to suppliers of components and equipment, and something else to suppliers of critical complementary innovations These various faces of one innovation at different stages of the innovation value-adding chain are what the authors call the *hypercube of innovation*. For many high-technology products, a technology strategy that neglects these various faces of an innovation and dwells only on the effects of the innovation at the innovator/manufacturer level, can have harmful effects This is especially so for innovations whose success depends on feedback coming from lessons learned at customers premises

Bass, Bernard M (1985) *Leadership and Performance Beyond Expectation* New York: Free Press

Bennis, Warren (1992) *Leaders on Leadership Interviews with Top Executives* Boston: Harvard Business School Publications.

Blades, Jon W (1986) *Rules for Leadership Improving Unit Performance* Washington, DC: National Defense University Press

Bogue, E. Grady. (1994) *Leadership by Design Strengthening Integrity* San Francisco: Jossey-Bass

Bray, Stuart (1995) *Total Innovation How to Develop the Products and Services That Your Customers Want* London: Pitman

Briner, Wendy (1990) *Project Leadership* New York: Van Nostrand Reinhold

Byham, William, and Jeff Cox (1990). *Zapp! The Lightning of Empowerment How to Improve Productivity, Quality, and Employee Satisfaction* New York: Ballantine Books.

Chemers, Martin, and Roy Ayman, eds (1993) *Leadership Theory and Research Perspectives and Directions* San Diego: Academic Press

Clark, Kenneth E (1990) *Measures of Leadership* West Orange, NJ: Leadership Library of America

Conger, Jay A (1993) *Learning to Lead The Art of Transforming Managers into Leaders* San Francisco: Jossey-Bass

Copp, Newton H , and Andrew W Zanella (1992) *Discovery, Innovation, and Risk Case Studies in Science and Technology* Cambridge, MA: MIT Press

> The authors introduce the concepts of discovery innovation, and risk The book presents brief descriptions of selected scientific principles in the context of interesting technological examples to illustrate the complex interplay among science, engineering, and society Case studies include telegraphy and the origin of telecommunications, hydroelectric power, the airplane, and others

Cortese, Amy, and Robert D Hof (1995) "Looking for the Next Netscape." *Business Week,* 23 October, p 58

Covey, Stephen R (1990) *The Seven Habits of Highly Effective People Restoring the Character Ethic* New York: Simon and Schuster

Cox, Danny (1992) *Leadership When the Heat's On* New York: McGraw-Hill

Crockford, Neil (1986) *An Introduction to Risk Management* Cambridge, England: Woodhead

Crosby, Philip B (1990) *Leading, the Art of Becoming an Executive* New York: McGraw-Hill

Dessler, Gary (1993) *Winning Commitment. How to Build and Keep a Competitive Workforce* Cambridge, MA: MIT Press.

> The author takes readers behind the scenes at 10 of America's top companies and provides actual company documents, such as mission statements and interviewing and training aids

The book focuses on tools, techniques, and battle strategies that managers and supervisors can use to develop and retain highly committed, motivated workforces essential for long-term, high-performance results *Winning Commitment* is based on extensive research and actual company interviews with managers and workers at IBM, Delta Airlines, 3M, Federal Express, Saturn Corp , Mary Kay, Toyota, and others.

Frankel, Ernst (1993). *In Pursuit of Technological Excellence Engineering Leadership, Technological Change and Economic Development* Westport, CT: Praeger.

In this book, the author attempts to evaluate engineering as a profession and engineers as individuals He offers suggestions on how the role and function of engineers in Western countries, particularly the United States, could be moved into the mainstream of both short-term and strategic decision making in government, industry, and society and how their contributions can be emphasized Most important, the link between technological excellence and engineering leadership in society is argued and a menu is proposed for a more effective, compassionate, environmentally conscious, and responsible technological society

Greiner, L E (1972) "Evolution and Revolution as Organizations Grow " *Harvard Business Review,* July–August, 31–46

Harmon, A , et al (1995) "Where Is Interactive TV? Not in Your Living Room " *International Herald Tribune*, 7 August 1995, p 14

Hein, Eleanor C , and M Jean Nicholson (1990). *Contemporary Leadership Behavior Selected Readings* Glenview, IL: Scott, Foreman

Helgesen, Sally (1990) *The Female Advantage. Women's Ways of Leadership* New York: Doubleday Currency

Hitt, William (1993) *The Model Leader A Fully Functioning Person* Columbus, OH: Battelle Press

Jain, R K , and H C Triandis (1991) *Management of R&D Organizations—Managing the Unmanageable* New York: John Wiley

Jones, Stephanie (1993) *Psychological Testing for Managers* London: Piatkus

Katz, Ralph, ed (1988) *Managing Professionals in Innovative Organizations* Cambridge, MA: Ballinger

Langdon, Michael J (1993). *Where Leadership Begins Key Skills of Today's Best Managers* Milwaukee, WI: QSQC Quality Press

Levinson, Harry (1994) *CEO Corporate Leadership in Action* New York: Basic Books

Levy, Steven (1995) "Waiting for Spielberg " *Newsweek*, 29 May, p 42

Martin, Michael (1994) *Managing Innovation and Enterpreneurship in Technology Based Firms* New York: John Wiley

Matsushita, Konosuke (1991) *Velvet Glove, Iron Fist, and 101 Other Dimensions of Leadership* New York: PHP Institute

Pinto, J K , and D P Slevin (1989) "Critical Success Factors in R&D Projects " *Research-Technology Management* 32 (January–February): 31–35

Roberts, Edward B (1995) "Benchmarking the Strategic Management of Techology—I " *Research/Technology Management*, January–February, p 42

This article examines the role chief technology officers play in some of the largest research and development companies in the United States, Western Europe, and Japan, and how their role affects the performance of these companies The study finds that Japanese chief executive officers are more heavily involved in integrating technology with overall corporate strategy Chief technology officers of Japanese companies have stronger board-level participation and greater influence on overall company strategy U S firms are rapidly decentralizing control of R&D activities to their business units, whereas Japanese companies are moving in the opposite direction In search of resource leverage, companies worldwide are experiencing major shifts to acquiring technology from outside sources, relying increasingly on universities for research and on joint ventures and alliances for development These and other findings on strategic management of technology arise from a global benchmarking study of the 244 companies that account for approximately 80 percent of the R&D expenditures in Europe, Japan, and the United States

Roberts, Edward B , ed (1987) *Generating Technological Innovation* New York: Oxford University Press

Roberts, Edward B (1990) "Evolving Toward Product and Market-Orientation: The Early Years of Technology-Based Firms " Working Paper 27 Sloan School of Management, Cambridge, MA

> Research studies of 114 technology-based firms within the greater Boston area indicate evolution over the first several years after founding toward more product-oriented businesses and away from consulting and R&D contracting, and increased orientation of the founders to sales and marketing, with lessened emphasis on engineering In this article, Edward Roberts reports that the character of many of these firms changes over time Evolution toward market-orientation is manifested in many ways Firms' use of direct sales forces and sales representatives grows over time, as does their adoption of more formal mechanisms such as marketing departments, sales forecasting, and analyses of potential markets Greater orientation toward marketing in all its dimensions is especially true for multifounder firms, the single founder company being slower to evolve in the characteristics cited

Slater, Stuart (1992) *Gambling on Growth How to Manage the Small High-Tech Firm* Chichester, England: John Wiley

Thomson, R , and C Maybey (1994) *Developing Human Resources* Oxford, England: Butterworth-Heinemann

Twiss, B C (1993) *Managing Technological Innovation* London: Pitman

Urban, Glen L , Bruce Weinberg, and John R Hauser (1994) "Premarket Forecasting of Really New Products," Working Paper 104 Sloan School of Management, Cambridge, MA

> The authors explore some of the challenges in forecasting customer acceptance of products that revolutionize product categories or define new categories They describe a new method based on multimedia computing technology that allows an innovative company to accelerate information to consumers so they can react to a really new product in a full-information setting The application of this technology to forecasting the sales of electric vehicles is given as an illustration of what has and what has not yet been accomplished After reporting on the managerial implications for the electric vehicle, the authors discuss other applications and initial data on external validity

Utterback, James M (1994) *Mastering the Dynamics of Innovation* Boston: Harvard Business School Press

CHAPTER 3

Creating a Favorable Environment for Inventors

I n the previous chapter, we explained and emphasized the critically important role
innovators or inventors play in a high-technology company Some of the odd behavioral characteristics of these exceptionally creative people were discussed and
the need to create conditions that optimize their productivity was briefly mentioned.

In this chapter, we concentrate on methods and approaches for creating an environment within the industrial organization that encourages and promotes innovation
We examine how successful, innovative companies have addressed the issue, as reported in recent literature, and add to this some lessons and personal observations

In *Innovation and Corporate Strategy*, Quinn (1986) reported the ways that some
of the world's most innovative companies stimulate innovation Van de Ven (1986) reviewed the literature and concluded that "of all issues surfacing in meetings with over
30 chief executive officers of public and private firms during the past few years, *the
management of innovation was reported as the most critical*" (p 104) Among the questions raised by the chief executive officers, the number one question was "How can a
large organization develop and maintain a culture of innovation and entrepreneurship?" In the following sections, we cite and explain the most relevant findings from
these and other publications First, however, we need to address an issue not well covered in the literature the paradoxical need to stimulate innovation in a high-technology company.

THE NEED TO STIMULATE INNOVATION

At first, it may seem strange that innovation needs to be stimulated in high-technology,
innovative companies Such companies consider innovation the heart of their business
Therefore, it should flourish there naturally For developing and maintaining a culture
of innovation and entrepreneurship to be a central issue in the management of such
companies may seem a paradox However, a number of factors play a negative role with

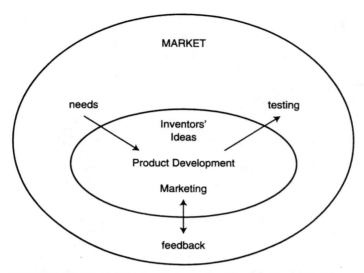

FIGURE 3 1 Typical Product Information Flow in a Start-Up High-Technology Organization

respect to encouraging innovation Those factors have to be fully understood and controlled by the management Otherwise, they may cause the extinction of all sparks of innovation, even in high-technology companies that critically depend on it

The first factor is associated with the growth and success of a start-up high-technology company into a larger, more organized firm Growth and success can create antibodies that fight innovation To understand the process, examine the start-up organization Figure 3.1 is a sketch of the informal, compact organization, typical in a high-technology start-up company

The inventor, the entrepreneur, or the small group of people with innovative ideas are in the center of the organization There are no formal boundaries between marketing, finance, development, and manufacturing Often the same individual takes part in two or more of those activities. For example, the entrepreneur may be in charge of securing financial support for the invention and at the same time of promoting its marketing Because the group is small in number, often less than 10 people, the information between members flows informally The feedback coming from market reactions has practically immediate impact on product development and manufacturing The people in the group are highly motivated and expect to be rewarded through the growing value of their equity in a successful company

Once the company has reached a market success, the situation changes, much as depicted in Figure 3 2 The bigger the success the company has with producing and marketing its product, the stronger will be the need to organize into a formal structure, with clear division of responsibilities Such a structure usually includes a number of departments, each responsible for performing a well-defined function Typically these functions are marketing, research and development (R&D), engineering, and manufacturing. The business success of the company becomes largely dependent on the performance of the marketing department. This department is headed usually by a se-

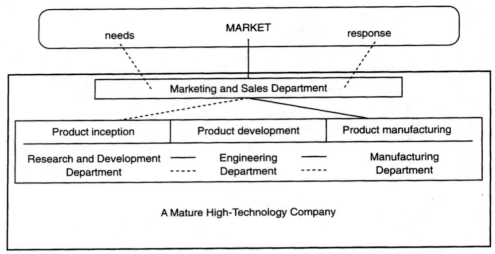

FIGURE 3 2 Typical Product Information Flow in a Mature High-Technology Company

Note ——— formal information flow

------informal information flow

nior executive, directly responsible for promoting and increasing the sales of the products The manufacturing department is headed by another executive whose main responsibility is to ensure smooth and efficient production of the products The innovators and inventors are then separated in yet another engineering department, if not set further apart in a research department, which hands the innovative ideas to engineering Engineering develops the ideas into working prototypes, these are handed to manufacturing for fabrication. Manufacturing in turn delivers the products to marketing, which moves them to the customers

Such an organization gradually develops a strong resistance to change, especially in the manufacturing division Indeed, the output of this division is optimal in terms of quality and quantity if the manufacturing process is repetitive, if materials arrive just in time from well-proven and reliable sources, and if no changes are introduced Changes tend to interrupt the process, to induce uncertainties, and to jeopardize the quality, the cost, and the delivery schedule of this department.

Because the company's income is strongly dependent on the quantity of products manufactured and sold, the power of the executives responsible for manufacturing and marketing in the organization grows stronger and stronger with the business success of the company Such executives, their divisions and the people working for them are perceived as the income generators, the money makers, research and development and engineering become "a necessary evil" that soak up company funding and valuable resources In more extreme cases the R&D and engineering personnel are perceived by the rest of the organization as "trouble makers" who never finish their tasks on time, always require additional changes, and disrupt the well-organized production process Comments like the following describe the attitude toward R&D and engineering typical in many high-tech companies "While we are sweating to generate some profit for the company, those guys in engineering enjoy playing with technology They exercise their hobby rather than concentrate on the business " "All we get from engineering are immature designs, impossible to manufacture in a smooth ordinary way," and so on

The second factor that creates an unfavorable environment for innovation is an incorrect management attitude and a skewed scale of rewards in the company Such attitudes and scales of values may develop gradually, without conscious direction

If the top management of the company does not have the competence and understanding necessary to put a stop to such attitudes, the situation may deteriorate to a stage where both monetary and nonmonetary rewards aggravate the problem even further People learn quickly to avoid taking any risk Managers and scientists involved with research and development begin to estimate conservatively the cost and the time necessary for the accomplishment of their tasks so as to look reliable in the eyes of top management Soon enough, such a process becomes a guarantee that the company will price itself out of any competitive innovative business

Solving these problems is certainly not a trivial matter As chief executive officer of a high-tech company, I have frequently asked myself what qualities I appreciated most in managers Over many years, I decided that one of the most important factors— one that helped determine the promotion of an individual to a position of higher responsibility—was the sense of reliability he or she could inspire, that the person would always deliver what was promised Talking to colleagues and observing the behavior of other managers confirmed the universal importance of this rule Clearly, the larger the organization, the more the manager has to rely on commitments made by other people Naturally, we appreciate those who do as they have promised and like even more the few who consistently do better than that

Rewarding high achievers for their better-than-planned performance is not only legitimate but most appropriate and motivating in almost any organization However, in high-tech, innovative companies, one has to take into account the difference between uncertainty and risk associated with planning of research and development activities as opposed to planning of more routine activities, such as manufacturing Manufacturing tasks are repetitive in nature and therefore relatively easy to measure and standardize, research and development tasks, however, are usually quite unique The uniqueness makes it much harder to compare estimates for future R&D work to any R&D tasks previously done in the company. The problem is further aggravated by the lack of internal or external standards for such tasks. Clearly, if research and development managers are measured by the same yardstick as manufacturing managers, they will have to take a much higher safety factor in their time and cost estimates to achieve a level of reliability similar to that of their manufacturing colleagues

The duty of top management in a high-technology company is to encourage research and development managers to avoid overly conservative estimation by adopting a more tolerant view toward delays and cost overruns for R&D tasks If an R&D manager accepts ambitious goals, the efforts made by his or her department to meet them can become a guarantee that the time and cost for performing such tasks in the company compare favorably with those of the competition On the other hand, if the R&D manager makes conservative estimates, to ensure meeting commitments, the manager may look reliable to top management, but that "good" performance may cause more damage than benefit to the business success of the company

MOTIVATION FOR INNOVATION IN A HIGH-TECHNOLOGY COMPANY

In large, high-technology companies, important, organizationally logical factors can work to suppress the motivation for change and discourage innovation The question of how to stimulate motivation for innovation in large companies has been treated by a number of authors. For example, Shapira and Globerson (1983) discussed an incentive plan for research and development workers Mito (1990) has described motivational factors for R&D employees in Japan Useful and relevant reading is provided by Loveridge and Martyn (1992) as well as Lowe and Lewis (1994) Treating the subject from a slightly different perspective, Drucker (1985) and Maidique (1980) described the role entrepreneurs and "champions" play in promoting innovation Analyzing these and other publications and comparing the views of their authors with what I have personally observed and experienced during the last three decades of managing high-tech employees leads me to the conclusions discussed in the following sections

How the Classical View on Motivation Applies to High Technology

The classical view on motivation examines the psychological needs of the individual, yet these needs have to be reviewed and adapted to the reality of the specific high-technology organization The classical view—as expressed, for example, by Maslow (1970)—suggests that there are layers of hierarchial importance of such needs In the first layer are the basic physiological needs such as food, water, and sleep. Once those needs are satisfied, the individual can pay attention to the next layer, which includes security—physical security, job security, and so on Then come the social needs, the need to be accepted and appreciated by others, followed by the next level, which includes ego needs such as the need for self-confidence. Finally, the highest layer includes the need for self-fulfillment and actualization, the desire to maximize self-development and satisfaction

For high-level people working in large high-technology companies, one can safely assume that the lower layers of Maslow's hierarchy are satisfied Therefore, effective motivating factors have to be found in the higher levels, with achievement, recognition, self-fulfillment, and so on The importance of the different factors, however, does vary with the age and seniority of the engineers, scientists, and researchers involved in the innovation process Therefore, we examine the different strategies appropriate for each case

Motivating Young Researchers

At the beginning of their careers, engineers and scientists aspire to be accepted in and belong to a prestigious work group where, normally, they are highly motivated to prove themselves as worthy members. The drive for achievement and professional recognition at this stage of their career largely exceeds their expectation of monetary rewards

Just being in an organization employing senior staff with excellent reputations, having the opportunity to work with and learn from people of recognized achievements, and, experiencing the professional challenge of the projects handled by the group are the primary drivers in the first five to ten career years The knowledge that they are engaged in an ambitious project, pushing the state of the art, provides ample motivation for truly creative and talented people

Another important factor for young engineers and scientists is the quality of life they can expect when joining a company The location of the company—how close it is to a winter or summer sports resort, to a prestigious university, or to other cultural institutions—plays a role that should not be neglected For example, Nathan Myhrvord, Microsoft's technology head, had this to say about the company's decision to open a research center in cooperation with Cambridge University in the United Kingdom "For some reason, not everybody wants to live in the rain-soaked, grunge-music-drenched environs of Seattle " (*Newsweek*, June 30, 1997, p 38) Hence, it is not merely by chance that many high-technology industries have sited their research laboratories near such amenities

Motivating Researchers in Mid-Career

For people in mid-career, factors such as status and organizational recognition gain more and more weight For them, material rewards become more important Even so, motivational drive depends on more than one element and the sum of the subjective weights the individual assigns to each of these factors is what finally matters Money, although very important at this stage, cannot substitute for personal fulfillment, recognition, and status for truly creative individuals On the other hand, the lack of adequate material reward can hardly be compensated by a combination of all the other factors

As explained in subsequent chapters, most high-technology companies go through cycles that include periods of financial difficulty During such cycles, managers must be concerned about retaining key creative personnel in the company rather than losing them to competitors Managers need to know how they can increase the probability of keeping the key people faithful and motivated, even in periods of company crisis

One family of methods aimed at increasing the attachment of key personnel to the company consists of stock option plans, pension plans, or similar designs granting substantial advantages to the individual who remains faithful to the company over a long period of time In periods of difficulty, when the company requests salary sacrifices from all its employees, a well-designed stock option plan may not only retain key people but may also become a strong motivator, mobilizing these personnel to work harder at getting the company out of its difficulty Such plans effectively link the fate of the company and its economic success to the material rewards, other than salary, that a key employee can expect

A temporary salary sacrifice has often been necessary, even in some of the best high-technology companies By some reports, for example, during the 1981–1982 recession, all the senior personnel in Intel agreed to add an extra working day, resulting in a 20 percent salary sacrifice, in order to bring new products to the marketplace faster This action helped to overcome the company's immediate problems while preserving the continuous employment of its key people

Another area that creates difficulties is providing sufficient organizational recognition to researchers who prefer, or are asked by the company, to continue their creative and innovative work rather than be promoted to prestigious managerial positions A company that fails to find effective solutions to this problem ends up promoting some of their most creative people who often become mediocre or even poor administrators A possible solution to this difficulty is discussed later in the chapter in the section titled "The Dual Ladder Reward Method "

To summarize, motivating researchers in mid-career is probably one of the most challenging and complex tasks for the manager of a high-tech company, especially those innovative people who have not moved to managerial positions Because of the complexity, no one single solution can be recommended Rather, the harmonized application of several of the methods mentioned here and those discussed in the next sections is more likely than any one method to bring the desired result

Motivating Senior Researchers

For our discussion, senior researchers are engineers and scientists approaching the end of their professional career This arbitrary definition does not include those young, outstanding, and bright researchers who reach senior position at mid-career and sometimes even earlier They are so strongly self-actualized that keeping their motivation high does not present a serious management problem

Motivating aging researchers who continue to perform mostly technical functions and have not moved to managerial positions is often a cause for concern to company management for several reasons First, considering the rapid pace of change in technology, keeping up to date with the latest developments is a formidable task Yesterday's know-how becomes marginally relevant today A vast amount of technological knowledge only a decade old may soon become totally obsolete and completely useless for gaining a competitive advantage in an innovative high-technology company Younger engineers with fresh knowledge and training are frequently more effective in applying the latest technologies than are their senior colleagues Naturally, these situations may lead to frustration, demoralization, and loss of motivation in aging researchers

Second, older researchers with a significant past performance record often compare themselves to colleagues their age who have been promoted to managerial positions of substantial power, influence, and respectability in the organization Frequently, these powerful individuals were encouraged to move to managerial functions precisely because their research performance was marginal compared to the performance of their more brilliant colleagues Later, individuals the company did not want to lose as researchers may become a problem for the company during their mid-career If management is unaware of, indifferent to, or just not sensitive to the existence of the problem, many formerly brilliant researchers become, by management's default, a liability to the company They are highly paid, frustrated individuals whose contribution to the company may become insignificant if not negative.

To minimize these problems and to keep the senior researchers in a high-tech company strongly motivated, management must actively address the issue and take concrete steps such as those described below

First, as employees enter the phase of senior researchers, they should be identified and tracked Because each individual in this group has probably been an important contributor to the company's success, he or she deserves special and specific attention by management

Second, although technology may have changed and the professional knowledge of the senior researchers may not be totally up to date, the experience accumulated by such individuals during a long career of successful research is extremely valuable Their methodology, their approach, and the lessons they have learned from success and failure in their technical activities remain highly relevant Hence, management should distinguish between technological know-how on one hand and experience on the other A younger researcher should be expected to have the most up-to-date knowledge, but his work should be supervised and reviewed by the more experienced, older researcher By formally requesting senior researchers to express their opinions and make recommendations on the work done by the younger fellows, the company makes the best use of the experience of these senior people By asking them to play a meaningful and important role, management promotes their self-esteem and motivation

Third, the company should find ways to show recognition and respect for senior researchers Emphasizing their achievements and contributions, using these as examples for the younger generation, is one way to proceed In this way, two desirable results can be achieved at the same time an increase in the motivation of senior researchers, and a signal to mid-career researchers that there is a meaningful role for them to play as they grow older themselves

CREATING A CULTURE OF INNOVATION AND ENTREPRENEURSHIP

Once we understand the motivating factors applicable to research and development personnel at different stages of their professional careers, we are ready to address the broader subject of creating a company culture that keeps, encourages, and promotes innovation In this section, some of the most important methods for achieving this goal are outlined

Scanning the literature, we can identify a number of approaches that have been applied by companies and organizations to promote innovation Because the problem is most acute in large companies and in big organizations, we concentrate here on approaches relevant for mature companies For example, Quinn (1986) reported on a two-and-a-half-year study of large, innovative companies and their strategies to achieve this goal Mito (1990) examined the experience of the Japanese Honda Motors, and Martin (1994) treated the entrepreneurial setting in small and large organizations These and other publications point out a large variety of specific solutions that have been applied in different business environments Nevertheless, one can detect some common trends that increase the probability of success

Identifying and Encouraging Champions and Entrepreneurs

The central figure in a start-up organization is naturally the inventor, the individual with the idea and the vision of creating a novel product In the case of mature high-technology companies, however, it is important to actively search for, identify, and encourage creative employees who propose new innovative products and are ready to fight for their realization

Many people from time to time have a good idea that could become successful if appropriately developed and introduced to the market Often, however, for lack of sufficient energy, enthusiasm, and perseverance, the practical realization of a good idea is postponed until some other company introduces the same or a similar product to the market In such a case, the only thing a frustrated inventor can do is tell his colleagues "Look, my idea was great "

The difference between an individual with a good, or even great, idea and a champion in a large high-technology company is the exceptional will power of the latter Whether the idea is original with that person does not really matter Often the innovator is not the champion Champions, however, are not only strong believers in an idea, whether theirs or not, they are also fighters, ready to "push walls" to see it materialized They are ready to work hard to overcome difficulties of any kind Champions will defend and protect the idea against all threats and convince everybody of the importance of its urgent realization for the best interest of the company, the customers, and sometimes for humanity

Good champions are often able to mobilize an army of believers in the idea or the product They can cut across the red tape and formal procedures of a bureaucratic organization and garner support to ensure that work for their project is treated with the highest priority in every department

Because many mature high-technology companies are in a stage of more or less advanced organizational paralysis with respect to innovation, the most frequent way an innovative product is developed successfully in such companies is by finding champions who will relentlessly overcome all the problems—technical, bureaucratic, and financial

In my conversations with colleagues in Europe and in the United States, I have often heard statements like these "In our company, there is always a champion behind every product" or "Why speak of long-term strategic planning? Our real product line is the result of sporadic or opportunistic initiatives of some *guru* in the company," or "It was obvious that our company should enter this or that field, but we could not find a champion, so today we are out of it " These expressions show the importance attached by top management in many high-technology companies to the role played by champions in their organizations.

Champions keep the spirit of innovation high in mature high-technology companies However, a few words of caution are due Sometimes the very useful characteristics of a champion, if pushed to the extreme, may become dangerous and even harmful for the company Many champions are indifferent to damage caused to other projects by the higher priority given to their own project "I am interested in my project; the company can go to hell" is a typical expression of this attitude If they become fanatically dedicated to their idea, they may develop mental blocks and subject blindness that prevent them from seeing and listening to objective reasons for reducing the pace or even dropping their favorite project altogether.

Entrepreneurs have many of the qualities of champions but usually have more realistic and balanced views of business realities They are generally more sensitive to the global needs of the company and take into account the economic, human, and commercial constraints while promoting an idea, product, or project In this sense, entrepreneurs are always preferable for the company unless the difficulties in creating a new product are so great as to require a champion's naivete and daring to launch an attack If this is the case, a champion may be the only solution, especially if success of the product is very significant to the company

Identifying champions and entrepreneurs even in a big company is not particularly difficult They find you, coming to you and to other members of management with all kinds of ideas and initiatives, you don't have to go looking for them The real problem might be distinguishing between the "enlightened" ones, or the true champions, and the empty shells The first type come with a proposal only after having done a significant amount of homework They have studied the problem and have convincing answers to most of the basic questions arising from their proposal They are ready to come with numbers, statistics, and technical solutions to defend their ideas

The second type, by contrast, usually start with some kind of "brilliant" idea or "very attractive" proposal but have vague or no answers to your second or third question Some time ago, one of the second type came to my office with the great idea for our company to diversify into the very lucrative field of ecology He pointed out that since the company was mostly active in defense electronics and the defense markets were shrinking, a move into the growing market of ecology would be a good idea Without telling him that the idea had already crossed my mind, I agreed with him and asked what particular field of ecology he proposed to enter

"Well," the answer came, "we have such a large spectrum of technologies in our company that it should not be too difficult to adapt some to the needs of ecology "

"O K " I said, "you must have some concrete idea in mind What is it?"

"This *is* the idea!" came the answer "Let's diversify into ecology!"

The real problem with champions and entrepreneurs in a high-technology company is providing effective management support and encouragement for their initiatives On one hand, you want them to be successful in fighting the rigidity of your organization, on the other, you do not want to break all rules and destroy the positive aspects of order and methodology in the company

One method that has met with success is to assign a senior manager with considerable power and entrepreneurial spirit as personal sponsor to the champion The champion should have direct access to the senior manager, whose door must always be open to the champion with little formality even if this means bypassing some intermediary level of management Getting managers to consent to this role will take attention, tact, and persuasive arguments from the highest level The role of the senior sponsor is extremely important This person must assume some of the responsibility for the unconventional shortcuts that help the champion achieve effective results At the same time, the manager must protect the global interest of the company He or she must be careful that the champion does not become prima donna.

This approach ensures effective support for the champions and encourages new initiatives to be brought to the management Soon, people learn that one efficient way to come closer to top management in a successful high-technology company is by becoming a champion or an entrepreneur for products and ideas that improve the competitive strength of the company

The High Management Involvement Method

One method that has been useful for both monetary and formal organizational recognition problems is high management involvement Any large organization usually has more than one hierarchy at the same time The most obvious one is, of course, the line-staff organizational hierarchy with the CEO or president at the top, the vice presidents, followed by the chiefs of departments and on down

Another hierarchy that exists informally in most organizations is the one established by management attention Some people in the organization have power and influence in the decision process because managers listen to their opinions This situation constitutes an informal power structure within many organizations The phenomenon can be purposely directed to show esteem and promote high motivation in researchers engaged in innovative projects, but because these researchers do not hold high positions of authority in the formal organizational hierarchy, management must be sensitive to the way this "open door" is perceived by those who are in official positions of power (Clutterbuck and Kernaghan, 1994)

There is one, straightforward way to achieve the goal of showing recognition and promoting researchers' motivation Managers at the highest reasonable level, and many times the CEO himself, should allocate a significant portion of their time to visit the researchers and the inventors, become genuinely interested in their work, try to understand their problems, and provide morale and effective administrative support Sometimes, high-level managers pretend they are too busy to get personally involved with the research and development work done by specialists Often, however, these managers have lost track of the rapidly changing technology and hide their apprehension of showing ignorance in a discussion with the researchers by consciously or unconsciously avoiding serious dialogue with them

My experience has shown me, time after time, that this is a groundless fear The specialists are quite aware that a CEO or a high-level manager knows less than they do in the narrow professional field of their specialization, they do not expect their managers to be up to date with the latest developments Specialists often are eager to explain their project and are proud to have someone of importance as their audience By asking pertinent questions, the CEO will not only create a feeling of involvement and participation but quite often will actually help resolve even professional problems Following are example questions that many times and in different circumstances have helped to create a constructive dialogue between the manager and the researchers

- What is the basic idea, "the heart," of the innovation, and what market needs does it address?
- What is the competition doing? What approaches are they taking?
- How is our product going to be better than the competition's product?
- Is our competitive advantage going to be stable for some time? How long before the competition can come up with a similar or better product?

- What are the risk areas? What are the major problems still ahead of us?
- What are we doing to reduce risk and resolve the problems?
- What are all the possible approaches for resolving these kinds of problems?
- Should we try two promising approaches at the same time?
- Is there anything I can do to help you?

In a number of cases, I have asked questions like these and helped researchers become more focused on the real problems that matter to the company Sometimes, by answering the questions, the researchers found solutions to problems that had been eluding them for weeks or months By describing to me alternative approaches, the solution all of a sudden became obvious to them

Often, the researcher needs assistance with some small administrative problem For example, the lab may need an accessory that could help the researcher significantly Trying to get the equipment through the normal channels may take months. With the help of the CEO, however, the accessory could suddenly arrive in the lab in days The result is a strong boost of the morale and the motivation of the entire research team and an effective speedup of the innovative process. Most important, the company learns by such examples that encouraging the innovative spirit is a major management objective, critical to the company's success

High management involvement has been applied in many successful high-technology companies Perhaps the most famous example is Soichiro Honda, from Honda Motors, who was known to participate directly with his researchers and engineers in design groups, discuss technical matters with them in detail, and enthusiastically support or disapprove engineering approaches (Sakiya, 1982) Such high management involvement does not have to go to the extreme of breaking all organizational rules On the contrary, if cleverly applied, this approach can be a formidable tool for promoting innovation and keeping the inventors in a large organization strongly motivated and inspired For further reading on the subject, see Lawer (1986)

The Dual Ladder Reward Method

Another method that has been applied—or at least attempted—in many large, high-technology companies is the "dual ladder " Kaufman (1974) noted that this approach "is generally formalized into parallel hierarchies: one provides a managerial career path, and the other advancement as a professional or staff member Ostensibly, the Dual Ladder promises equal status and rewards to equivalent levels in both hierarchies" (p. 24)

Sooner or later, the management of almost any high-technology organization that has reached a certain size and maturity is faced with the need to keep creative scientists and engineers happy without moving them to managerial positions Most naturally, the idea of creating a different scale of rewards for such people is raised However, the practical results have in many cases been rather disappointing Even so, we should discuss the merits and drawbacks for at least two reasons First, the idea is basically sound If applied without illusions and unrealistic expectations, it can contribute to the creation of a favorable environment and a company culture that promotes and encourages innovation Second, if managers are aware of some of the disenchantment of this method, they should be better prepared to avoid some of its problems

Supporters of the dual ladder method point to aspiration differences between people interested in bureaucratic versus professional careers as the basic justification for establishing two different scales of rewards They claim that professional employees are motivated by the desire to move their professional field forward whereas bureaucrats are motivated by the desire to move upward in the organizational hierarchy Professionals acquire status from their colleagues; bureaucrats acquire it from their superiors and subordinates

Although these arguments are quite true, we have seen that the motivating factors do change with age and seniority of the employees Hence, the important reason for using a dual ladder method is the need to convince creative, highly valued engineers and researchers to continue their contribution to the company as professionals despite their desire to take managerial positions and by doing so gain power, status, and respect. It is the company management, therefore, that strives to keep and to motivate its most valuable research people and to prevent them from moving out of R&D work and into the company bureaucracy The major push does *not* come from the theoretical desire of research workers to continue their contribution to a field of knowledge or their indifference to hierarchy and status

This distinction is extremely important if managers are to avoid some of the disappointments resulting from a misguided application of the dual ladder method If it were true that research personnel are self-motivated and uninterested in the company hierarchy, all a company would need would be a parallel ladder of professional titles. The professionals could "climb" their side of the dual ladder as the management and bureaucrats climbed theirs

In reality, the professional ladder has to be a true compensation for the research employee's consent to forsake hierarchical power and status In the *Columbia Journal of World Business*, L M Roth (1982) proposes a critical examination of the dual ladder approach to career advancement and makes the following recommendations for its successful application

1 The career paths defined by the Dual Ladder structure should be achievable and not just available on paper If the rewards associated with top-level positions are to motivate good performance, then individuals on the professional ladder must witness that their colleagues actually advance to the highest positions

2 Positions on the professional ladder should extend high enough to give professionals a truly challenging job

3 The rewards that are associated with the various ladders should be meaningful and appealing to the groups they aim to motivate In addition, they should be distributed equitably on the various ladders To insure some measure of equivalence between the different ladders, compensation packages for the parallel ladders should be identical at each of the levels

4. Organizational recognition of outstanding performance should go beyond well-publicized promotions Organizations should work at enhancing their professional environments with a variety of non-cash forms of recognition

5 The organization's performance appraisal system should be tailored to evaluate both individual contributor and managerial positions Unfortunately, most performance appraisal systems focus primarily upon management skills and are ill-designed to assess the skills of individual contributors

6　To insure that technical ladder promotions are based upon technical performance, a formal peer review committee should oversee the promotion consideration process for technical ladder positions

7　High-level specialists on the technical ladder should not be isolated from the top management decision-making group They should be actively involved in planning and decision-making activities of a technical nature Such a change in the traditional power bases of an organization will not only raise the status of technical contributors and improve their morale but will also lead to more balanced decisions.

8　It is essential that both management and specialists view the technical ladder as a legitimate and prestigious avenue of a career advancement Cultural commitment to the professional ladder implies recognition of the critical contributions of technical specialists to the achievement of organizational objectives

9　The Dual Ladder structure should be clearly communicated to employees early in their careers so that they will be aware of formal career paths and can use this information for their own career planning Employees should also be aware of long- and short-range job opportunities, as well as job requirements, so that they can take an active role in their career development

10　Finally, the Dual Ladder program should be evaluated regularly A close monitoring of the system will help to identify general problems that need to be addressed *

In our view, Roth's recommendations are certainly sound but not easily applicable in real life—especially recommendations 3, 5, 6, and 7 Roth himself points out in 5 that "unfortunately, most performance appraisal systems focus primarily upon management skills and are ill-designed to assess the skills of individual contributors " Overcoming this and other difficulties is not a simple task Managers should strive to apply these recommendations to the extent possible, combining them with some of the other methods recommended in this chapter

The Listen-to-the-Customer Method

It may sound trivial, but many important inventions came from sensing customers' needs and by creating a product that answered those needs Barnard and Wallace (1994) advocate using the voice of the customer as a strategic edge for breakthroughs in innovation We would not have to discuss something so obvious if there were not so many large, high-technology companies that consciously or unconsciously isolate their creative people and their research and development departments from direct contact with customers

Usually, the phenomenon begins with the creation of a marketing and sales department Gradually, all the responsibility for contact with the customers is assigned to this department In the same spirit, the after-sales service organization is soon recognized as an important factor for future sales, therefore, it is attached to marketing and sales All that is needed now is a minor personal conflict between the director of marketing and sales and the director of research and development—or even just the usual organizational bureaucratic rigidity This event will assure that an R&D engineer or scientist will never see another customer

---

* © 1982 *Columbia Journal of World Business* Reprinted with permission

Putting a buffer between the innovators and their potential customers is a mistake, even if the buffer is your best-intentioned sales department We know that a direct dialogue between the users and the engineers has often stimulated not just significant product improvements but also some totally new, sometimes revolutionary and different products—especially in the more specialized high-tech areas, such as medical electronics Here, fruitful dialogues between users and engineers has created an array of revolutionary new tools such as lasers for surgery, laparascopical interventions, ultrasound scanners, magnetic resonance scanners, and many more Without direct dialogue, users would not seek an innovative product out of ignorance of new technological possibilities Without the dialogue, even the most innovative minds could not guess a very specialized need that may be turned into a novel line of high-tech products

Managers must understand the importance of keeping close contacts between R&D personnel and the present and potential customers of the high-tech company The practical implementation of this principle has to be adapted to the company's specific strengths and markets Different companies have used varying approaches in applying this principle, as illustrated in Case 3 1

Hardware- and systems-oriented high-technology companies have also used the Beta-Site approach to get useful feedback from "friendly customers" before they begin quantity production and distribution of a novel product Usually, Beta customers receive significant incentives from the high-technology company for their consent to "suffer" the inconveniences of a not-yet-mature product These benefits range from the prestige of being the first in the marketplace to have the new product, the possibility to

---

CASE 3.1

An Example of Maintaining Close Contact with Customers: Microsoft

Microsoft—one of the most successful high-technology companies in the last decade—has devised a very effective method to maintain close contact with its worldwide customers Every new, innovative software package it develops is first distributed, free of charge, to a network of enthusiastic customers willing to serve as Beta-Sites or pilot-plants for Microsoft They are the first to try, apply, and benefit from the most up-to-date software, but at the same time, they provide an invaluable service to Microsoft First, with all the care the company takes to put out a "bug-free" product, the best way to assure that a new product has no problems is to subject it in a statistically significant quantity to real-life testing Microsoft does this and collects the feedback and criticism from these first users Then, the company corrects the problems identified by the Beta-Site users before the actual commercial release takes place, thus preserving its reputation as a reliable source of bug-free software Second, in the feedback received from the Beta-Site customers, there is a bonanza of comments, suggestions, and proposals for improvements These play an important role in the design of the next-generation product

An Example of Keeping Close Contact with Customers: Sony

Another method used by many high-technology companies consists of rotating its engineering staff from research and development to sales, to after-sales service, and then back to research and development Successful examples of this kind have been reported mostly by Japanese companies Lyons (1976), in *The Sony Vision* noted. "Soon after technical people are hired, Sony cycles them through weeks of retail selling Sony engineers become sensitive to the ways retail sales practices, displays and non-quantifiable customer preferences affect success" (p 74)

influence and adapt the product to their specific needs, up to a straightforward price reduction—all for being a friendly customer Again, the benefits for the high-technology supplier resulting from direct dialogue between its engineers who created the product and the real-life users are certainly worth all the advantages granted to the Beta-Site customers As with Microsoft, this company can then introduce a better, bug-free product to the market as it collects user ideas for the next-generation products

A different way to maintain connections with customers is illustrated in Case 3.2 For cultural and other reasons, this method has been less popular in the West Instead, companies in Europe and the United States usually form mixed teams of personnel from research and development and sales, these teams are then tasked with special assignments to make periodic visits to a significant sample of present and potential customers The teams collect and report the users' opinions, satisfaction, or criticisms on performance of the company's products together with suggestions for their improvement

Many companies rely on professional shows, exhibitions, and congresses for opportunities to strengthen the dialogue between the designer and the customer Meeting customers and looking at the competition fully justifies sending some of the most creative and imaginative people in the company to participate in such events When a company's management fails to understand the importance of this principle, they may limit company participation to only marketing and sales personnel This action may save the company some petty cash but deprive it of most valuable information about current needs and trends

Blue Team–Red Team

Another approach that has been applied in large companies and organizations is the creation of two competitive teams for development of the same product The idea here is to increase motivation by creating the challenge of competition, which in turn stimulates innovation

Although this approach requires a significantly higher initial investment and cannot be applied in general situations, in a number of cases it may be an effective and worthwhile approach For this to be so, a number of prerequisites are usually needed

First, there must be a significant reward for the company that achieves higher performance and early market appearance Second, the company must have enough human resources and competence to be able to field two genuinely capable teams with roughly equal chances for success Third, the company must have established the right "sportive spirit" whereby the losing team is easily reintegrated into the organizational structure and genuinely appreciated for having given the winner a good fight

Unless these conditions are met, applying this approach can be not only expensive but also counterproductive It can create serious morale problems, or worse, acceptance of compromise solutions so as to "keep everybody happy "

A variant of the Blue Team–Red Team approach, which we shall call the "Red Competitor," avoids to a large extent the drawbacks of the teaming described earlier This approach uses the strongest real competitor as the Red Team Indeed, in a nonformal way, that is what happens naturally during the development of any innovative product. The team responsible for the development of a product always tries to improve on the existing products or to come out ahead of the competition, which may be developing a similar product

The difference between the informal competition and the Red Competitor is the creation of a small, in-house Red Team that monitors and "represents" the work being done at the same time by the real competitor This Red Team, which may be as small as just one person, is assigned the formal task of obtaining as much information as possible on the technical and tactical approaches adopted by the major competitor. In addition to information gathering, the Red Competitor is to simulate possible competitor moves and present a constant challenge to the Blue Team, which actually develops the novel product in the company Periodic design reviews are scheduled in order to compare advantages and disadvantages of the company development with what might be the performance and status of the product developed by the major competitor

This variant avoids the problems associated with the classical Blue–Red Team approach In addition, it performs an extremely important function by increasing the awareness of the R&D team to what their major competitor is doing or is capable of doing—within reason. In this very competitive world, the probability of having a real competitor for almost every innovative product is quite high; therefore, the cases are rare in which management resorts to creating and financing two full-size competitive teams in the same organization for lack of a real external competitor The only pitfall to be avoided with this approach is to choose a weak Red Competitor The person or the small team representing the work done by the competition must be highly professional, analytical, imaginative, and with a proven record of competence in the field if they are to be respected and sufficiently influential in the game-playing decision process The more realistic the Red Competitor is, the more this role player will motivate the in-house development group, the Blue Team

Entrepreneurial Greenhouses

The next management approach—the entrepreneurial greenhouse method—if not unique to high technology is surely more commonly found there than in more traditional industries In the high-technology industry, a relatively larger number of top-level managers come from entrepreneurial backgrounds Some remember the not-sodistant past when they began their careers as pioneers in a successful start-up company From their positions of responsibility in a large, high-technology corporation, they can easily compare the favorable environment of the small, start-up organization—that breeds innovation and supports inventors—to the one in a large, formally organized company with all its rigidity It is understandable that a number of large, high-technology companies such as Hewlett-Packard, 3M, and others have attempted to recreate a kind of greenhouse within the big organization to encourage innovation.

This approach is characterized by a number of cost centers with relatively low overhead burdens, each responsible for the development of an innovative product The number of personnel in each cost center group is kept small At the heart of the group is usually an entrepreneur, an inventor, or a champion This central individual plays the critical role of keeping the small team highly motivated and enthusiastic, similar to the case in a start-up company Just as a greenhouse helps small plants thrive, the nurturing effect of the corporate greenhouse can enhance the chances for growth of innovative products when each gets individual and appropriate attention

The advantages of this approach are obvious However, there are some significant differences between a real start-up and an artificial greenhouse

First, in a real start-up, both the penalties and the rewards for failure and success are much higher When they are successful, the members of a start-up can reasonably expect to become wealthy in a relatively short time When they are unsuccessful, their company is out of business, sometimes with significant losses to the people involved In a greenhouse within a large organization, the individual rewards for success are usually limited and modest On the other hand, if the product developed by the group is not a commercial success, no individual is expected to pay a personal price for the failure

The Start-Up Subsidiary Method

The start-up subsidiary is a variant of the entrepreneurial greenhouse method, designed to resolve most of its drawbacks It can be applied independently or as a continuation of the greenhouse method

The basic idea is simple Why not combine the creativity and flexibility of a start-up organization with the financial stability of the large company by creating a separate subsidiary devoted to the development and marketing of a new product? The resulting entity should have the best of both worlds On one hand, an independent business entity can emulate much better the conditions existing in a genuine start-up, where rewards for success of key personnel are closely linked to the business success of the subsidiary On the other hand, the subsidiary can count on and use all the know-how and industrial infrastructure available in the mother company to accelerate the development and industrialization of its product

Some large companies prefer to "grow the seeds" of an innovative product in a greenhouse exactly as described in the previous section, but as soon as the concept is proven and the first prototypes are successful, a new subsidiary is created for the exploitation and commercialization of the product If the researchers and the staff working on the innovative product in the greenhouse stage—within the mother company— know from the beginning that they will be offered stock options or another appropriate form of equity in the subsidiary, the situation can approach the same kind of motivation for success that exists in a real start-up To strengthen the similarity even further, the greenhouse team must understand that it has no personal future in the company if the product is a commercial failure. From the beginning, there will be only two outcomes for the greenhouse personnel: if the product is a success, they join the subsidiary; if the product is a failure, they leave the mother company and start looking for other jobs

In practice, the success–failure provisions are not easy to implement In Europe, with its strongly unionized labor force, it is much easier to implement the "carrot" without the "stick " Even in the United States, managers should expect serious difficulties if people working on a greenhouse project are not willing to move from a stable and secure company into a start-up subsidiary unless they can insure their social benefits, pension plans, and other perquisites If the idea for a new product comes from within the large company's organizational structure, there is little one can do to avoid such problems However, companies have been successful in transferring a greenhouse into a subsidiary, especially if the market success of the product seems assured and if truly lucrative conditions are offered to the personnel transferred from the mother company to the new subsidiary

To avoid the problems we've discussed, some companies prefer to buy a start-up or create an independent start-up company for the specific purpose of developing a new product. This is typically the case with large corporations that have developed a holding type of structure, that is, the corporation controls a large number of independent entities—some big, some small—but all fitting the overall corporate strategy This approach has been implemented by more centralized companies, such as IBM and others, with the purpose of creating a start-up-like, favorable environment for inventors and innovators that is as authentic as possible

When the operation begins in an entirely new entity such as a specially created subsidiary, most of the personnel problems described earlier can be avoided However, this method does not contribute to the motivation and encouragement of personnel in the mother company to generate innovative ideas and promote new initiatives In addition, with all the help the mother company offers the new subsidiary, there is generally a large degree of duplication in the subsidiary of laboratory and other capacities already existing in the mother company The management of a high-technology company interested in implementing this method should be aware of these pitfalls and reduce their impact as much as possible

Using the Greenhouse Method to Transfer Military High Technology to Commercial Use

The transfer of military high technology for use in commercial markets became particularly important after the disintegration of the Soviet Union in the early 1990s The defense high-technology industry, in both the West and the East, used to employ hundreds of thousands employees and produce sophisticated products for a trillion dollar market In the mid-1990s, the drastic cuts in military budgets in most countries created an urgent need to restructure and transform this industry The problem is so huge that the process of restructuring is far from finished in the West In the East, where most of the high-technology industry served the needs of the military, a decade may be needed to resolve the problem

The topic is of interest here because creating a new, separate entity has proven to be one of the most effective ways to transfer military technology to commercial use Many defense-oriented companies that have been successful in producing military high-technology products have had extreme difficulty in transferring their technology to the needs of the civil market The false starts, disappointments, and wasted resources are a roadmap for how not to accomplish the transition from military to commercial high technology Among the most common reasons for failure is the attempt to diversify from within—merely to reassign part of the defense company personnel to deal with commercial products

For many reasons, diversification from within usually fails Among the most important ones are the lack of sufficient flexibility, the lack of an appropriate culture, and the lack of a thorough understanding of the market. Most successful examples of transfer from military to commercial high technology have avoided or substantially reduced those problems by creating start-up subsidiaries specifically devoted to the commercial market

By being small and separated from the mother company, the subsidiary reacts much faster than the heavy, bureaucratic, defense-oriented high-technology company The people in the subsidiary know that their fate depends on their business success and they adapt faster than their counterparts in the mother company to the needs of the market In a relatively short time, they develop a culture that allows them to think, act, and behave like other commercial organizations In such a greenhouse, the spirit of innovation grows much more easily than in a large company. Finally, being separate, they have a better chance to attract a partner who has an understanding of and connections in the commercial market and who can bring them marketing experience—a most important factor for success

SUMMARY

This chapter was devoted to problems of creating a favorable environment for inventors and preserving the spirit of innovation The discussions and the solutions offered apply mostly to large and mature high-technology companies, as the problem rarely exists in young, start-up companies. The basic reasons for suppression and discouragement of innovation in large organizations were identified and explained The effect of wrong management attitudes in aggravating those problems even further and jeopardizing the future of the company was examined

Next, we explored how to motivate people and how to encourage new ideas and initiatives in a large, high-technology company, noting that the motivating factors playing a strong role at the beginning of a researcher's career should be complemented and replaced by other factors later in his or her professional life Hence, the appropriate management attitudes applying to young researchers, to researchers at mid-career, and to senior researchers were discussed and recommended

Seven of the most important methods for creating a culture of innovation and entrepreneurship were described and illustrated with practical examples First, we described the role of a champion and his or her critical importance for moving an innovative idea through the rigidity of a formal organizational structure Then, we looked at other methods for fostering a young, dynamic, innovative spirit the high-management involvement method and the dual ladder method. Their promises and drawbacks were shown, together with suggestions for improvements

A fourth, the listen-to-the-customer method, was shown not to be as trivial as it might seem at first glance Practical ways for a high-technology company to implement this method in real life were given The fifth method—Blue Team–Red Team—exploits the creativity stimulated by competition Such friendly competition has both advantages and difficulties, which were explained so that the reader could make an educated use of the method

Finally, the greenhouse and the subsidiary methods were shown to have a lot in common. They both try to emulate the favorable environment that exists in a small, start-up company environment, which encourages inventors and innovation Whereas the entrepreneurial greenhouses remain within the mother company structure, the subsidiary takes the method a step further in trying to reproduce the same motivating forces that are powerful and effective in a real start-up This seventh and last method was shown to be of particular relevance and interest to large, defense-oriented high-technology companies wishing to diversify and move into the commercial market.

To conclude, we recommend and emphasize the combined use of the methods examined in this chapter. They are by no means mutually exclusive. On the contrary, they are very complementary Each one is better adapted to certain situations than others and should be used in harmony with the others in different contexts Whereas some of the methods can and should be applied permanently, such as the high-management involvement method, others—Blue Team–Red Team—are more appropriate in specific time frames to address particular needs under well-defined circumstances

For Further Reflection

1 Why may a high-technology company, based on innovative products, have a problem with keeping an innovative spirit among its employees? What are the major factors working to the detriment and suppression of innovation in a high-technology company?

2 How do classical views on motivation apply to high technology? What are similarities and differences between motivating in the high-technology environment and in the traditional one? Outline the basic approaches for increasing the motivation of researchers during the different phases of their professional careers.

3 Why are champions so important in the high-technology industry? What are the negative aspects of champions' typical inclinations and actions, and how can a manager contain them within acceptable limits?

4 What are the major problems in applying the high management involvement method? What are its advantages?

5 What major problem is the dual ladder reward method supposed to solve? What conditions have to be observed to obtain effective results from the application of this method?

6 Doesn't every company always listen carefully to the needs and wishes of its customer base? Why and when is it appropriate to apply a "listen-to-the-customer" method in high technology? Enumerate and explain a few practical ways to implement this method

7 Describe situations appropriate for the Blue Team–Red Team method as a tool for promoting innovation in a high-technology company. What are some practical ways to structure these teams? Of what should one be careful when applying this method?

8   What is an entrepreneurial greenhouse? Comment on the motivating factors and compare those existing naturally in a true start-up company with those of a created greenhouse

9   What problems is the start-up subsidiary method designed to solve? Is there a difference in the approach if the initiative comes from outside the mother organization as opposed to initiative coming from within the large, high-technology company?

10 Prepare a summary of situations that call for the application of each one of the seven methods described in this chapter Are these methods mutually exclusive? Develop a scenario of a practical situation and propose the appropriate mix of some of the methods described.

References and Further Reading

Barnard, William, and Thomas F Wallace (1994) *The Innovation Edge Creating Strategic Breakthroughs Using the Voice of the Customer* Essex Junction, VT: Oliver Wight

Clutterbuck, David, and S Kernaghan (1994) *The Power of Empowerment Release the Hidden Talents of Your Employees* London: Kogan Page

Drews, T R (1977) "Motivational Factors Relevant to R&D Employees " *Industrial Management,* July–August, pp 37–39

Drucker, Peter F (1985) *Innovation and Entrepreneurship Practice and Principles* London: Heinemann

Kaufman, H G (1974) *Obsolescence and Professional Career Development* New York: AMACOM

Lawer, E E (1986) *High Involvement Management* San Francisco: Jossey-Bass

Loveridge, Ray, and Martyn Pitt (1992) *The Strategic Management of Technological Innovation* Chichester, England: John Wiley

Lowe, Phil, and Ralph Lewis (1994) *Management Development beyond the Fringe A Practical Guide to Alternative Approaches* East Brunswick, NJ: Nichols

Lyons, N (1976). *The Sony Vision* New York: Crown

Maidique, M (1980) "Entrepreneurs, Champions and Technological Innovation " *Sloan Management Review* Winter

Martin, Michael J C (1994) *Managing Innovation and Enterpreneurship in Technology Based Firms* New York: John Wiley

Maslow, A (1970) *Motivation and Personality* New York: Harper

Mito, Setsuo (1990). *The Honda Book of Management· A Leadership Philosophy for High Industrial Success* London: Kogan Page

Quinn, J B (1986) "Innovation and Corporate Strategy: Managed Chaos," in *Technology in Modern Corporations*, ed Mel Horowitch Elmsford, NY: Pergamon Press.

Roberts, Edward B (1991) *Entrepreneurs in High Technology Lessons from MIT and Beyond* New York: Oxford University Press

The ingredients for success in starting and developing a technology-based company aren't obvious In *Entrepreneurs in High Technology,* Edward Roberts, a professor at the MIT Sloan School of Management, offers entrepreneurs information on starting, financing, and expanding a high-tech firm His book reveals the results of research conducted over 25 years on several hundred high-tech firms; it reflects the author's own insights gained from first-hand experience as a company founder, director, and venture capitalist

Roth, L. M (1988) "A Critical Examination of the Dual Ladder Approach to Career Advancement," in *Readings in the Management of Innovation,* second edition, by Tushman, M L, and Moor, W L New York: HarperCollins Publishers Section 4, pp 275–292

Sakiya, T (1982) *Honda Motors The Men, the Management, the Machines* Tokyo: Kodansha International

Shapira, R, and S Globerson (1983) "An Incentive Plan for R&D Workers " *Research Management* 26, no 5: pp 17–20

Van de Ven, A H (1986) "Central Problems in the Management of Innovation " *Management Science* 32, no 5: pp 103–107

CHAPTER

Minimizing the Research and Development Cycle

In the life span of a high-technology product, one can normally distinguish between four distinct cycles research and development (R&D), manufacturing, marketing, and after-sales support. Each of these cycles may be subdivided into several stages Research and development, for example, usually includes an inception or concept definition stage and a development stage

The research and development cycle is probably the most critical phase in the entire life of a product Much as the life of an individual is affected by the months preceding birth and by early infancy, so does the R&D cycle determine to a large extent the market success or failure of a product (Chase and Aquilano, 1985) During the R&D cycle, the most important product parameters are determined the basic characteristics of the product, its performance compared to competitor products (Utterback, Meyer, Tuff, and Richardson, 1992), its future manufacturing cost, and other critical parameters

Because of the importance of this cycle for putting a competitive edge on the product, logically, it should be allowed all the time necessary to achieve the best possible advantage over the competition (Meyer and Utterback, 1995) Unfortunately, in the dynamic business of high technology, for reasons explained later, allotting unlimited time to development is inappropriate. If the high-technology product arrives too late on the market, it will lose most if not all the market advantages it is designed to achieve

THE NEED FOR SHORTER TURNAROUND TIMES

Unlike the goods of traditional industries, which commonly have life cycles extending over a number of decades, the products of high technology have much shorter market life spans. The real product of the high-technology industry might be considered innovation, which by nature does not last long. Innovation is what captures the marketplace,

---

CASE 4.1

The Computer Life Cycle Example

The first generations of commercial computers introduced by IBM in the 1950s had a useful market life of more than a decade After the introduction of the System 360 in the mid-1960s, IBM maintained its dominant market position until the arrival of the minicomputers Then, companies like Digital, Data General, and others started challenging IBM from the low end of the business The pace of competition continued to accelerate, and the viability of machines shrank from 10 years to 8 years, then only 5 years, then 3, and 2 Finally, in the early 1990s, with the massive success of the desktop and laptop computers, it dropped to less than a year

---

with many products being replaced by newer models in an ever increasing pace Probably the best example of this phenomenon is the rapid evolution in the computer market (see Case 4 1)

In the competition to lead the market, the situation with other high-technology products may be somewhat better: Communication systems or radar systems, for example, may remain viable for several years On the other hand, software products like the popular spreadsheet of LOTUS have seen more and more frequent updates in order to face the competition of MS-EXCEL, QUATRO-PRO, and similar products coming to the market with newer versions every several months Even the more traditional industries are shortening the time between models by exploitation of computer technology, automation, and robotics The Japanese industry was among the first to sense the trend and introduce the concept of continuous innovation Under this concept, between two revolutionary models are many evolutionary improvements, with new features coming to the market almost continually Such concepts are in strong contradiction with traditional organizational thinking, which strives for product lines that are steady, long term, and without modification Now, many companies in the West are rethinking and reorganizing in order to meet the Japanese challenge

For any high-technology product, and especially for market-driven innovative products, there is a window of opportunity for market exploitation that is constantly shrinking in length as the competition brings new products more and more frequently This window of opportunity is the period in which the new product faces no or low competition in the marketplace Comparison of respective opportunities for market exploration can be seen by looking at the product cash flows overtime The typical traditional industry product cash flow is illustrated in Figure 4 1

After the investment made during the research and development cycle, represented in Figure 4 1 by a negative cash flow, the product begins to return a positive income As long as it has only limited competition, the window of opportunity remains open If the window stays open long enough, the product returns a nice profit on the investment

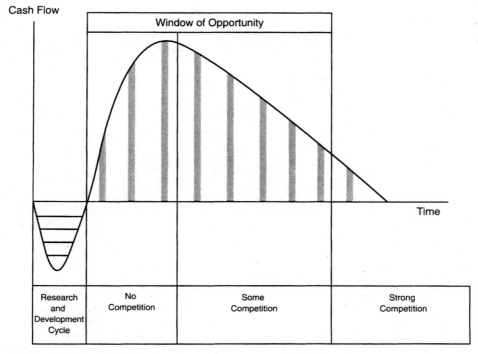

FIGURE 4 1 The Classic Product Cash Flow

For a high-technology product, one usually sees a shorter window of opportunity, as shown in Figure 4 2 Here Project A and Project B represent the development and the marketing phase of the same product Project A, which was introduced before the competition came up with an equivalent or better product, has been able to generate a positive cumulative cash flow, with a good return on the investment made during the R&D cycle Project B, on the other hand, shows that exactly the same product, introduced into the same market but at a time when some competition already existed, results in a negative cumulative cash flow. Note that the investment made during the longer R&D cycle of Project B is no higher than the one for Project A

The lesson to be learned from Figure 4 2 is that in high technology, a concentrated R&D effort is worthwhile It pays to invest whatever is necessary—money, equipment, and people—to shorten the R&D cycle and introduce the high-technology product to the marketplace much before the competition makes a viable entry of its own This procedure can be formulated in quantitative terms as follows

If *Inv[dT]* is the investment necessary to advance the time to market a product by the amount *dT*, the investment is justified if

$$Inv[dT] \text{ is smaller than } dP * dT$$

where *dP* is the profit differential between what the product can return before the level

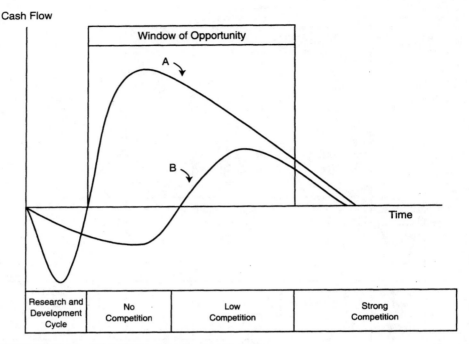

FIGURE 4 2 The High-Technology Product Cash Flow

Note: A = cash flow of a product launched early to the market
   B = cash flow of a product launched late to the market

of competition is increased and what the product can return after the competition is ready with a competing product

A good lesson on the "window of opportunity" notion and its importance for the commercial success of a high-technology product can be learned from the PowerPC case (Case 4 2) This illustration demonstrates that three of the most competent high-technology companies in the world may pay the price for missing the window of opportunity for their PowerPC.

Another factor that also emphasizes the need to move into the market rapidly with a high-technology product is the phenomenon of "vanishing need" This phenomenon is illustrated in Case 4 3.

Despite these and other examples, some authors still challenge the idea that to stay competitive, a high-technology company must organize for shorter R&D turnaround times (Meyer and Utterback, 1992) Others accept the need but warn that a company that has not made the effort to learn and apply the appropriate methods for successful R&D cycle time reduction may find itself facing a financial disaster Utterback et al (1992) noted the need for balance "While faster may be better, speed brings with it pressures that, for certain types of technological ventures, can lead to failure if they are not clearly understood and managed Speed is relative to the capability of the venturing company and to the nature of the venture it is attempting" (p 5) This

---

CASE 4.2

The PowerPC Example

In 1991, IBM, Apple, and Motorola joined forces to break Intel's hold on the microprocessor market For that purpose they established a joint venture known as Somerset By taking advantage of the design and manufacturing powers of Motorola and IBM and the volume purchase potential that Apple and IBM could guarantee, the partners were virtually assured of success

In an article, "Time May Have Passed the PowerPC" (*Business Week*, 4 March 1996), Ira Sager and his colleagues raised serious doubts regarding the PowerPC's future

> As it is, Somerset hasn't even come close to its goal of posing a serious challenge to Intel Corp 's dominance in microprocessors . Somerset fell behind schedule on more powerful versions of the PowerPC chip. "Three years ago, they had it in their hands," says Jon Rubinstein, president of Firepower Systems Inc , one of the few companies outside the Somerset trio to use the PowerPC But technical difficulties, internal bickering, and management upheavals delayed successor chips by 18 months Says Sun CEO Scott G McNealy: "The PowerPC is on really shaky ground "

Clearly, if the companies involved had made it their priority to keep the project on schedule, the probability of missing the window of market opportunity for the PowerPC would have been much lower

---

CASE 4.3

The STACKER–IBM Example

At the beginning of the 1990s, many P C users found their hard disks, which then typically had 40 million byte (MB) capacities, too small to contain newer generations of powerful software Instead of replacing their hard disks with disks of higher capacity, a relatively expensive operation at that time, thousands of P C users chose to buy a software product that proposed to double the disk's holding power Software packages, offering this expansion, like the STACKER package, became so popular that by 1993 IBM found it necessary to introduce such a package, called "Double Space," in their MS-DOS 6 0 version This program was subsequently improved in the newer MS-DOS 6 2 and 7 0 versions launched a year later At the same time, however, driven by the need for higher disk capacity and using the advances in relevant technologies, the manufacturers of hard disks came to the market with products of 500 MB, 1000 MB, and 2000 MB so competitively priced that the need for double-space software vanished

observation underscores the need to understand what factors are responsible for the length of the research and development cycle and how to reduce its duration

MAJOR FACTORS INFLUENCING THE LENGTH OF THE RESEARCH AND DEVELOPMENT CYCLE

The amount of time necessary for research and development is affected by a number of elements Among these are the size of the innovative jump desired—how ambitious the project is Clearly, the more ambitious the project, the larger will be the number of problems the company must resolve to be ready for production and the longer the time necessary to do so Another factor is the experience and talent available in the R&D team of the company In general, all the critical factors for success that were presented and discussed in chapter 2 play a role and influence the amount of time that must be spent in the research and development cycle

In this chapter, we focus on three elements that have direct implications for management policy and on the approaches a company may take to shorten the research and development cycle First, we deal with *technological uncertainty and innovation risk* This was introduced in chapter 2 and recognized as a critical factor for success. The second factor, *supply of critical materials and parts*, was also explained in chapter 2 Here we concentrate on how this element affects the length of the R&D cycle The third factor, *bottlenecks in the R&D organization*, has not been discussed previously, so we examine it in depth here, especially as it is not well understood by managers in many high-technology companies

Technological Uncertainties and Innovation Risk

Innovation implies uncertainties and risks Even if, to reduce risk, a company attempts to develop an innovative product by using proven technologies, the very act of combining these technologies in a new manner creates risk It is the *combination*, which has never been tried before, that may generate unexpected surprises

Anything done for the first time may not work right away, and the more time the inventors need to fix it, the longer will be the R&D cycle The length of the research and development cycle grows as the number of innovations in the development process increases (Smith and Eppinger, 1992) The process may become extremely complex as interdependencies are introduced A modification introduced in one part of the product can demand modifications in other parts, which then have to be adapted to the new configuration

Examining some typical situations can help us distinguish between technological uncertainties and innovation risk This distinction can help us devise methods for reducing the length of the research and development cycle

Technology Uncertainties

Uncertainty is associated with a lack of sufficient information This is the case when the research and development organization lacks adequate information on the successful performance of certain elements that are critical for achieving the competitive edge in a new product Typically, this happens when such components are produced by outside vendors. Development of the product may require a new technology, a new material, or a new process (Smith and Eppinger, 1992), until these pieces are truly available and reliable, the project must deal with technological uncertainty The technological uncertainties in this situation are external and outside the control of the company developing the product In such cases, the research and development organization does not have enough information to quantify the uncertainty and to assign it a probable risk level For an example of technological uncertainties, refer again to Case 2.4 in chapter 2.

Innovation Risk

Risk is associated with the probability that a given event will occur In the strictly mathematical sense, one can assign a valid probability only when dealing with large enough populations or with some kind of repetitive process. In our case, we are dealing with the development of a product having rather unique qualities. Therefore, we have no statistically significant population or repetitive events However, if the research and development organization possesses sufficient information about the development process, it should be in a position to assign some subjective probabilities to the success of the process and thereby quantify the risk Such subjective probabilities are normally based on previous experience with similar events Although using *similar* experience is not as rigorous as applying exactly *identical* experience, assigning subjective probabilities and quantifying the risk are important contributions to managing it

Innovation risk is therefore associated with cases for which the organization has reasonably good information and control of the situation. This happens, for example, with in-house development of a new product architecture or a new software algorithm If the device, the material, or the process is developed internally, the R&D team in the company should have adequate information on the status of development They should know what alternative routes are available to achieve the desired objectives All such activities, if analyzed carefully, can be assigned a probability of success Thus, the risk can be quantified Most often this quantification relies on subjective assessments of probability for success, made by knowledgeable and experienced people Even if such probabilities are not strictly valid in the pure mathematical sense, they may be important in pointing out the steps to take to reduce those risks

Most real-life cases of development of a new product have a combination of technological uncertainties and innovation risks, all of which can contribute to the length of the R&D cycle They have to be tightly controlled and reduced where possible to minimize the time between the inception of a new product and its introduction to the marketplace (Meyer and Utterback, 1995)

Supply of Critical Materials and Parts

Earlier we examined delays that may be caused by the late availability of state-of-the-art technologies However, even if one uses only proven parts and components, shortages of some critical material can occur because of normal supply problems that can be exacerbated by wrong inventory policies

An innovative product might have thousands of different components. Any reasonable research and development organization will try to keep the number of technologically innovative components to a minimum However, any of the "normal" components can also delay the project and lengthen the R&D cycle if it is not available when needed. In the last decade, many American businesses have begun imitating Japanese inventory policies, such as the just-in-time (JIT) policy (Plenert and Best, 1986, Schonberger, 1982). In the surge to cut costs, management in many R&D organizations ordered an indiscriminate reduction of inventories The JIT method and others are indeed very effective for improving competitiveness in the fabrication of mature equipment in large quantities, but they are totally inappropriate for the development of only a few prototypes This wrong application of a good method has caused serious delays in the R&D cycle in high-tech companies because of unwarranted shortages of some regular, standard components

There is no economic or other justification for causing the R&D department to wait for standard components Maintaining a minimum stock level of these, as might be required by the research and development department, is totally justified Their immediate use in a small number of prototypes not only helps to shorten the R&D process but also reduces significantly the total cost of research and development in the company A rational high-technology management should never allow a critical shortage of a standard part to develop Then, the only shortages can be limited to the technologically innovative components and materials

Bottlenecks in the Research and Development Organization

Exactly as the strength of a chain is determined by its weakest link, the output of any organization is determined by the throughput of its bottlenecks Taking a favorite example from the school of Optimized Production Technology (OPT) (Fox, 1982a, 1982b), imagine a three-stage production process consisting of three personnel who perform separate but related functions at different rates. One assembles an electronic circuit at a capacity rate of 10 circuits per shift A second person tunes these circuits but at a maximum pace of 8 circuits per shift Finally, a third person inspects and ships these circuits with a capacity of 12 circuits per shift Clearly, the throughput of this operation is limited by the second person at a maximum 8 circuits per shift If the first person on the chain was allowed to produce to his capacity, over time, a huge stockpile of assembled circuits would accumulate in front of the second person The second person would be busy all the time, whereas the third person would be idle during significant periods of his or her shift.

The School of OPT (Goldratt and Fox, 1986) teaches how to identify the bottlenecks (in our example, the second stage of the circuit manufacturing process) and how to optimize the available production technology to achieve a maximum throughput from the operation We discuss this topic in more depth in the next chapter

As one should expect, a similar situation exists in any R&D organization where a large amount of people and functions are involved in the development of a new product The throughput of the organization is determined by the maximal capacity of its bottlenecks, much as in the simpler case of a manufacturing organization described earlier In the R&D environment, however, the bottlenecks are not determined just by machine capacity or by the number of people doing simple tasks, such as assembly work

The typical R&D bottlenecks are more complex. They are often determined by specific know-how, by experience or talent that resides in particular individuals. Therefore, R&D bottlenecks are much harder to identify and resolve

In the research and development environment, often only one person has the precise knowledge, experience, or talent to do a job. When a firm struggles to advance the state of the art in a given professional field, the number of people in the company capable of major contributions is always quite limited They often become bottlenecks in the R&D process but are seldom recognized as such by management This slowdown occurs, even though it is management's duty to find ways to assist such people and to allocate whatever they need to open those human bottlenecks The situation in the R&D environment may, unfortunately, be made even more complex than managing a few special personnel In the dynamic process of developing new products, the bottlenecks are not constant. They shift from one person to another, from a work group to a design center, and so on

The real output of the R&D organization is not just a prototype but also the knowledge and information that accompany it Until the work is finished and well documented, most of this information is in the heads of the people involved in the process Therefore, almost anyone may become a critical bottleneck if he or she is absent for some reason—suddenly hospitalized or simply gone on vacation This situation creates many more opportunities for unexpected bottlenecks in an R&D organization than in a manufacturing one

Bottlenecks not only limit the throughput in any organization but also have a strong influence on the time a product stays in the research and development cycle The fewer the bottlenecks in the R&D organization, the shorter will be the turnaround times and the total time needed to launch a new product into the market

METHODS FOR REDUCING UNCERTAINTY AND INNOVATION RISK

In the previous section, we examined the way innovation uncertainty and risk may affect the length of the research and development cycle. In the following paragraphs, we explore some methods to reduce the negative impact of these factors to a minimum Again we stress that, given the critical importance of the R&D cycle in the life of any high-technology product, this cycle must be allowed the time necessary to ensure that the product has a strong competitive advantage However, if innovation uncertainty and risk are not managed correctly, they may prolong the R&D process beyond the time absolutely necessary The resulting delays could jeopardize the market success of the product by letting it miss its window of opportunity

Procedures for Early Identification of Risk Areas

We have made a distinction between uncertainty and risk We have seen that uncertainty comes from having too little information about an event Risk, on the other hand, concerns the probability that an event will occur Dealing with risk permits more reliable predictions than dealing with sheer uncertainty Therefore, the first significant step for shortening the research and development cycle of a high-technology product is to identify formally all the uncertainties and risks involved

The identification process should begin no later than the end of the concept definition phase of the product (Shtub and Globerson, 1994, offer details on projects and product phases) At this stage, which precedes actual development of the product, many of its characteristics are at least roughly defined Product architecture, its work breakdown structure, the list of components and necessary materials, processes, and technologies—all these are specified Managers can therefore establish at this time a formal list of uncertainties and risks that have a strong impact on the product's performance, compared to that of the competition The list must then be reviewed to separate the technological and other uncertainties from the innovation risks, which are under the control of the R&D organization

The second step is to make a critical examination of the resulting list of uncertainties The objective is to reduce it to the absolute minimum. All items on the list should be reexamined for alternatives. Once they are identified, it might be prudent to purchase some of the technologies, together with their alternatives, that are most critical to the project In many cases, this additional investment will later be justified as it will prevent schedule delays in the product development caused by exclusive dependence on a single source of supply. To be truly effective, the work of deciding which technologies are critical must be done by a task group of researchers and purchasing people who will call in specialists as required

Remember that if the competitive advantage of a new product is achieved by the use of some novel component or technology purchased from an outside vendor, the stability of the competitive advantage obtained will be somewhat uncertain When a competitive edge is obtained through outsourcing components, sooner rather than later they will be advanced by some other vendor or the same vendor may develop a new generation of the component The new generation normally outperforms the first, and the competition can then use it to produce a better and often cheaper product If the company chooses to build an unstable competitive advantage in this way, its management should know that they are in a merciless run against time to get their product to the market before someone else Otherwise, the window of opportunity to recover the investment and realize some profit will most certainly be closed

The third step consists of quantifying risk areas by assigning a subjective but educated probability for the success of reaching the required performance on each of the developmental tasks A formal list of such tasks should be established in decreasing order of risk. Tasks with the highest risk factors should be attacked first All resources necessary for the speedy and successful reduction of risk should be allocated by the company Concentration of effort and management attention during this technological battle is as critically important as is concentration of effort in a military operation Half measures usually result in too little, too late This is what IBM, Apple, and Motorola may soon find out, as illustrated in Case 4 2

Reducing Risk by Measuring and Monitoring

After the risk areas have been identified and each separate risk has been quantified, the company should apply the appropriate combination of risk-reduction techniques If the process of assessing risks in a given project is by itself lengthy, the management of the research and development organization should establish a formal risk-reduction review (RRR) schedule These reviews should be in addition to the various PDRs (product design reviews), PMRs (project management reviews), and other normal management procedures The importance of focusing on risk reduction is obvious Once the tasks of highest risk have been successfully developed, there is much less room for bad surprises and uncontrollable delays

The most straightforward technique consists of formal tracking and monitoring of risk until it is decreased to zero This technique is illustrated in Case 4 4.

CASE 4.4

The Cellular Transmission System Example

At the beginning of the 1990s, Europe experienced an explosive growth in mobile cellular communications. To keep mutual interference under control, the European agency issued strict regulations for stability and spectral purity of all transmission equipment authorized for deployment One of the companies competing for this market reduced its risk by applying the monitoring technique briefly described here Reportedly, the application of this formal risk-reduction method helped the company to arrive first to the market, obtain official approval, and win a substantial market share

The company identified some nine areas of risk They were arranged in descending order and a risk-reduction review schedule was established to track and monitor the progress made in solving critical problems in each of the nine areas The highest priority, management attention, and resources were given to the area of highest risk. the development of a "clean frequency synthesizer " This device generates the required communication frequencies and must be sufficiently stable and noise free for the system to perform as required The quantitative part of the risk-assessment process had identified five important steps of risk reduction Each step represented the successful achievement of a significant risk-reduction event. The company preferred to work in terms of probability of success, which is of course equivalent to risk reduction The probability (Pr) of success was defined to reach the levels indicated below for each of the following events

1 Pr = 50 percent when a successful computer simulation of the synthesizer shows a 20 percent spare margin on the required performance

2 Pr = 60 percent when a successful layout shows the feasibility of a realistic packaging within the size constraints

3 Pr = 80 percent after the first prototype in its final size package has been tested successfully

4 Pr = 90 percent after the receiver and the system power supply have been integrated

5 Pr = 100 percent after the product has passed all system acceptance tests

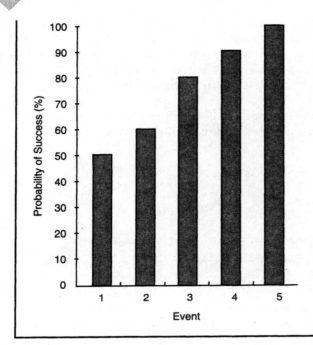

FIGURE 4.3 The Probability of Reaching the Required Performance

The risk-reduction reviews for the examination of the risk-reduction status must be scheduled in advance, according to the program development plan The total project probability of achieving the performance goals is of course a function of the joint probability of solving the problems in all risk areas If the milestones are not reached on time, the management has to consider all the alternatives available, including cancelling the whole project As in other risky businesses, a manager in a high-technology company must know when to cut the losses in order to avoid an economic disaster

The development of a complex high-technology product requires hundreds, sometimes thousands, of tasks Accomplishing all these tasks requires a significant investment of resources Only a small number of the tasks represent significant development risk Hence, a concentrated effort to reduce risk at the very beginning of an R&D project has numerous advantages It assures that most of the research investment is made at a stage of low project risk This increases the likelihood that most of the research and development money and company resources will be invested in products with a high probability of success This successful risk reduction is illustrated in Figure 4 4

A formal risk-management procedure allows the company to cut investment in projects that remain risky too long If the development risk is not reduced below a certain figure—perhaps 20 percent—after a reasonable amount of time, management can decide to stop throwing good money after bad This decision process is illustrated in Figure 4 5.

Another risk-reduction technique can be applied in both technology uncertainty and innovation risk We examine it next

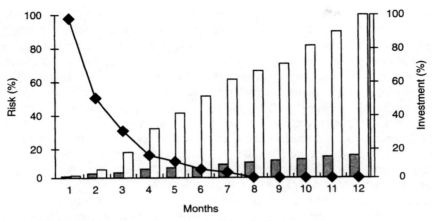

FIGURE 4 4 Successful Risk Reduction

Parallel Development: Friendly "Shoot-Outs"

The technique of parallel development has been applied by many high-technology companies, mostly for reducing uncertainties and risk in vitally important projects If the future of the company depends on the success of a particular project, or if the market returns are especially generous for the company arriving first with a successful product, it makes sense to launch parallel efforts for the development of critical components

This approach reduces innovation risk significantly Clearly, if the probability of success for each of two parallel approaches is perhaps 70 percent, the combined probability that at least one approach will yield the expected performance is more than 90 percent

FIGURE 4 5 A Nonsuccessful Risk Reduction

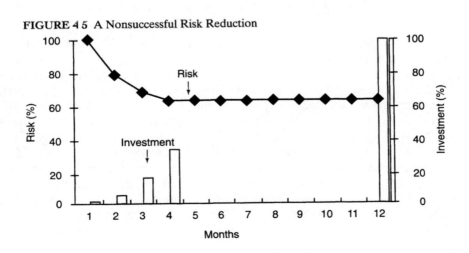

Sony reportedly launched 10 different options in developing the VTR (video tape recorder) program Without doubt, Sony's market rewards greatly compensated the company for redundancy in the effort Another application of the parallel development method has been reported recently by Mitsubishi Motors In their work to develop an environmentally "clean" car, the researchers could not find one single path to meet their ambitious requirements, but they claim to have found a combination among their parallel paths that promises to fulfill the specifications (see Case 4 5)

Another advantage of the parallel development method, sometimes called "friendly shoot-outs," is that it can create a constructive competition between the teams in the company In the past, this approach has been used by many high-technology companies just for the sake of increasing the motivation of the competing teams In the future, this strategy will probably continue to be applied, in view of the growing importance of timely marketing of high-tech products within their window of opportunity Hence, it is important also to outline some of the most important drawbacks of this

---

CASE 4.5

The Mitsubishi Motors Electric Vehicle Example

In the race to gain a strategic position in the prospective "clean vehicle" market, Mitsubishi tried a number of parallel aproaches, including these:

1 An improved vertical vortex engine This is a lean burn engine, which means it burns at higher air-to-fuel ratio than conventional engines, making it more fuel efficient and thus lowering its carbon dioxide emissions

2 An innovative electronic control engine with modulated displacement. Basically, the engine runs in three modes depending on driving conditions This flexibility translates into a 17 percent improvement in fuel efficiency

3 An efficient electric power engine, developed jointly with Tokyo Electric Power Company This engine operates in combination with solar power and returns energy to the battery when the car is braking

In an article that appeared in *Business Week*, October 31, 1994, Mitsubishi Motors declared: "When we set out to create an extremely low-emission, energy efficient car to meet 21st century standards, we knew there were many obstacles ahead So we tried different approaches What we found, after years of researching and testing various technologies, was that not one of them worked. All of them worked Together The result is a high performance, spacious car that is practically as clean as an all-electric vehicle And infinitely more practical " (p 49) The new experimental car, called "ESR," is an electric powered hybrid design that employs a high-efficiency, low-emission internal combustion engine (to recharge the battery) in combination with solar and even kinetic energy from the braking system The car has demonstrated quite promising performances indeed a maximum speed of 200 km/h (125 M/h), a battery operated range of 500 km (300 miles), and a range of over 1000 km (600 miles) in the hybrid mode

method A management should try to minimize these pitfalls when applying the shoot-out approach

First, the teams formed to compete must all have a fair chance for success If the company does not have sufficient human and other resources to ensure this equality, the result will probably be a significant waste of effort In such a case, the wiser course might be to concentrate the scarce resources in one group only, but support it by all means available to increase the probability of its success

A second concern with this method is the problem of how to compensate the losing teams This issue requires special management attention. As discussed in previous chapters, the company must have a culture honoring high performance of teams whether they win or lose in a friendly shoot-out Naturally, the winning team will assume responsibility for implementing the results of their development effort Ideally, the company as a whole will gain sufficient momentum in the marketplace to create opportunities for the losing teams members to reintegrate in future research and development efforts

The third method for reducing uncertainty and risk, which we find appropriate to describe here, is gaining more and more popularity with the advances made in powerful computer modeling and simulation

Simulation and Rapid Prototyping: Right the First Time

Several advances have created opportunities that were not available earlier. Two of the most important are the tremendous progress made in computer simulation and modeling, and the arrival of powerful, affordable workstations capable of doing billions of operations per second Judicious use of simulation and modeling can shorten the research and development cycle by very significant amounts as well as conserve other resources However, in applying this approach, managers should be aware of some pitfalls, as reported in the literature (Murotake and Thomas, 1991) Today, it is quite possible to simulate the operation of a complex system and optimize its performance long before the first hardware prototypes are built Compared to the old "trial and error" procedures, this approach can save substantial time and money

Validation of this concept was first made by researchers and engineers working in the field of semiconductor high technology In this branch, there is no possibility for building and trying prototypes in any way but by computer simulation Driven by the need to miniaturize complex integrated circuits, mass memories, and microprocessors, which involve thousands of components packed into a minuscule surface, companies were forced to invest in the development and perfection of powerful simulation techniques These techniques take into account a huge amount of information about the electrical performance of different components, on possible couplings and resulting interference between a number of elements on a given substrate, and other effects From the very beginning, designers of such circuits knew that the circuit must work right the first time, otherwise the entire lot would be lost without any possibility of changing or tuning a tiny component in such a high density package

Another very important advantage of the computer modeling and simulation method is that it generates, as by-products, all the tools necessary for the manufacturing and testing of the element designed The time to manufacture and test the actual equipment can thus be substantially reduced A well-controlled computer-aided design (CAD) process assures a good degree of reproducibility and reliability in the subsequent manufacturing process, as we discuss in the next chapter.

Compared to conventional prototype building and testing, products built after successful computer simulation have a better chance to work correctly much sooner if not the first time One important reason for this difference is the concentration of information In conventional prototyping, the work is usually divided among a number of professional groups. The division of work requires a stringent definition of the interface between the different modules In the development process, the need to keep those interface specifications rigid often complicates and prolongs the research and development cycle Because the different teams involved in developing each module know little about the impact of changing the interface parameters, they have no choice but to stick to the original definitions In many cases, however, even slight modifications of some of the interface parameters may help greatly to improve the product's performance or significantly shorten the development time

Computer modeling and simulation, by contrast, is usually done by one group of people under the close supervision of the chief designer During the simulation process, if some parameters need to be relaxed to optimize others and achieve optimum product performance, the decision can be made on the spot The time and cost of the classic sequential process will thus be further reduced

By applying an appropriate risk-reduction process from the beginning of any ambitious project, a high-technology company focuses on solving the major problems first Usually this effort costs only a fraction of the total research and development cost Hence, the company may follow an ambitious innovation policy, which includes cancelling some projects if they do not take off successfully during the risk-reduction phase The projects that do will largely compensate for the loss of those that do not as the successful ones will generate revenue due to their superior performance, compared to the competition A strong competitive advantage usually means a long period of time before the competition catches up, so success in an ambitious project generally also has the benefit of a widely opened window of market opportunities

Having examined some appropriate uncertainty and risk-reduction techniques, we need to investigate the remaining significant factors affecting the length of the research and development cycle We explore this in the remainder of the chapter

APPLYING RATIONAL INVENTORY POLICY FOR RESEARCH AND DEVELOPMENT ORGANIZATIONS

Shortages of materials and components can prolong the research and development cycle and need to be avoided Yet, emphasizing inventory management as one of the main contributors to reducing cost and improving competitiveness, many U S and European companies with great enthusiasm began imitating the just-in-time (JIT) methods employed with such telling effect in Japan. In adopting JIT, however, many Western corporate and plant managers focused their attention on emulating the Japanese inventory levels without considering the quite different nature of their businesses The just-in-time method was developed to serve mass-production companies, it doesn't apply as well in the research and development environment As yet, little attention has been given to raw materials management in research and development organizations typical for the high-technology sector

The Basic Difference between a Mass-Production Environment and a Research and Development Environment

The most important characteristic of a mass-production process is its repetitiveness Everything in the process has been specified, stabilized, and fixed There should be no changes or variations for this process to perform at its best

Another important characteristic of a mass-produced product is the high proportion of the total product cost that is represented by the cost of parts and purchased material Today, most of the manufacturing and assembly tasks in such processes are automated and robotized, so the cost of labor is kept very low compared to the cost of purchased parts and materials

In contrast, the most prominent characteristic of the research and development process is its uniqueness Many steps in the procedure are being done for the first time Nothing is certain or stable, and changes and variations are not only permitted but form an integral part of the process.

The second important way the research and development process is different from mass production is in the very high proportion that labor costs represent in the total cost of the R&D product itself This product consists of a few prototypes and a considerable amount of information and documentation The personnel working in research and development are almost all highly qualified and hold academic degrees, characteristics that also contribute to the high labor content of the total product cost

There are many other differences between a mass-production and an R&D environment, but the two just discussed are sufficient to demonstrate that totally different inventory policies are needed for these cases In particular, managers need to consider the following points when establishing an inventory policy for R&D organizations

1. In the product development stage, the cost of components and other raw materials as a percentage of total product cost is relatively low, usually less than 15 percent This figure contrasts sharply with large quantity manufacturing, where the same proportion may reach 85 percent to 95 percent.

2. The competitive race forces the engineers to use state-of-the-art components The lead time of nonstandard components is long and uncertain; it may vary from item to item and over time

3. The development cycle is not finished until the last product component is assembled and successfully tested

4. The cost of waiting for the last component can easily exceed the component cost by a factor of 100, 1000, or more

To clarify the last point, consider the direct cost of keeping a large team of scientists, engineers, and technicians waiting for the arrival of a very inexpensive component—one that may cost no more than $100 Often in high-tech companies, a few hundred dollars worth of missing components have blocked the delivery of systems and equipment worth millions

Establishing a Rational Purchasing Policy for Research and Development Organizations

Our discussion should have made clear that the just-in-time purchasing policy, which advocates near-zero inventory coupled with supply of all components just before their assembly, is totally inappropriate for an R&D organization However, the pressure to implement JIT in the mid-1980s was so strong that we had to develop a mathematical model to prove this point (Levy and Ronen, 1984) The model appears as an appendix to this chapter

The analytical model investigates the total cost of the research and development project as a function of the purchasing policy. It answers these questions in two steps Should one order components with a lead time exactly equal to the promised delivery interval (JIT), or should one allow some spare time? If yes, how much spare time should be allotted?

First, the model analyzes the simple case of a project containing just one purchased component. The model looks for the minimum project cost as a function of timing the placement of the order for the component. An early order results in a holding cost for the component until it is needed for assembly. A late order results in a penalty cost, which is a function of the cost of waiting until the component arrives

- If delivery time of the component can be determined, as is most often the case in the manufacturing of mature products using stable sources of supply, the optimum time to purchase is indeed just in time This procedure results in no holding and no penalty cost
- If the delivery time is a random variable, however, as is most often the case with state-of-the-art components, the model clearly shows that the minimum cost requires the order to be placed with sufficient spare time to allow for variability in delivery time

Next, the model is extended to the more realistic case of a project that has a large number of components with random delivery times Here, it shows clearly that the minimum project cost is directly tied to the cost of components—that is, to the proportion of the total project cost that is represented by component cost

- The higher the ratio of purchased components to total cost, the larger will be the holding cost If this ratio approaches 100 percent, as is the case for mass-produced products, then the most cost-effective policy may well be the JIT policy
- In contrast, if the ratio of purchased components to total cost is below 10 percent to 20 percent, the optimal policy requires purchase orders to be placed as early as possible This is generally true for research and development projects, for which the waiting penalty largely exceeds the cost of holding materials

To summarize, the optimum inventory policy for a research and development organization may be formulated as follows

1. Maintain in stock all inexpensive, frequently used standard components An R&D project should never wait for the arrival of such components
2. Keep a reasonable, minimum amount of more expensive but "moving," nonobsolescent components in stock Adjust the quantity to keep the holding cost low, but monitor the stock to ensure that no shortage of such components occurs

3. Order as soon as practicable all state-of-the-art components and any other component with uncertain delivery time

4. Periodically dispose of all stock that is not moving or is "dead " Such stock contains mostly obsolescent components that your R&D department does not need Salvage such stock and cut the holding costs

---

METHODS FOR REDUCING BOTTLENECKS IN RESEARCH AND DEVELOPMENT ORGANIZATIONS

We have seen that one factor that can lengthen the time a product spends in the research and development cycle is the bottlenecks in the organization that create waiting lines and delays We learned that the output of any organization is no greater than the throughput of its most stringent bottleneck

One peculiarity in research and development organizations is the presence of nonphysical bottlenecks In an R&D environment, often the critical bottleneck is not a machine or a process but the know-how and the particular experience of specific individuals In the following paragraphs, we examine the methods for identifying and opening critical bottlenecks in R&D organizations

Identifying the True Bottlenecks in Research and Development Organizations — The Know-How Bottlenecks

The methods for identifying bottlenecks in a manufacturing environment are quite straightforward: You measure the throughput of each of the machines or stations in the manufacturing chain of a given product Those with minimum throughput can be immediately identified as bottlenecks

A slightly different but equally effective approach is to walk through the workshops and look for piles of parts waiting in line before a machine or a station can be released to process them The longer the waiting line, the narrower the bottleneck This approach has the advantage of taking into account not just the measured throughput of the machines and the stations but also their real-life performance in the specific environment of a given workshop

The second method is much better adapted to the research and development environment To identify the true bottlenecks in the R&D department, look for work in progress waiting in line "on the desk" of each key researcher Here the task becomes more complicated There are seldom physical piles of work waiting in line before a researcher begins to process them Research and development organizations rarely keep a formal record of future tasks or files to be worked on by the different researchers In organizations that do try to keep such records, people often complain about senior researchers refusing to accept or even to talk about future work, as they are drowning in more tasks than they can handle

To get around these difficulties, one way to assess the situation is by assigning a "smart guy" to conduct an in-depth investigation A "smart guy" is a person who knows what he is looking for, who knows how to formulate appropriate questions and how to read the answers This person should devote a couple of days to on-the-spot interviews to help him identify the most critical bottlenecks It is unnecessary to spend additional time and effort identifying second- and third-order bottlenecks The situation will probably change once the main blockages are opened If a problem remains after that, a subsequent bottleneck analysis using the same approach may be useful and necessary Once the critical bottlenecks are identified, management must take appropriate action to open them and thus speed up the process and shorten the R&D cycle

Methods to Open Know-How Bottlenecks

Opening industrial bottlenecks is generally associated with investing to increase capacity, thus improving the throughput of a critical resource machines, manpower, and so on For opening *know-how* bottlenecks, this type of approach won't work. In most cases, the scarce resource turns out to be a specific individual with special skills, know-how, and experience Attempts to add another individual with similar knowledge and skills to "double the capacity" will likely fail for a number of reasons First, it is difficult to find a person with exactly the same skills and experience Second, the division of work between two equally competent individuals creates personal problems (see the "prima donna" effects in chapter 2), resolving these issues may use up so much creative energy that the bottleneck may "shrink" and become even worse than before

A much better approach is to relieve "bottleneck specialists" from routine tasks that can be performed by others When the workload of these people is analyzed, the results often show that they are performing tasks that require their unique skills only a fraction of the time Most of their time is spent on trivial tasks that someone else can do

Nevertheless, there are sometimes social obstacles in assigning such help These can include a negative interpretation of the management's intent by other researchers, or a misunderstanding of the behavior of the specialist whose workload the management is trying to reduce Releasing the specialist from performing routine tasks may look as if the management is creating a superior class of aristocrats or that the person is behaving like a prima donna Other than that, the approach can work quite effectively and should be used to reduce the bottlenecks when appropriate

Opening one bottleneck is just the beginning of what is needed to speed up the R&D process Theoretically, this task has no end Any time one bottleneck is opened, the next becomes critical However, when the most damaging bottlenecks are opened, the throughput of the R&D organization will significantly improve

Opening the bottlenecks in the R&D organization, together with the other methods discussed here for reducing delays and minimizing risks, are among the most important actions management can do to shorten the R&D cycle to the minimum When these steps are taken, the competitive position of the high-technology company will be significantly strengthened

---

SUMMARY

In this chapter, the paramount importance of the R&D cycle for the success and market performance of a high-technology product was explained If a company is to create a thoroughly "debugged" and fully performing product before the beginning of the manufacturing cycle, it must allocate sufficient time to research and development

In spite of this wisdom, a clear trend toward shorter and faster development cycles has emerged in the last two decades We discussed the primary reasons for shortening the R&D cycle and showed that the window of market opportunity for commercial success of a high-technology product is brief To be successful, a high-technology company must get organized to introduce its products as closely as possible to the beginning of this time window

Next, the major factors determining the length of the research and development cycle were examined Those that most frequently cause delays in this cycle were analyzed with the purpose of identifying effective ways to avoid them Some of the methods that are effective in reducing cycle times in the mass-production industry must be modified significantly to work in a high-technology company

In particular, the rational inventory policy adapted to the specific needs of the R&D organization was examined in some depth so as to avoid inappropriate application of the just-in-time method An analytical model for a purchasing policy adapted to the needs of the R&D organization was defined and proposed.

Special attention was given to the unique phenomenon of know-how bottlenecks in research and development organizations We discussed the possibility that individuals with specific know-how and experience may themselves become bottlenecks and thus create serious obstacles to the smooth flow and progress of work in the organization Some methods for identifying such bottlenecks were proposed We explained why adding personnel with similar qualifications can be counterproductive Effective methods for opening the know-how bottlenecks were introduced together with some warnings regarding particular situations

Finally, we should stress again that all the methods described in this chapter are complementary They should be applied in the right proportion to reduce the research and development cycle without injuring its purpose to develop a reliable, stable, and highly competitive innovative product

For Further Reflection

1 Describe and explain the phenomenon of a window of opportunity for a high-technology product List and elaborate the principal factors that determine the width of this time window

2 What is the importance of the research and development cycle and its significance in the life cycle of an innovative product?

3 How do technological uncertainties influence the length of the R&D cycle? What methods can reduce the impact of those uncertainties on the length of this cycle?

4 What distinguishes uncertainties from risk in the R&D cycle of an innovative product? What are some effective methods for reducing risk?

5 Draw a parallel between the application of just-in-time inventory policies to manufacturing and to R&D organizations

6 Compare the rational inventory policy proposed in this chapter to the purchasing policy applied in your company or a high-technology company you know What conclusions can you draw from this comparison?

7 What types of bottlenecks may exist in the work flow of an R&D organization? Which types are found in any general organization and which are specific to research and development?

8 Describe methods for opening general bottlenecks Explain why some of these methods may be counterproductive in the R&D environment

9 What are some effective methods to identify the "know-how" bottlenecks in an R&D organization? Can all the bottlenecks be opened?

10 Describe effective methods for opening "know-how" bottlenecks in R&D organizations. Can these be used simultaneously with methods for risk reduction?

References and Further Reading

Chase, R B., and N J Aquilano (1985) *Production and Operations Management· A Life Cycle Approach* 4th ed Homewood, IL: Richard D Irwin.

Cusumano, Michael A., and Richard W Selby (1995) *Microsoft Secrets· How the World's Most Powerful Software Company Creates Technology, Shapes Markets, and Manages People* New York: The Free Press

> In this book, the authors, Michael A Cusumano and Richard W Selby claim to reveal many of Microsoft's innermost secrets They draw their conclusions from almost two years of on-site observation at Microsoft headquarters The report is based on 40 in-depth interviews with individuals who had access to confidential documents and project data Cusumano and Selby identify the following seven complementary strategies that characterize how Microsoft competes and operates: Bill Gates's "Brain Trust" of talented employees; exceptional management; "bang for the buck" competitive strategies; clear organizational goals; an orientation toward self-critiquing, learning, and improving; a flexible, incremental approach to product development; and a relentless pursuit of future markets

Fox, R E (1982a). "MRP, Kanban or OPT, what's best?" Part I *Inventories and Production,* July–August 1982

Fox, R. E (1982b) "OPT, An Answer for America," Part II. *Inventories and Production,* November–December 1982

Goldratt, E M , and R E Fox (1986) *The Race.* Milford, CT: Creative Output

Levy, N. S , and B Ronen (1984). "Purchasing and Raw Material Management in Science-Based Industry." *International Journal of Material and Product Technology* 4, no 1, pp 2–7

Meyer, Marc H , and James M Utterback (1992) "Moving Ideas to Market and Corporate Renewal," Working Paper 69 Cambridge, MA: Sloan School of Management

> This paper presents a different opinion on the prevailing view that a firm will be most successful if its development times are shorter and its high-quality products are generated faster than those of its competitors The authors argue that intensive research in *one* firm shows that rapid development times are not correlated with expected commercial success, and that forcing rapid development when technological and market uncertainties are high may produce failure Difficulties in technology integration, which occur when multiple core technologies must be combined, slow the speed of developing new products We recommend reading this paper, despite our disagreement with its conclusions. As recommended in this chapter, if a company's management concentrates on reducing technological uncertainties, the market results can only benefit from shorter R&D cycles

Meyer, M H , and J M Utterback (1995) "Product Development Cycle Time and Commercial Success," *IEEE Transactions on Engineering Management*, November 1995

Mitsubishi Motors (1994) "The Power of Positive Thinking " *Business Week*, 31 October, p 49

Murotake, David K , and Thomas J Allen (1991). "Computer Aided Engineering and Project Performance: Managing a Double-Edged Sword " Working Paper 47 Cambridge, MA: Sloan School of Management

> The authors warn about the inappropriate use of computer-aided engineering (CAE) They assert that computer-aided engineering tools are like a double-edged sword Properly employed, CAE tools improve engineering productivity and help keep technical projects on schedule and under budget For some kinds of work, CAE tools can also stimulate creativity However, they can also have detrimental effects. For less-structured engineering tasks, such as preliminary analysis and problem solving, the use of inappropriate or inadequate tools can severely constrain performance By encouraging the "cloning" of old solutions, computer tools can stifle creativity and yield suboptimal designs through negative biasing

Plenert, G , and T D Best (1986) "MRP, JIT, and OPT: What's Best?" *Production and Inventory Management*, Second Quarter

Ronen, B , and D Trietsch (1986) "Optimal Scheduling of Purchasing Orders for Large Projects," Working Paper CRIS no 127, GBA no 86-64 New York: New York University, Graduate School of Business Administration

Sager, Ira et al. (1996). "Time May Have Passed the PowerPC By " *Business Week*, 4 March, pp 43–45

Schonberger, R J (1982). *Japanese Manufacturing Techniques Nine Hidden Lessons in Simplicity* New York: The Free Press

Schonberger, R J (1986) *World Class Manufacturing· The Lessons of Simplicity Applied* New York: The Free Press

Shtub, A , J. Bard, and S Globerson (1994) *Project Management Engineering, Technology and Implementation* Upper Saddle River, NJ: Prentice Hall

Smith, Robert P , and Steven D Eppinger (1992) "Identifying Controlling Features of Engineering Design Iteration," Working Paper 72 Cambridge, MA: Sloan School of Management

> This working paper examines one important factor for lengthening the research and development cycle: engineering changes When a product is designed, this generally involves a large number of coupled elements with a very complex set of relationships The authors claim that it is this complex coupling that leads to iteration among the various engineering tasks in a large project The Design Structure Matrix (DSM) is shown to be useful in identifying where iteration is necessary The Work Transformation Model developed in this paper is an extension of the DSM method It can predict slow and rapid iteration within a project, as well as those features of the design problem that will require many iterations to reach a technical solution

Tyre, Marcie J , and Wanda J Orlikowski (1992) "Windows of Opportunity: Temporal Patterns of Technological Adaptations in Organizations," Working Paper 66 Cambridge, MA: Sloan School of Management

> Contrary to what is often argued in the innovation literature, the authors contend that the

process of technological adaptation is not gradual and continuous but is instead highly discontinuous They draw their conclusions from observations of three manufacturing and service organizations Their findings indicate that there is a relatively brief window of opportunity to explore and modify new process technology following initial implementation Afterward, modification of new process technologies by users tends to stagnate as the organization gets used to certain routines that come with experience Thus, the technology and its context of use tend to freeze, often embedding unresolved problems into organizational practice. Subsequent changes appear to occur in an episodic manner, triggered either by discrepant events or by new discoveries among users

Utterback, James M , M H Meyer, T. Tuff, and Lisa Richardson (1992) "When Speeding Concepts to Market Can Be a Mistake," Working Paper 45 Cambridge, MA: Sloan School of Management

This paper warns about speeding the R&D cycle beyond a reasonable limit The authors ask these questions: Is rapid development from concept to market vital? What pressures are induced by the urgency of product introduction, and can they lead to poor decisions? Can a more deliberate pace be recommended? The paper argues that widely diverse new business ventures outside a company's core business areas can prove problematic Although faster may be better, speed brings with it pressures that, for certain types of technological ventures, can lead to failure if they are not clearly understood and managed Speed is relative to the capability of the venturing company and to the nature of the venture it is attempting The studied company's experience shows that successful ventures, particularly the more risky and potentially rewarding, require commitment and persistence Although we believe that rapid development from concept to market is vital, we agree with the need to adapt speed to the capability of the company In this chapter we describe methods for increasing such capability

APPENDIX 4 A

An Analytical Model for Establishing
a Rational Purchasing Policy for Research
and Development Organizations

First, we introduce the one-item model and show a heuristic solution for the n components model Then, we modify the model and apply it to the case of a typical research and development organization

For introduction, consider the following special case A project requires one purchased component, which must be on hand at a specific time, t^* If the item is received earlier, the project will be completed in time—that is, without penalties—but an inventory holding (carrying) cost C will be incurred for each time unit the item is held in inventory after arrival and until t^*. On the other hand, if the component is late, a penalty P is incurred for each time unit of delay, as the whole project will consequently be delayed In a high-tech company, the penalty has a tangible component (contract penalty for late delivery) as well as many intangibles: loss of goodwill, ill-conceived and hasty attempts to catch up by avoiding good engineering rules, and so on

Assume the following The lead time of the component has a given stochastic distribution, and the project manager has to decide when to place the order so as to minimize the inventory holding cost and delay penalty The project manager is responsible for all the costs associated with the purchasing decision; therefore, it is in his or her interest and power to minimize (*MIN*) the expected total costs The component's lead time is a stationary stochastic variable with a given distribution The element to be manipulated to the best advantage is scheduling of the order placement, which is the decision variable under the project manager's control

The objective function is this:

$$\underset{T}{MIN} \; [E \, (\text{Penalty Cost}) + E \, (\text{Holding Cost})] \tag{1}$$

where *T* is the time the order is placed Figure 4A 1 illustrates the relationship between *t**, *T*, and the lead time distribution

Note that the distribution starts at *T* (the item cannot arrive before it is ordered) Consequently, the area to the right of *t**—the penalty probability—increases with *T*, as expected Expanding the objective function (1), we have this

$$\underset{T}{MIN} \; \left[C \int_{T}^{t^*} F(t - T)dt + P \int_{t^*}^{\infty} [1 - F(t - T)]dt \right] \tag{2}$$

where *t* is the current time, *F*() is the Cumulative Distribution Function (CDF) of the lead time, *C* is the holding cost per period, and *P* is the penalty cost per period

Note that these costs are assumed to be linear The lead time distribution *F*() in a high-technology company has a much larger standard deviation than in the repetitive assembly lines

FIGURE 4A 1 The Relationship between *t**, *T*, and the Lead Time Distribution

f(t-T)

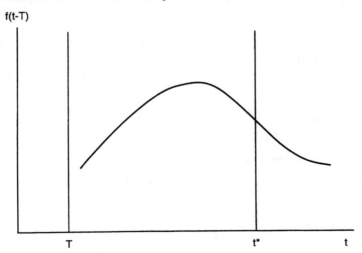

Note: f = probability of arrival
    t = time
    T = time of order placement
    t* = time component needed for assembly

Solving equation (2) yields an optimal order point T^*, satisfying

$$F(t^* - T^*) = P/(P + C) \tag{3}$$

Rewriting this equation in a slightly different form leads to some quite revealing results:

Let a be the proportion of the purchased items contained in the total project cost
Let Ct be the total project cost
Let Ch be the holding cost portion of the total cost
Let Cp be the penalty cost portion of the total cost Then

$$C = Ct * Ch * a \tag{4}$$

$$P = Ct * Cp \tag{5}$$

Incorporating equation (3) into equations (4) and (5) yields

$$F(t^* - T^*) = Cp/(Cp + Ch * a) \tag{6}$$

or

$$F(t^* - T^*) = 1/\{1 + a * (Ch/Cp)\} \tag{7}$$

We can run a simple sensitivity analysis of the optimum lead time distribution F as a function of a—the proportion of the total cost that is represented by the cost of purchased items Immediately, we see the difference between the optimum policies appropriate for research and development and those suitable for mass manufacturing

In research and development, a is small, typically around 10 percent For the sake of simplicity, let us assume that a approaches 0, if so, then

$$F(t^* - T^*) \text{ approaches } 1$$

Therefore, $T^* = 0$, a result that reflects the tendency of many project managers to release purchase orders at the first possible opportunity Moreover, in certain cases, for a to approach 0 may even yield a negative T^* In real-life situations, it is common for project managers to feel that they should have released the orders to purchase "yesterday "

On the other hand, as in the case of mass production of mature products, if a is very large, typically around 90 percent, we can assume that a approaches 1, or

$$F(t^* - T^*) \text{ approaches } 1/(1 + Ch/Cp)$$

In this case, the ratio between the holding costs and the penalty cost determines the optimal timing Usually, in mass manufacturing Ch is much larger than Cp, a situation that leads to

$$F(t^* - T^*) \text{ approaching } 0, \text{ or } T^* = t^*$$

Thus, better results will be obtained if the purchase orders are released at the last possible opportunity This is the usual case when the just-in-time (JIT) purchasing policy is applied, not surprisingly with great success in repetitive assembly lines

The complete model involving n purchased items rather than only one item is much more complicated to solve Ronen and Trietsch (1986) suggested a good approximation for optimal scheduling by computing a simple lower bound for the n model They achieved this by treating each item separately Their end results only strengthen and confirm the conclusions derived from the simplified model, namely, two completely different strategies apply for research and developing and mass manufacturing In the first case, ordering components well ahead of the last minute as well as holding a certain amount of them in stock is rational and economically justified. In the second case, just-in-time is the best policy to follow

CHAPTER

Organizing for Smooth Transition from Research and Development to Production

The previous chapter presented the need to shorten the research and development cycle of a high-technology product and offered some effective methods for doing so The next step for most high-technology products is the production cycle

The production or manufacturing department of a high-technology company usually has the responsibility for establishing procedures and providing resources for serial production of the product The first prototypes developed by the research and development organization are generally manufactured using soft tooling or manual methods, the next steps, however, are more complex The larger the series of units to be produced, the greater will be the need for a totally defined and stable manufacturing process that uses the most efficient tools, machines, jigs, and fixtures

The transition period between the end of the R&D cycle and the beginning of serial production is often rich with problems As long as the width of the market opportunity window for the product was large, those problems could be tolerated—if at the end of the discussions and changes an efficient product manufacturing line would be established With the shrinking of the market opportunity window, many high-technology companies have realized that they have less time to act effectively (Schonberger, 1982, 1986) They must face the transition problems early, analyze those specific to their organization, and find methods to smooth and speed up the passage between research and development and efficient manufacturing They must change the way they view manufacturing (Pisano and Wheelwright, 1995) and include manufacturing process innovation as an important ingredient in their competitive strategy.

Fortunately, this task is becoming easier and more manageable because of innovative organizational concepts such as group technology and optimized production technology (OPT), and Kanban along with advances made in computer information technology In this chapter, we first examine the classical transition problems from development to manufacturing This step should help the reader already working in a high-technology company to identify similar problems in his or her organization Next, we describe some of the methods to help resolve those problems Finally, we explore the concurrent engineering approach, which seems to be one of the most promising ways to make the transition from research and development to manufacturing

CLASSICAL TRANSITION PROBLEMS FROM RESEARCH AND DEVELOPMENT TO MANUFACTURING

In the classical high-technology company, a product goes through five distinct stages

1. Concept definition or inception
2. Product development
3. Product manufacturing
4. Marketing and sales
5. After-sales service and support

These stages involve four different departments in the company, as shown in Figure 5 1

Concept definition of a new product is usually accomplished by close collaboration between marketing and research and development personnel At this point, the product is still in its inception phase, if interface problems exist, they can be solved easily by further dialogue between marketing and R&D personnel responsible for its definition

Product development is usually done in the research and development department in close cooperation with the reliability and quality department The R&D department is responsible for producing one or more working prototypes together with full documentation describing the product Responsibility for manufacturing the product in large quantities is usually assigned to the production or manufacturing department The manufacturing process is overseen by the reliability and quality assurance department The marketing department is usually responsible for distribution and sales of the product The after-sales service is usually the responsibility of the marketing department

The most significant transition problems, which have caused frequent delays in the introduction of a new product to the market, occur in the interface between re-

FIGURE 5.1 The Classical High-Technology Organization

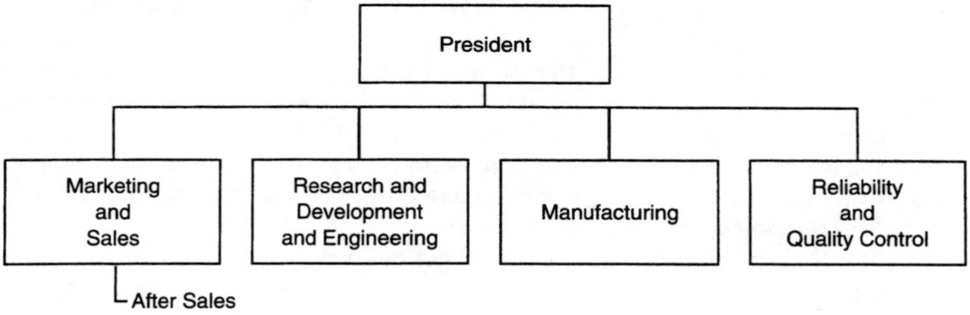

search and development and manufacturing In the following paragraphs, we examine in detail the most important reasons that the interface between these two departments is so difficult

The Responsibility Factor

In the classical high-technology organization, responsibility for a new product shifts from one functional department to another at the end of each cycle of the industrial process Such transfers of responsibility are always problematic, but the most significant problems usually occur during the transition from development to manufacturing

The task of the R&D department is to develop a number of prototypes of the product, together with all the information necessary for its problem-free fabrication and reliable operation The responsibility for organizing a smooth chain of volume manufacturing, assembly, and testing, using the most efficient fabrication process and procedures, lies with the manufacturing department The reliability and quality control department must ensure an adequate level of reliability and stop any defective product from reaching the market Therefore, it interfaces with research and development in the product inception and development phases, and with manufacturing during the production phase

Quite often, however, the people in the R&D department lose interest in a product once the prototypes successfully demonstrate the principle of operation and reach the desired degree of performance They see subjects such as the cost of fabrication, the use of readily available parts and materials, or almost any other aspect that paves the way to problem-free manufacturing as being of secondary importance At that stage, the minds of the R&D personnel are already busy with the inception and development of a new, more challenging product They see work related to smooth manufacturing as trivial—a burden they have to perform, but with a minimum of energy There is often a perception in many R&D departments that all tasks related to manufacturing are none of their business

The manufacturing department expects to receive a fully developed and debugged product from research and development, with all the necessary error-free documentation and drawings When they have unambiguous information on the new product, the people in manufacturing are able to concentrate on what most concerns them—designing the most appropriate production methods, preparing the necessary jigs, tools, and fixtures; and then, beginning the pilot runs followed by serial manufacturing

Any mistake in the documentation or inconsistencies in the drawings provided by the R&D department can be a major cause in interrupting the manufacturing process and become grounds for hot disputes between the research and the manufacturing representatives The usual claim of the manufacturing people is that producing the item on the basis of the documentation provided by research and development is impossible In counterclaim, research often accuses manufacturing of hiding their own internal problems behind minor flaws in the documentation They take the view that the problems could have easily been resolved by production engineers in the manufacturing department had they shown sufficient will to do so

We could bring many more examples of quarrels and disputes between representatives of the R&D and manufacturing departments of a classic high-tech organization

That both arguments have elements of truth only complicates the issue For example, in the case above, it is true that the R&D department should provide an error-free file of documentation to the manufacturing department It is also often true that some of the mistakes in documentation are easily solvable and that such mistakes are used as excuses for hiding deficiencies in the manufacturing department However, the division of responsibility between these two departments makes it very difficult for the management of the company to judge in every case who is right. The company as a whole suffers the consequences resulting from delays in the time to market the product, no matter which department is responsible for the problem

The Maturity of Design Problem

Another problem, somewhat linked to this one, has to do with maturity of the design The design of a product is considered mature when no additional changes or modifications are necessary to assure the desired level of performance, reliability, and reproducibility Because designs mature over time, it takes a good amount of management experience to decide when the transfer should take place Transferring an immature design of a product to manufacturing, or worse, to customers, can lead to very unpleasant situations, as shown in Case 5 1

Driven by the desire to meet a promised delivery date to a customer or by the need to make best use of the window of market opportunity, many high-technology companies launch their new product prematurely They may release a product before they have all the necessary information and feedback from testing and from the performance of the product in its real operational environment Often as a result, a large number of engineering changes are necessary before the manufactured product reaches the degree of performance and reliability required.

Any engineering change introduced after the manufacturing process has begun is clearly disruptive It may have a major impact on the cost and time of availability of the modified product For example, consider the implications of a change requiring the modification of an electronic circuit Typically, such change involves these steps:

1. Redesign of the circuit
2. A new layout of the printed circuit (PC) board
3. New fabrication and assembly tooling
4. New test procedures, jigs, and fixtures
5. New integration procedures for the modified PC
6. Update of all manuals, documentation, and configuration control drawings
7. Assurance of timely arrival of the new parts procured
8. Scrapping or salvaging the old parts and assembled PCs

This list represents the implications of just one engineering change

For changes required to solve a significant performance or security problem, in addition to the steps listed, there is also the cost of recalling all the products already sold, as was the case in our example Sometimes, the company may even be required to bear the cost for introduction of the modification at the customer's premises

CASE 5.1

Intel, the Pentium Flaw Example

The maturity of design problem is well illustrated by the story of the first-generation Pentium microprocessors, introduced to the market by Intel On October 30, 1994, Dr Thomas R Nicely, a mathematics professor at Lynchburg College in Virginia, published a note on the Internet about a flaw in the then-new Pentium chip On December 22, 1994, the *International Herald Tribune* printed an article by John Markoff, from which we quote

> It was during the weekend after Thanksgiving that Paul Otellini, Intel Corp 's senior vice president for worldwide sales, first realized that his company had a crisis on its hands Customers were angry about reports of a flaw in the company's Pentium chip that caused errors in some division calculations
>
> Even as he was discussing the problem with his boss, Andrew S Grove, the president and chief executive officer of Intel, a message was coming out of Mr Otellini's home facsimile machine, his computer was receiving electronic mail and his cellular phone was ringing It was at that moment, he said, that his wife threw up her hands and walked out of the room "I thought to myself, Thank God I don't have another phone line," he said
>
> One immediate result of the teleconferencing after Thanksgiving was that Mr Grove composed an apology to be posted on a computer bulletin board on the Internet At 8 A.M the following Monday, inside the company's headquarters in Santa Clara, California, Intel executives set to work on the crisis
>
> During the following days the committee grew to several dozen Intel employees, drawn from all parts of the company Throughout the next two weeks, the company continued to believe that its customers were listening to its explanation that the Pentium's computational errors were so infrequent that ordinary users did not need to worry
>
> Then disaster struck again On Monday, Nov 12, International Business Machines Corp abruptly announced that its own researchers had determined that the Pentium flaw would lead to division errors much more frequently than Intel had indicated IBM said it was suspending shipments of its personal computers containing the Pentium chip Ten days later, Intel announced that it will replace all flawed Pentium chips

Intel was able eventually to overcome the problem and to reestablish its standing as a world leader in the microchip business However, for smaller, and financially weaker companies, a similar crisis could prove fatal

Clearly, the larger the number of engineering changes and modifications necessary in the life of a product, the larger will be the cost and number of problems a high-technology company must face In some cases, if the problems get out of hand, they can jeopardize the existence of the company, or at least cause very serious damage to its financial health and reputation

The trade-off decision between the need to shorten the time to market and making reasonably sure that a product has reached maturity is among the most difficult to make. Before we examine some methods for reducing the magnitude of this problem, we need to look at the third aspect of the transition between research and development and manufacturing—namely, the problems created by the need to redesign for manufacturing

The Problem of Redesigning for Manufacturing

Problems with a new product's reproducibility are often a major cause for a large number of engineering changes As explained, prototypes produced in the R&D department are often built with components and materials as available, without too much concern about their cost or long-term availability Also, the manual or soft tooling techniques used by the research and development department for production and assembly of the prototypes can create problems of reproducibility They may require substantial modifications for adaptation to more automated, lower cost, and larger quantity production

In addition to the direct cost for making such modifications, redesigning for reproducibility can degrade the product's performance to a degree inconsistent with the product's specification or with the good reputation of the company Production engineers, who are only partially aware of all the research and development considerations, remain focused on cost and reproducibility Tempted by the availability of less expensive components or by faster tuning and testing procedures, they may overlook some less obvious characteristics of a part or a component In the presence of such an event, the right thing to do is to call the original designers for help.

However, group prestige and pride have often led production engineers to make a number of unsuccessful and expensive attempts to solve the problem within the manufacturing division before seeking help If the problem gets out of hand, a meeting between research and manufacturing may be set as a last resort Typically, such meetings begin with mutual accusations The manufacturing engineers claim that the new product is not economically producible in large quantities despite their best efforts Research and development, having succeeded in creating a good product that meets all established requirements, counterattacks by accusing manufacturing of incompetence—and on it goes Only the intervention of competent management can refocus such meetings on solving the problem to field a product that meets all requirements and that is economically producible

Redesign for reproducibility may be expensive and time-consuming, but it has some advantages compared to the maturity of design problem The process is entirely internal, meaning that there are no disappointed customers, this condition eliminates questions of confidence or problems with the company's reputation Also, as most redesign for smooth and efficient manufacturing is accomplished by engineers and technicians within the manufacturing division, their ideas are generally accepted and applied by their division with low or no friction, especially if the changes come at the beginning of product manufacture

To summarize, we have seen that a product is viewed with somewhat different considerations by engineers in research and those in manufacturing This discrepancy of viewpoint calls for special management attention during the transition of responsibility between departments The process must be closely monitored because the transition problems can be quite complex and interlaced The organizational responsibility factor reflects on both the product maturity problem and the need to redesign the product for efficient and trouble-free manufacturing In the next section, a number of methods for resolving these problems are described and discussed

METHODS FOR SMOOTHING THE TRANSFER

The problems of transfer between research and manufacturing are of such importance that many high-technology companies have tried different methods for their reduction and solution Some of these solutions can create new problems, therefore, their application has to be adapted to the particular culture of the people and the company involved This is particularly true with the first methods we discuss.

Organizational Methods

At the beginning of this chapter, we diagrammed the classical functional organization of a high-technology company (see Figure 5 1) To avoid some of the transition problems discussed earlier, some high-technology companies prefer to concentrate responsibility in one business unit from start to finish for a family of similar products In different companies, such units are called by different names groups, divisions, strategic business units, and so on. In this type of organization, the emphasis is on total and continuous responsibility Here the business unit is responsible through the entire life span of a product product inception, development, production, marketing, and after-sales service Figure 5 2 illustrates such an organization In this example, a high-technology company is engaged in diversified communications product lines

At first glance, it would seem that a company organized by product line units could eliminate completely the transition problems found in traditional organizations The vice president (VP) of any of the business units has full responsibility for the products in his group from inception to after-sales service Hence, his people should design the product from the beginning, with a view toward easy manufacturing and reproducibility Also, feedback coming from marketing or from after-sales service flows more smoothly into the same organization, without having to cross the organizational

FIGURE 5 2 Organization by Business Units

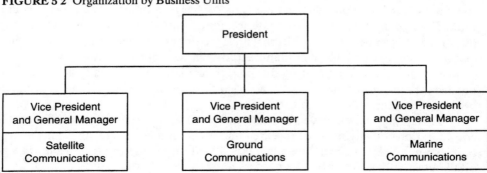

walls of the functional traditional organization Everyone in the same group should act as a team player driven by the same motivation—the business success of the product and of the group

However, even within the independent business units, there is again a more or less formal group of people in charge of research and development, and others in charge of manufacturing, of marketing, and so on If the business unit is sufficiently large, it may ultimately have a totally formal functional structure, much like the one described in Figure 3 1, with all the problems previously discussed Therefore, to avoid transfer problems, the most important consideration is to keep the "walls" between the different functions (which exist formally or informally) as low and as transparent as possible

The basic factors responsible for the walls that can develop between the different functions are the divergence of interests and the divergence in motivations driving the members of the different groups, amplified by the personal ambitions of dominant individuals Some of those factors are objective but others are more imaginary and subjective A competent management should be capable of removing the imaginary factors, such as the divergence of interest between the groups Clearly, the common interest to make the product successful is much stronger than an individual interest in showing who is right and who is to blame for some of the difficulties in the transition process

In the business units type of organization, the walls of conflicting group motivations can be lowered by avoiding separate performance evaluations of the various parts, such as the research and development department and the manufacturing department Such evaluations, originally designed to increase the performance of the whole company by promoting creative competition, can easily degenerate into conflicts of group interests and destructive competition Measurement of performance, however, is a strong motivating factor for groups and individuals The answer is not to abandon all performance evaluation but to devise appropriate criteria that will further the interest of the company—by strengthening motivation and aligning individual goals with those of the organization

One organizational variant of the business units approach is depicted in Figure 5 3 This structure enhances motivation for better group results without creating conflicts of interests among the groups.

In this type of organization, the professional business units have complete responsibility for research and development, manufacturing, and marketing of well-defined families of products, much like the units in Figure 5 2 Some important differences, however, exist between the two organizations In the modified variant, the professional groups are kept smaller, thus, they are more compact and manageable than those in Figure 5 2 This sizing is achieved by separating the major manufacturing resources from the professional units and allocating these to the production technology units This variant is quite satisfactory in providing a good balance between group performance and company performance

One question that might arise with a modified business unit organization is whether it would reintroduce some of the old interface problems we wanted to avoid Indeed, there is similarity between its production technologies units and the manufacturing division of the traditional organization However, by defining appropriate crite-

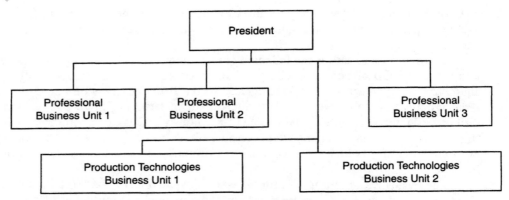

FIGURE 5 3 A Modified Business Unit Type Organization

ria for measuring performance of the business units in this organization, management can eliminate much of the undesirable confrontation between the production technologies and the professional business units Before we discuss these performance evaluation criteria, we need to explain more fully how such an organization functions

Using Figure 5 3 as an example, note that the whole responsibility for the "ground communication" products, including the responsibility for manufacturing, is completely in the hands of the professional business unit This unit may subcontract with one or more of the production technology business units to manufacture the entire product or parts of it This subcontracting may imply giving out authority for manufacturing decisions, but the professional business unit always retains responsibility It may even choose to subcontract with outside vendors if they offer better quality, delivery, or price than can be obtained from the company units After a product is manufactured, it normally returns for final assembly and testing to the professional unit before being sent to the customers by the marketing personnel in that same unit

The production technology business units (see Figure 5 3) like a machine shop or a printed circuits manufacturing shop are not limited to accepting work only from the professional business units of the company They have the privilege and the duty to compete in the open market for any work suitable to their infrastructure, capability, and capacity. Such an open market policy helps these units establish fair and competitive prices for the work they do, whether for the company's professional units or for outside customers By organizing the technological services in centers as described, the company gains a number of additional advantages

1. There is no duplication of investment from creating the same type of production technology in each of the professional business units Some modern manufacturing equipment and machines are quite expensive and duplicating them just so each unit has its own equipment is not cost effective

2. Because the technology unit is expected to function as a business unit, the local management takes care to invest in new machines and adjust capacity so as to adapt it to realistic demands. Temporary excess of demand can be handled by subcontracting excess work to outside vendors

3. The quality of work and services provided by the technology centers must be equal to or better than what is available elsewhere Otherwise, the professional units of the company may choose to subcontract production tasks to external contractors Also, competitive quality is an obvious prerequisite if these centers are to attract external orders.

This background on how the company functions can help to explain the performance evaluation criteria If performance evaluations are to stimulate motivation in such an organization, clearly two slightly different sets of criteria are needed

1. For the product business units, all the criteria should be used that are applicable to any business: sales, sales per employee, profit and loss, added value, cash flow, inventory, work in progress, and so on In addition, managers must also consider criteria designed to measure the long-term stability and profitability of the business unit Among such criteria is product diversification, measured by the share of income attributable to each product A stable business unit should not depend on any single product for more than 10 percent of its income Most important, some criteria should be used to measure the innovative dynamism of the business unit Examples of such criteria are time between inception of a new product and its introduction to the market and number of novel products introduced per year

2. For the technology business units, some specially adapted measures are necessary in addition to the normal business criteria First, managers should measure the cycle time on each of the production processes and strive constantly to reduce those Second and simultaneously, the quality of the different production processes has to be constantly monitored and improved Third, the number of man hours per manufactured part has to be reduced below the level found in the competition

Organizational methods such as these, when properly applied and adapted to the specific needs and cultural environment of the high-technology company, may significantly reduce the transition problems of a product from research and development to production With these methods, the number of conflicting interests between the designers and innovators on one hand and the manufacturers on the other are more easily kept to a minimum By establishing appropriate success criteria, managers encourage each of these professionals to focus on their respective principal tasks, thus smoothing the transition and shortening the time to market of innovative products

Computer-Aided Design and Manufacturing Methods

The enormous advances made in the last decade in computer and information technology have created new opportunities never before available to smooth the transfer from research to production In the previous chapter, we discussed the impact of computer simulation, modeling, and testing as a way to minimize the R&D cycle This same approach has significant potential for reducing the classical transition problems from research and development to manufacturing A well-organized computer-integrated manufacturing (CIM) system, which encompasses computer-aided design (CAD) and computer-aided manufacturing (CAM), contributes to a smooth transition in a number of ways

First, during the design phase of the research and development cycle, computer-assisted design can generate, as a by-product, many of the tools subsequently necessary for manufacturing It can also provide test programs and procedures necessary for checking and verifying the performance parameters of the manufactured part A vast amount of error-prone, manual work, traditionally done by the production engineers in the manufacturing department, can now be done by computer Computer-assisted design thus helps avoid misunderstandings between the R&D and production engineers because it makes the work more graphic rather than abstract and open to interpretation

Second, because the CAD method concentrates responsibility for design of the manufacturing and testing tools in the hands of a single, competent individual—the product designer—the quality of the results is much improved The original designer of a part or of a product usually has all the information about the functions the part or product has to perform Also, when the product is faced with some constraints, the designer is usually the most suitable person to make the necessary trade-off Using traditional methods, a number of individuals, each overseeing a part of the process and belonging to different departments, had to work together to solve a complex problem Now, the best-informed individual can handle the job alone Clearly, such a procedure not only speeds up the process but also generally improves the end result

Without going into detail on computer-integrated manufacturing, which is beyond the scope of this text, we should caution that for the method to work effectively, a certain number of prerequisites must be fulfilled One important prerequisite is the insertion into the computer-assisted design system of all the pertinent data on the machines and the processes that may be used during manufacturing and testing These data are usually generated cooperatively between the R&D and the production engineers Once the data are installed and debugged in the computer-assisted design/manufacturing system, their presence in the system usually proves useful in a large variety of situations

Today, most managers agree that a soundly designed CAD/CIM system that is well tailored to the specific needs of the high-technology company can greatly improve performances (Gerwin and Kolodny, 1992, McDermott and Marucheck, 1995, Song and Dyer, 1995) Nevertheless, inappropriate use of CAD/CIM has reportedly caused problems in high-tech companies (Murotake and Allen, 1991, Robertson, Ulrich, and Filerman, 1991) The reader is encouraged to refer to the publications cited in this paragraph for more details on the subject

With the help of computer-integrated design and manufacturing, high-technology companies are significantly shortening the transition from research and development to manufacturing and marketing This shortened time improves their competitive stand and opens a wider window of market opportunity for an innovative product The method greatly improves the possibility for quickly introducing variations and useful modifications to a given product. Hence, it increases flexibility and adaptibility to a specific customer's requirements This flexibility gives an important market advantage to companies that use these methods well To illustrate this trend, we quote from an article by Bruce Nussbaum, published in *Business Week* on September 25, 1995 (see Case 5 2).

The Computer-Assisted Design (CAD) Revolution

It is not "sex, lies and videotape" but the drama of CAD, cost, and cycle time that is generating a revolution in the business of design Pressure to install computer-aided design technology, cut project costs, and sharply reduce time to market for new products is revolutionizing in-house design departments, from IBM to Rubbermaid, from AT&T to Steelcase

A new survey by *Business Week* and the Industrial Designers Society of America of 53 design departments in America's largest companies reveals that decentralization is in, budgets are up, staffing is down, high-tech spending is up, and time to market is down

Adapting Optimized Production Technology (OPT) and Just-in-Time (JIT) Methods to High Technology

In the first decades of the twentieth century, the industrial process was revolutionized by the introduction of mass-production, assembly line methods In the last decades, another cycle of radical change has taken place in industry This came with the introduction of innovative production approaches that helped to reduce cost, increase quality, and shorten the manufacturing cycle times by significant amounts Among these methods, two are of special interest for their potential adaptability to the R&D community and to the nonrepetitive manufacturing found in many high-technology companies We first discuss the just-in-time (JIT) method and its adaptability to high technology Then, we complement the JIT methodology with the optimized production technology (OPT) approach Finally, we see how these methods can help to smooth the transition from research and development to production and marketing of new products and systems

The just-in-time method has received extensive publicity and acclaim as one of the major factors in Japan's industrial success in the 1980s Essentially, companies using JIT profess holding few or no parts in stock and reducing work in process (WIP) to a minimum [1] Parts come to assembly lines just when they are needed. Thus, inventory and other costs can be minimized Most of the JIT literature discusses the benefits that are gained by implementing these methods in mass production Most often cited are gains in reducing inventory levels, work in process (WIP), shortening of lead time, and increasing the quality in large-scale, repetitive manufacturing (see Schonberger, 1982, 1986) [2]

However, the JIT literature gives little or no attention to the special needs of a research and development organization or the job-shop production environment, typical

---

[1] Work in process (WIP) designates assemblies or sub-assemblies waiting for parts or processing before they can be finished and delivered to customers

[2] Quality is improved by use of new, up-to-date parts and fresh materials

in most high-technology companies In the previous chapter, we discussed the basic difference between a mass-production environment and an R&D environment We concluded that a blind application of the just-in-time techniques is inappropriate for the research and development environment Therefore we introduced an analytical model for determining a rational inventory policy for R&D organizations (see chapter 4) However, by thoroughly analyzing just-in-time principles, a distinction can be made between Big JIT—the philosophy and strategy of the JIT methods—and Small JIT—the scheduling mechanism. Small JIT is the famous Japanese Kanban technique, which should not be applied to the R&D environment

The philosophy of the just-in-time method rests on a number of very sound principles that can be applied almost universally to any industrial environment The idea of just-in-time arrival of materials and components that are used for the immediate needs of the assembly line can lead to disaster if simply copied and applied to the R&D environment This was explained in the previous chapter However, the principle of JIT in its broad sense can be interpreted as meaning to *avoid large investments in anything not necessary to assure the smooth flow of work tasks in the organization* This definition, while precluding large inventories in parts and in work in process, allows the flexibility necessary to accommodate the uncertainties and variations typical in the R&D environment

Applying the redefined principle for inventory control of parts in an R&D organization, the smooth flow of work is clearly better served if the company keeps a certain level of standard parts in stock However, keeping a larger than necessary inventory not only increases the inventory cost but causes another problem due to the fast obsolescence of components in the high-technology industry It forces a choice of either frequently scrapping stocks of obsolete components, or worse, using them in the development of a new product. Such outdated parts may then reflect negatively on the product's overall performance

Looking into the problem of work in process (WIP) in an R&D environment, the Big JIT principle is quite applicable Although not as obvious as in the mass-production environment, an observer can still identify quantities of work in process being done by different individuals and departments This work has little to do with the smooth progress of the real projects and tasks, it often consists of tasks the individual believes will become necessary at some time in the future Investing in such tasks, up to a certain level, may make sense, especially if the individual does not have an immediately necessary task waiting that is related to concrete commitments of the company The more frequent case is to find people working on noncritical tasks—tasks that are not immediately necessary but will be needed only after a number of other project tasks are ready and completed For a more detailed definition of critical tasks and work packages, see chapter 6

In addition to other disadvantages, investing in work in process, which must wait until other critical tasks are accomplished before becoming useful, may be a total waste This will be true if the original specification of the task in question has to be significantly changed because of modifications in other tasks and work packages

An appropriate application of the just-in-time principles in a high-technology, innovative organization calls for focusing on the swift and smooth execution of the critical tasks first while keeping minimal amounts of inventories of both parts and work in process This minimum level should be adapted to specific needs, case by case, to allow for flexibility and account for the uncertainties typical in the R&D environment

The second method—optimized production technology (OPT)—was first developed by E M Goldratt (1980) as a computerized model for allocating and scheduling production resources It is in some sense complementary to the JIT approach Goldratt introduced analytical thinking to the manufacturing community and contributed a number of very useful ideas for optimizing production flow, especially in a job-shop type environment This type of environment is similar to the one found in the manufacturing departments of many high-technology companies The most interesting and probably the best application to high-technology companies is his suggested idea for bottleneck control.

Goldratt saw that if the demand for goods manufactured by a company exceeds the supply, the monetary income generated by the company is determined by the narrowest bottleneck in the manufacturing process. To illustrate, let us take a simplified example The manufacturing process in a company goes through three sequential stages A, B, and C, A is a resource that can process five products per hour, B can do three products per hour, and C can handle six products per hour The number of finished products the company can deliver to the market is therefore no more than three in any one hour If the income resulting from the sales of one end product is $100,000, the maximum per hour income is $300,000, determined by the resource bottleneck B From here, follow the important logical conclusions

1. The real cost of an hour lost on a bottleneck equals the value of one hour of the entire company's output ($300,000 in the example)

2. Any work done for a period of time on a bottleneck other than for processing immediately deliverable goods results in lost income for the company equal to the value of the entire company's throughput during this same period

3. A resource bottleneck should never develop because of a lack of materials or parts necessary for the continuous, smooth flow of work through this type of resource In particular, any bottleneck machine or process should be serviced, as much as possible, only during periods of company shut-down time so as to retain maximum utilization

4. A company should exercise stringent quality control of all materials and parts going into a resource bottleneck *before* they enter it Any rejects, after the bottleneck, lose the entire company's income for the period of the bottleneck

5. If there is an alternative for planning the work flow in the company to decrease the workload of a bottleneck resource, it should be exploited For example, if the resource bottleneck is a process, it can often be replaced by an equivalent, non-bottleneck process, if only sufficient attention is given to the problem

6. If possible, subcontract to outside vendors work that is designated to a bottleneck resource Often, wrong but widely accepted accounting methods hide the true picture and lead to improper management decisions For example, the accountants may determine that processing a part in the company costs only $300 an hour whereas subcontracting the work would cost $400 an hour For this reason, the accounting department often recommends disapproval of subcontracting the work However, if the work has to be done on a bottleneck resource, this type of decision logic is totally wrong The $400 an hour subcontracted work would allow the company to increase output and generate an additional $300,000 an hour of income, as shown in our example

The progress of an innovative, high-technology product from research and development through manufacturing is a sequential process, much like the one treated by Goldratt Therefore, wise application of the OPT approach in the high-technology sector can significantly increase the output of this industry

In the previous chapter we discussed how to identify bottlenecks in the R&D cycle and described methods for opening such bottlenecks To smooth the transition from research and development to production, managers must examine the entire sequence for bottlenecks The bottlenecks in the manufacturing job shops are easily identifiable by the stacks of items waiting to be processed by the bottleneck machine, facility, or process By concentrating their attention and investment on widening the bottlenecks, managers can shorten the total cycle time of research and development and manufacturing by very significant amounts

THE CONCURRENT ENGINEERING APPROACH

Earlier, we described and discussed some of the transition problems resulting from segregation of responsibility and from erection of organizational walls between various functional groups such as research and development, engineering, manufacturing, marketing, procurement, quality control, and after-sales service We also discussed several organizational methods for handling the problems Another approach, which has been gaining popularity since the beginning of the 1990s, is the concurrent or simultaneous engineering approach (Cleland, 1991; Katzenbach and Smith, 1993)

The concurrent engineering approach (CEA) first appeared in the late 1980s, inspired by the then-prevailing sense of decreasing competitiveness of European and U S industry, compared to the industry of Japan and the Far East (Schonberger, 1982, 1986) After studying the Japanese industry example, a large number of Western high-technology companies began organizing task force teams (Ancona and Caldwell, 1992, Katzenbach and Smith, 1993), accepted the need to implement a continuous innovation process, and applied the total quality management (TQM) approach (Cusumano, 1992, Deming, 1982; Gavin, 1988, Ishikawa, 1985) In the following sections we explore these procedures and explain how they help to smooth the transition from research and development to production

The Japanese Industry Example

In the beginning of the 1980s, numerous attempts were made to study and compare the Japanese industrial methodology to the one generally accepted in the West, and more specifically in the United States This effort resulted in a number of publications comparing the ways of designing, developing, and manufacturing products in the West to the significantly different approach taken by Japanese companies (Cusumano, 1991, Ken-ichi et al, 1988, Whitney, 1996) For the field of manufacturing, Schonberger (1986) summarized in *World Class Manufacturing* most of the lessons learned from this comparative analysis These writings show that contrary to initial misconceptions, the Japanese have significant ability to innovate There is strong evidence of the advantages of some methods applied in Japan for managing innovation in the research and development cycle and for the transition to large-scale manufacturing (Cusumano and Takeishi, 1991, Cusumano, 1992, Song and Dyer, 1995)

Most if not all the publications comparing the Japanese to the U S ways of conducting research and development and managing the transfer to production agree on at least one point: Much tighter links exist in Japan between the people doing research and development and the groups responsible for manufacturing For example, Westney and Sakakibara (1985) write "One of the most striking differences between the U S and the Japanese firms was that U S development and design groups were much less closely linked to manufacturing than their Japanese counterparts, at all levels: the corporate level, in terms of R&D funding and the physical location of research activities, the level of the project group and internal technology transfer, and the level of the individual engineer, in terms of career patterns and significant reference groups" (p 332)

In an article by Ken-ichi et al (1988), first published in Japanese and then translated into English, the authors reported on their investigation of the innovative behavior of Japanese companies with respect to new product development Two major points were highlighted: "(1) The speed with which new product development takes place and (2) the flexibility with which companies adapt their development process to changes in the external environment" (p 534) These two factors were recognized as being most significant contributors for gaining a competitive advantage in the international markets Further, the same authors noted, "The key to identifying the various factors that make speed and flexibility possible is to view the product development as a dynamic and continuous process of adaptation to changes in the environment" (p 534)

The practical application of this approach in Japan involves six intrafirm management principles and a seventh element a quite unique relationship that major Japanese companies develop, having a wide infrastructure of external primary and secondary subcontractors The six intrafirm principles applied are these

1. Top management involvement
2. Self-organized project teams (task forces)
3. Overlapping development phases
4. Multilearning
5. Subtle control
6. Organizational transfer of learning

Because of cultural and other differences, it would probably be a mistake to try to copy the Japanese approach directly, as successful as it might be in Japan Instead, managers could usefully adapt some of the innovative ideas to the Western socioeconomic and industrial environment Probably the ideas that have been adapted most successfully in the West in recent years are the organization of task force teams, the continuous innovation process, and the total quality management approach, which are discussed in the following paragraphs A number of principles are common to these and other Japanese approaches

First, top management must be involved in changing a company's process of product development and manufacturing It is impossible to overemphasize the importance of this factor Without total management commitment, it would have been impossible—especially in Japan, where organizational rigidity and decision hierarchy are traditional—to promote ideas such as self-organizing product development teams Such teams, by purpose and by definition, bypass hierarchical obstacles They apply a self-contained, flexible, and speedy decision process that, to be effective, must receive firm backing from the top

In most cases, the only way such an approach can be accepted in an organization is for the organization to experience a real sense of emergency The team is given a mission, sometimes a "mission impossible," and the entire organization is requested by the top management to help in bringing the mission to success in view of its critical importance to the company's future Reportedly (Ken-ichi et al , 1988), this has been the case in development of the Fuji-Xerox FX-3500 plain paper copier, Canon's Auto Boy automatic camera, the Honda City car, and others. All were developed by special task force teams in record time, with the total and unconditional support of top management of the companies involved

Another significant difference between the Japanese approach and the practice in the West concerns the way large industry treats subcontractors (Cusumano and Takeishi, 1991) Japanese industry gained notable flexibility by using a wide base of small and medium-size subcontractors, and between the leading contractor and the subcontractors in Japan there is a high degree of loyalty and interdependence Such relationships are exceptional in the West, where major companies are likely to "squeeze" their subcontractors in difficult times, asking them to reduce prices and accelerate deliveries Examples of large companies compensating subcontractors for past performances when the situation improves is extremely rare As successful as it might be, this Japanese example cannot be very useful in the West until a basic change takes place in the way we do business

Organizing Task Force Teams

The organization of task force teams to achieve important objectives quickly and effectively is certainly not a new idea. Despite the obvious advantages of the team idea, the West had to experience a number of years of sluggish productivity growth in the United States and a deep sense of profound crisis in Western industry to make the idea widely acceptable "In the particular area of manufacturing leadership, moreover, the use of an alternative organizational design, vis-à-vis, the use of product design teams, can make dramatic improvements in a company's global competitiveness These teams provide a multi-disciplinary integration of organizational effort through a simultaneous product and process design strategy" (Cleland, 1991, p 24)

In *The Wisdom of Teams* (1993), two senior McKinsey & Company partners, Katzenbach and Douglas, claim, "We cannot meet the challenges ahead, from total quality to customer service to innovation, without teams Teams are turning companies around. Motorola relied heavily on teams to surpass its Japanese competition in producing the lightest, smallest, and highest-quality cellular phones. At 3M, teams are critical to meeting the company's well-publicized goal of producing half of each year's revenues from the previous five years' innovations" (p 2)

Task force teams can be organized in a number of possible ways In Japan, they are called self-organized project teams and consist of members from diverse backgrounds Often, the members of the team are hand-picked by top management and given freedom to create something new. The performance of such teams is expected to be commensurate with the confidence they have been voted by the management This expectation often risks team members' reputations and sometimes their careers In the United States, some companies have reorganized their activities, placing the design and the manufacturing functions in the same physical location and under one senior manager. Another method used is "to appoint a key individual as an integrator, responsible for working and coordinating with the organizational interfaces, so that a unified approach is taken in the design, with due consideration of the design, manufacturing and marketing factors" (Cleland, 1991, p 25) However, some research shows that selecting the team may not be a simple task (For details, refer to Ancona and Caldwell (1992))

Some of these strategies resemble to a considerable degree those described earlier in the chapter in the section titled "Organizational Methods " Others are similar to the old "matrix" form of organization familiar to project managers It is therefore important to stress the slight but significant differences that distinguish task force teams from other organizational forms Among the most noteworthy are the following

1 *Sense of Purpose and Urgency* A task force must receive a mandate to perform a mission generally accepted as critically important to the company The companywide perception that the team's assignment is to resolve a crisis situation in the most expeditious manner gives the team the legitimacy to bypass some of the company's bureaucratic structures

2 *The Autonomy and Power to Simplify the Approval Process* Because the team members from all the relevant disciplines work in close collaboration, all information necessary for the approval of different steps in the process is constantly shared Therefore, when a team concludes its deliberations on a certain topic, the logical decision becomes readily evident Formal approval in such a case is a natural extension of the same process

3 *Top Management Attitude* Last is the power and backing the team receives from the top There is no substitute for total commitment of the entire company's management to assure success of the task force Only if such consensus can be achieved and implemented in a Western company can the concept bring the expected positive results

The Continuous Innovation Process

Another concept that was first widely used by Japanese industry to achieve competitive advantages in world markets is the continuous improvement strategy Under this strategy, called Kaizen (Imai, 1986), the Japanese place a high priority on continuous incremental improvements that, over time, leapfrog competitors who practice the traditional sequential approach. In the traditional approach, as soon as the R&D cycle is considered finished, the product goes into production and the research and development effort for that product is ended

Once a company has adopted the task force teams approach, described in the previous section, it is relatively easy and natural to implement the Kaizen method as well Unlike the sequential cycles approach, in which the R&D team responsible for the product's development is practically dispersed after the end of the research and development cycle, the task force teams continue to follow the product during its entire lifetime Thus, feedback coming from customers, information on competitive products, new market trends, and other information can receive adequate, timely, and professionally competent attention that can be translated into product improvements as necessary. Figure 5 4 is a graphic representation of the continuous improvement (or Kaizen) method Note that product performance level includes also improvement in reliability, reduced cost, and any other parameter that increases the competitive advantage of the product in the marketplace

The time between two product generations depends on many factors Although the trend is toward shortening the time between two generations of high-technology products, a second major research and development cycle would not normally start before some significant breakthrough idea or technology had justified the beginning of such an effort Any major R&D cycle requires a significant investment, which companies can usually afford only periodically Between two R&D cycles, the company can maintain its market share much better if the structure for continuous incremental innovation is held in place. Top management must, of course, require and foster the continuous innovation process, making it an integral part of the company's strategy

The Total Quality Management Approach

Probably one of the most significant conceptual innovations in recent years in the management of industrial organizations is the total quality management (TQM) approach The pioneering work of such visionaries as Deming, Juran, and Fiegenbaum, which was first applied with remarkable success in Japan by Ishikawa, Taguchi, and others, is now widely accepted in most of the industrialized world (Deming, 1982; Gavin, 1988, Ishikawa, 1985)

Prior to the acceptance of TQM, quality was treated in many industries as an added burden that required an added cost Management often failed to understand that

FIGURE 5 4 The Continuous Innovation Process

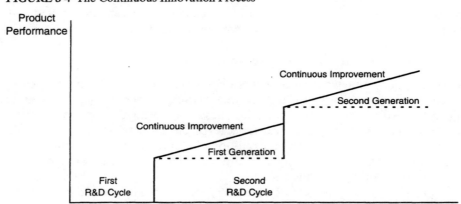

high quality in every process can actually reduce cost, increase profitability, and guarantee or even expand the company's market share. The thinking was flawed, concentrating on inspection of the product for conformance, with emphasis on detecting and managing defects

If you consider all the cost and effort necessary to correct noncompliance in a company as a wasted output, it is useful to describe the company as containing two factories The first is the factory that delivers goods to customers, the second throws materials and work hours into the garbage Often, the output of the "garbage" factory can reach 20 percent to 30 percent of the company's output! Total quality management could in this sense be seen as a concentrated management effort to close the garbage factory This is achieved by shifting emphasis from defect correction to defect prevention. It comes from closely monitoring every process in the company and ensuring immediate action if the process goes out of its control limits

The objective of total quality management is to broaden the focus on quality and to embrace the concept of continuous process improvement Management must change their concept from quality that is inspected into the product to quality that is designed and built into the product Managers must move from acceptable levels of defects to nontolerance of defects, a system in which employees strive for continuous process improvement and reduction of defects to the absolute minimum level Companies practicing TQM have reported orders of magnitude reduction of defect levels by applying the TQM approach and methodology [3] Today, the concept of TQM is seen extended in many companies. For example, Houser, Simester, and Wernerfeld (1995) in *Internal Customers and Internal Suppliers* describe and analyze one such extension (See also Griffin and Hauser, 1993)

The TQM methodology consists of applying a well-defined, step-by-step procedure for continuous product and process improvement, and use of a set of tools and techniques to measure and identify problems This is followed by on-the-spot corrective action to achieve the desired improvement (U S Department of Defense, 1989)

The Total Quality Management Procedure

Figure 5 5 is a graphic representation of the TQM procedure Typically, it consists of six steps, most of which are recursive in a way that leads to continuously improved performances lower defect level, lower cost, reduced cycle time, and improved quality

The first step, and probably the most critically important one, is to establish true, genuine management commitment and support for an in-depth implementation of the TQM strategy Management has to be exposed to and convinced by real-life examples, relevant to their company's type of business, of the advantages that can be gained from total quality management This conversion requires training at all levels of management, starting from the very top Then, management has to create the vision of what the organization wants to be and where it wants to go

Because any significant change in an organization is usually met with resistance, management must find ways to modify the existing culture and institute a new, more flexible, and cooperative attitude that encourages and accepts innovation Adequate financial and human resources must be allocated for the implementation of total quality

---

[3] Defects level reduction from few parts per thousand to few parts per million are not exceptional

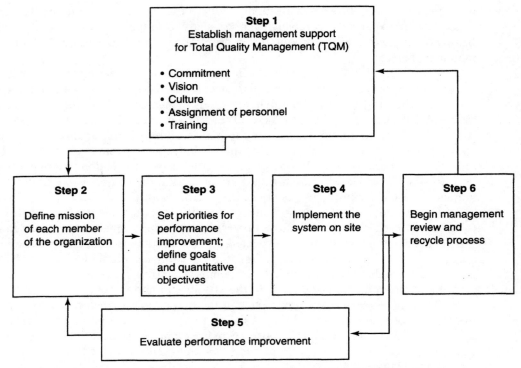

FIGURE 5 5 The Total Quality Management (TQM) Stepwise Recursive Procedure

management These investments will later be returned to the company with a generous margin, coming from the improvement in results At the beginning, however, assigning key people to the effort and providing them with all necessary support are essential

The second step consists of defining the mission of every member of the organization. Logically, this effort should start with deciding first on the mission of the key people and subsequently making this determination for all personnel in the company Everyone in the organization is viewed as both a customer and a supplier Almost every job requires the holder to provide some goods, services, or information to someone else in the organization This someone is the "customer," whether external or internal To provide the required output to his or her customer, the individual normally must receive some goods, services, or information from suppliers, whether external or internal For these suppliers, this individual plays the role of "customer "

The mission of each individual in the TQM spirit involves adding value and providing customers with products and services that consistently meet their needs and expectations Everyone must know his or her customer's requirements Everyone must also make suppliers aware of his or her needs and maintain with them a constant dialogue aimed at increasing the satisfaction of these needs and requirements

The third step consists of establishing quantitative goals and objectives for performance improvement These goals must reflect the process capabilities of the organization so that the goals are realistic For example, if a process generates a 0 1 percent defect level, a realistic goal may be to reduce this level to less than 500 ppm (parts per million) A well-accepted technique for setting quantitative goals is to establish the cost of quality (COQ). This is the total cost of scrap caused by nonconformance plus the cost of conformance—the investment to ensure high quality.

The goals should first be set at the senior management level They should reflect strategic choices about the processes most critical to the organization's survival Middle and line management set both functional and process improvement goals to achieve the strategic goals set by the top management The hierarchy of goals establishes an architecture that links improvement efforts across the organization Within traditional organizations, performance improvement teams provide cross-functional orientation and the employees on these teams become involved in the process issues. Thus, the entire organization is effectively mobilized to form an ideal setting for improving performance.

The fourth step consists of on-site implementation of the previously selected performance improvement processes, using the TQM tools described in the next section After the performance improvement goals have been established, a systematic statistical measurement of the process performance is necessary The causes of variation from the control limits are carefully analyzed by competent problem-solving teams A logical order of priorities for actions to be taken by such teams is established on the basis of cause-effect breakdown examinations After a corrective action has been implemented, the process continues to be measured and monitored The results recorded are again analyzed and further improvement action is taken as necessary

The fifth step consists of evaluating the longer-term results of the improvement process Elements in this comparison are not only the "before" and "after" process performance level but also such important factors as the customer's satisfaction, the savings in wasted materials and hours spent redoing work, the reduction in cycle time, and so on The period between two such evaluations depends on the nature of the process, in any case, it must be long enough to allow the evaluators to collect statistically significant data Most organizations have existing instruments for measuring these factors that can be used as is or modified if necessary. The key is to select measures that can be used by work units to manage and evaluate their products and services so that continuous process improvement can take place

The sixth step consists of management review and recycling To ensure that the continuous improvement process becomes integral to the company's work style, stagnation must be avoided After seeing the first symptoms of diminishing returns from implementation of the previous steps, management must intervene, review the situation, establish new and more ambitious goals, allocate the necessary resources, and start the process again—and again.

The Total Quality Management Tools and Techniques

To help managers implement the stepwise procedure described in the previous paragraph, a set of generic tools and techniques has been designed and applied with considerable success. Here, we outline only the most popular ones (For more detail, see Ishikawa, 1985, Gavin, 1988; or Department of Defense, 1989)

1 *Control Charts.* Probably the most basic of all TQM tools, the control chart was first introduced by Deming (1982) as part of statistical process control (SPC) This tech-

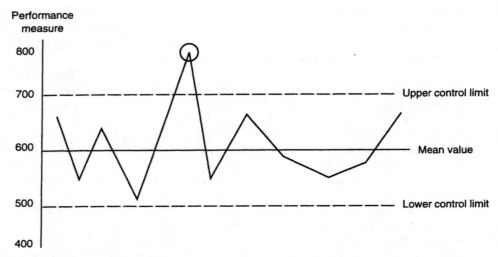

FIGURE 5 6 Typical Control Chart

nique has been successfully applied, first in Japan and then throughout the industrial world Figure 5 6 illustrates a typical Control Chart

    Control charts are usually displayed on centrally visible boards They plot the variation of the measured process performance over time Every time the process goes outside its control limits, the process is stopped, analyzed, and not restarted until the problem-solving team recommends appropriate corrective action

FIGURE 5 7 Typical Fish-bone Diagram

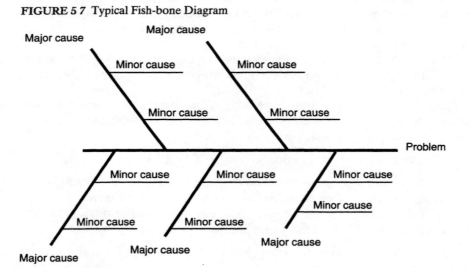

2 *Cause and Effect Diagrams* Sometimes called "fish-bone" diagrams, cause and effect diagrams provide effective help in analyzing a defect (problem) and its potential causes Figure 5 7 illustrates a typical fish-bone diagram

In this diagram, all potential major causes for a problem are shown as main branches Potential minor causes associated with each major cause are depicted as a leaf of a branch With the help of such a tool, the problem-fixing team is able to identify the problem quickly and to take corrective action

3 *Pareto Charts.* The relative contribution of each subproblem to the total problem can be displayed in a Pareto chart Based on the Pareto principle, which states that usually 20 percent of all possible factors are responsible for 80 percent of all given phenomena, it allows management to concentrate their attention and priority in treating these factors first Figure 5.8 is an illustration of a typical Pareto Chart

This diagram shows that factor A is responsible for 50 percent of the cost of waste, Factor B accounts for roughly 30 percent, and all other factors, C to I, contribute the remaining 20 percent In reality, of course, the ratio may not be exactly 80 percent to 20 percent, but the principle is valid in most practical situations

To summarize, total quality management is now being applied in many high-tech companies with great success This is illustrated in Case 5 3

The results obtained by Dowty reflect the degree of management commitment in this company In the small number of exceptions in which introduction of total quality management has not led to satisfactory results, there is usually a lack of total commitment, which can only come from the top down. Other failures occur in companies that, instead of a flexible, "no nonsense" approach, have taken a rigid, almost "pious" implementation of the method, without proper adaptation to the existing company's environment

FIGURE 5 8 Typical Pareto Chart

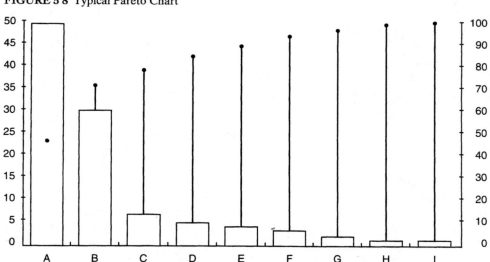

CASE 5.3

The Dowty Example

Dowty is an aerospace firm based in the United Kingdom The company was having severe problems in the early 1990s According to its managing director Tony Belisario, despite its high reputation, the company's management was complacent and the customers dissatisfied. The company failed to win significant business on the European Fighter (a major European fighter aircraft program) because it did not listen to its customers Belisario believes that this rejection, although a major blow at the time, was the catalyst for change It was critical for the company to get back on course. But how?

The solution A total quality management program was instituted The majority of Dowty Fuel Systems' senior executives "bought in" to the TQM process from the outset, following their participation in an off-site awareness day run by a competent consultant From this group, a steering committee was set up, this committee then put many TQM executive techniques into practice One of the first was analysis of the cost of quality (COQ). This is the measure of the cost of conformance—deliberate investment made to ensure good quality—weighed against the cost of nonconformance, or the price of getting it wrong This analysis showed that Dowty, a 50-million British pound business, was losing 6 million pounds annually through nonconformance—and this was a conservative estimate.

Just four weeks after analyzing the cost of quality, Dowty put corrective action teams (CATs) in place to determine key processes and methods for improvement and to implement corrective measures This swift action was a vital part of the plan to gain quick results Each CAT was given a major objective A team in the machining department, for example, was required to reduce errors by half in six months The team met its target in the required six months, after 10 months they had achieved an 82 percent improvement Other statistics are equally impressive In three years, Dowty Fuel Systems has improved already healthy margins by 50 percent and trebled its return on capital Service to customers has also improved significantly

SUMMARY

In this chapter, we discussed the most important classical problems associated with the transition of a high-technology product from research and development to manufacturing The discussion showed that in the traditional, phase-sequential approach, organizational "walls" of responsibility are often built between the R&D department and the manufacturing department, thus obstructing the smooth transfer of the product between the research and development cycle and the manufacturing cycle Another associated problem that occurs frequently was described the maturity of design problem

The importance of this problem has grown recently with the increasing pressure to shorten the R&D cycle The two problems were shown to lead to the third classical problem the need to redesign for manufacturing Redesigns require additional time and investment, which add to the complexity of the transition from research to production

Next, some effective methods for smoothing the transfer period were described and discussed, including the ways that new organizational thinking may contribute positively to lowering the division-of-responsibility barrier Different forms of organizations were compared and their advantages and drawbacks were examined Then, the impact of recently available computer-aided design and manufacturing technology was discussed These new tools were shown to have great potential for solving the interface problems and thus shortening the time to market for a new, innovative product At the end of this section, some of the most successful approaches used in manufacturing organizations (just in time and optimized production technology) were shown to be adaptable to the high-technology environment and specifically to the research and development and job-shop production typical in many high-technology companies.

Finally, the most recent version of concurrent engineering, which was inspired to a significant degree by the striking success of Japanese industry during the 1980s, was presented in some detail After a review of the Japanese industry example, the organization of task force teams was described The discussion showed that such task force teams can lead naturally to the creation of a flexible work environment that accepts and adapts to the continuous innovation process Continuous innovation was shown to bridge the gap between two generations of a product, allowing the companies practicing this method to extend their market share. The last topic discussed, the total quality management approach, was presented in some detail because of its vital importance to the high-technology industry. The TQM procedure was outlined and the most important TQM tools were described so the reader could quickly grasp this increasingly accepted philosophy, which has transformed the culture in many high-technology companies

For Further Reflection

1 List and discuss briefly all the factors hampering the smooth transition of a high-technology product from research and development to manufacturing in a functionally organized high-technology company

2 Compare the advantages and disadvantages of a traditional high-technology organization versus a business units type organization

3 Is computer-aided design and manufacturing more important for companies producing long lines of high-technology products or for companies engaged in small quantity production? Explain why

4 Describe basic principles of just in time (JIT) and optimized production technology (OPT) What are appropriate ways for employing these techniques in the high-technology environment?

5 List the most important lessons learned by comparing the Japanese manufacturing approaches to those practiced in most Western high-technology industry during the 1980s

6 What are some of the most important problems associated with organizing task force teams? How can these problems be avoided or solved?

7 Is continuous innovation practiced in your company? If not, why not? If yes, describe the contribution of this approach to your company

8 Describe the most important total quality management (TQM) tools Who should be responsible for updating the data while using these tools? Why?

9. Why has total quality management gained such widespread acceptance in recent years? Is TQM practiced in your company? If yes, describe some real-life improvements achieved after its introduction Are there disappointments with the method? Describe and suggest solutions

10 Describe the typical TQM procedure for continuous process improvement What are the quality methods practiced by your company? In what way are they different and why?

References and Further Reading

Ancona, Deborah G , and David F Caldwell (1992) "Demography and Design: Predictors of New Product Team Performance," Working Paper 36. Cambridge, MA: Sloan School of Management

> This working paper examines the composition of task force teams appointed by company management to do more complex tasks and to cross functional boundaries within the organization The authors performed a study using 409 individuals from 45 new product teams in five high-technology companies They investigated the impact of diversity on team performance, challenging the conventional wisdom that suggests that teams be composed of more diverse members. Their study found that functional and tenure diversity each has its own distinct effects. The greater the functional diversity, the more team members communicated outside the team's boundaries This communication was with a variety of groups such as marketing, manufacturing, and top management: the more external the communication, the higher were the managerial ratings of innovation As use of task force teams becomes increasingly popular, this paper provides an interesting insight for managers in high-technology firms

Cleland, D I (1991) "Product Design Teams: The Simultaneous Engineering Perspective " *Project Management Journal* 22, no 4:5–10

Cusumano, Michael (1991) *Japan's Software Factories A Challenge to U S Management* New York: Oxford University Press

Cusumano, Michael (1992) "Japanese Technology Management: Innovations, Transferability, and the Limitations of 'Lean' Production," Working Paper 75 Cambridge, MA: Sloan School of Management

> The author is an active contributor to the "Japan Program" at MIT, a program that over several years has examined and compared management approaches in Japan to those in the United States and the West This paper examines factors that have helped Japanese industry to achieve competitiveness in a number of industries Among the most important is a series of innovations and practices in manufacturing and product development that have been referred to as lean: aimed at high productivity as well as high quality, and thus high price-performance in the value of products delivered to the customer The paper outlines some innovations and practices, particularly as they exist in Japan It then brings up two other is-

sues: how transferable these practices are outside Japan, and what limitations the Japanese themselves have encountered

Cusumano, Michael, and Akira Takeishi (1991) Supplier Relations and Management: A Survey of Japanese, Japanese-Transplant, and U S Auto Plants, MIT Japan Program Working Paper Series (1991)

> This paper presents the results of a questionnaire survey sent to a sample of automobile manufacturers in the United States and Japan (including Japanese-managed plants in the United States) during the spring of 1990 The data support observations that Japanese and U S practices tend to differ in key areas Japanese suppliers perform better in dimensions such as quality (defects) and prices (meeting targets, reducing prices over time); and that Japanese-managed auto plants established in the United States have, in general, adopted Japanese practices and receive extremely high levels of quality from Japanese as well as U S suppliers *These findings provide evidence that Japanese practices and performance levels are transferable outside Japan and suggest that considerable improvements are possible for U S suppliers supplying U S auto plants* In addition, the survey indicates that U S firms have adopted at least some practices traditionally associated with Japanese firms, apparently reflecting some movement toward Japanese practices and higher performance levels in supplier management

Deming, W E (1982) "Improvement of Quality and Productivity through Action by Management " *National Productivity Review*, Winter, pp. 12–22.

Gavin, D A (1988) *Managing Quality* New York: The Free Press

Gerwin, Donald, and Harvey Kolodny (1992) *Management of Advanced Manufacturing Technology Strategy, Organization, and Innovation.* New York: Wiley-Interscience

> The authors deal with complex issues and problems involved in the planning, organization, and implementation of plantwide control reprogramming of automated manufacturing systems, or CIM (computer-integrated manufacturing) The topics covered include the process of introducing programmable automation into manufacturing organizations; programming vast numbers of independent machines to function in harmony; problems of integrating manufacturing centers using both quantitative and qualitative approaches, and more

Griffin, Abbie, and John R Hauser (1993) "The Voice of the Customer," Working Paper 56 Cambridge, MA: Sloan School of Management

> This paper focuses on the "voice-of-the-customer" component of quality function deployment (QFD)—that is, the tasks of identifying customer needs, structuring customer needs, and providing priorities for customer needs In recent years, many U S and Japanese firms have adopted quality function deployment in a total-quality-management process in which the "voice of the customer" is deployed throughout the R&D, engineering, and manufacturing stages of product development For example, in the first "house" of quality function deployment, customer needs are linked to design attributes, thus encouraging the joint consideration of marketing issues and engineering issues

Hauser, John R , Duncan I Simester, and Birger Wernerfeld (1995) *Internal Customers and Internal Suppliers,* Working Paper 194 Cambridge, MA: Sloan School of Management

> In implementing total quality management, many firms have adopted systems by which internal customers evaluate internal suppliers The internal supplier receives a larger bonus for a higher evaluation The paper examines such incentive systems and shows that under fairly general conditions, the internal supplier will normally share any gains with the internal customer in return for a higher evaluation However, the firm, without loss of profit, can

design incentive systems that anticipate this "gainsharing " Then two simple incentive systems are examined For either system, the firm can select parameters for the reward functions that will lead both the internal customer and the internal supplier to choose the same profit-maximizing actions that the firm would choose if it had the power and knowledge to dictate actions In each incentive system some risk is transferred from the firm to the employees and the firm must pay for this; but in return, the firm need not observe either the internal supplier's actions or the internal customer's actions The authors claim that the incentive systems are robust, even if the firm guesses wrongly about what employees perceive as costly and about how employee actions affect profit

Imai, M (1986) *Kaizen* New York: Random House

Ishikawa, K (1985) *What Is Total Quality Control?* Englewood Cliffs, NJ: Prentice Hall

Katzenbach, Jon R , and Douglas K Smith (1993) *The Wisdom of Teams Creating the High-Performance Organization* Cambridge, MA: MIT Press

In *The Wisdom of Teams,* two senior McKinsey & Company partners argue that we cannot meet the challenges ahead—from total quality to customer service to innovation—without teams Emphasizing the role that teams play in turning companies around, the authors examine the use of teams in U S industry For example, Motorola relied heavily on teams to surpass its Japanese competition in producing the lightest, smallest, and highest-quality cellular phones At 3M, teams are critical to meeting the company's well-publicized goal of producing half of each year's revenues from the previous five years' innovations

Ken-ichi, Imai, Ikujiro Nonaka, and Hirotaka Takeuchi (1988) *Managing the New Product Development Process How Japanese Companies Learn and Unlearn, Readings in the Management of Innovation,* edited by M L Tushman and W. L Moore New York: Harper Business

Markoff, John (1994) "Inside Intel: Saga of Chip Switch " *International Herald Tribune,* 22 December, p 9

McCord, Kent R., and Steven D Eppinger (1993) "Managing the Integration Problem in Concurrent Engineering," Working Paper 95 Cambridge, MA: Sloan School of Management

This paper deals with problems that arise when more than one task force team has to work together on large research and development programs Concurrent engineering in such projects generally involves multiple cross-functional teams working simultaneously on separate aspects of the overall development effort The often complex technical coupling among such teams makes integrating their activities an essential yet difficult task for project management The authors refer to this challenge of integrating teams as the integration problem in concurrent engineering The paper presents a methodology for determining the needs for integration and coordination by studying the underlying technical structure of a project It uses a project modeling tool known as the design structure matrix (DSM) to depict the patterns of required information flow in a project This matrix representation allows managers to identify where coordination is most essential and then to design integration mechanisms based on the specific technical information needs of the project

McDermott, C M , and A Marucheck (1995). "Training in CAD: An Exploratory Study of Methods and Benefits " *IEEE Transactions on Engineering Management,* November, pp 57–61

Murotake, David K , and Thomas J Allen (1991) "Computer Aided Engineering and Project Performance: Managing a Double-Edged Sword," Working Paper 47 Cambridge, MA: Sloan School of Management

The authors warn about inappropriate use of computer-aided engineering (CAE) They assert that computer-aided engineering tools are like a double-edged sword. Properly employed, CAE tools improve engineering productivity and help keep technical projects on schedule and under budget For some kinds of work, CAE tools can also stimulate creativity However, computer tools can have equally detrimental effects For less-structured engineering tasks, such as preliminary analysis and problem solving, the use of inappropriate or inadequate tools can severely constrain performance By encouraging the "cloning" of old solutions, computer tools can also stifle creativity and yield suboptimal designs through negative biasing

Nussbaum, B (1995) "Is In-House Design on the Way Out?" *Business Week,* 25 September, p 31

Pisano, Gary P , and Steven C Wheelwright. (1995) *The New Logic of High-Tech R&D* Boston, MA: Harvard Business School Publishing Corporation

In *The New Logic of High-Tech R&D,* Gary P Pisano and Steven C Wheelwright assert that managers of high-technology companies should view manufacturing as a primary source of gaining competitive advantage They warn of conventional thinking that is often costly and potentially dangerous to the competitive health of high-technology companies They show, in fact, that it is not only possible but also necessary to excel at developing new products and new manufacturing processes simultaneously In many high-technology markets, manufacturing process innovation, according to the authors, is becoming an increasingly critical capability for product innovation.

Robertson, David, Karl Ulrich, and Marc Filerman (1991) "CAD and Cognitive Complexity: Beyond the Drafting Board Metaphor," Working Paper 31 Cambridge, MA Sloan School of Management

Computer-aided design (CAD) systems can and should support and enhance the product development process Unfortunately, the benefits delivered by current systems have not met users' expectations. This is largely because of two closely related problems: These systems have historically been designed to support the drafting function, not engineering design, and CAD systems often have interfaces that are difficult to use Computer-aided design systems should be designed to minimize the cognitive complexity facing the engineer; they should be easy to use and should help the engineer manage design-related complexity The systems must move beyond the drafting board metaphor In this article, a series of five propositions are developed that expand and refine these ideas

Schonberger, R J (1982) *Japanese Manufacturing Techniques Nine Hidden Lessons in Simplicity.* New York: The Free Press

Schonberger, R J. (1986) *World Class Manufacturing The Lessons of Simplicity Applied* New York: The Free Press

Song, X M , and B Dyer (1995) "Innovation Strategy and the R&D-Marketing Interface in Japanese Firms: A Contingency Perspective." *IEEE Transactions on Engineering Management,* November

Ulrich, Karl T , and Steven D. Eppinger (1995) *Product Design and Development* New York McGraw-Hill.

The authors employ detailed examples to illustrate key concepts—a different product in each chapter, including the Apple Powerbook, specialized mountain bike suspension fork, and General Motors 3 8L V6 engine They provide structured, step-by-step methodologies in each chapter, making the book suited for use by teams engaged in ongoing project work The book uses an interdisciplinary approach, including the perspectives of marketing, design, and manufacturing It treats contemporary design and development issues such as identifying customer needs, design for manufacturing, prototyping, and industrial design

Urban, Glen L , and John R Hauser (1993) *Design and Marketing of New Products* 2d ed Englewood Cliffs, NJ: Prentice Hall

U S Department of Defense (1989) "Department of Defense Directive on Total Quality Management," DOD 5000 51 G - Final Draft Washington, DC: U S Department of Defense.

Warner, Malcolm, Werner Wobbe, and Peter Brodner, eds (1990) *New Technology and Manufacturing Management Strategic Choices for Flexible Production Systems* New York: John Wiley

> Concentrating on microelectronics and information technology, this text explores the ways in which progress in these fields can be expected to give rise to new types of production facilities, work organization, and manufacturing management Supported by numerous case studies, the book also discusses topics with titles such as these: Towards the Fully Automated Factory, Strategic Options for CIM Integration, Flexible Manufacturing Systems and Cells in Europe, The Factors behind Successful Technology Innovation

Westney, E D , and Sakakibara, K. (1985) "The Role of Japan Based R&D in Global Technology Strategy," *Technology in Society*, Vol 7 New York: Pergamon Press

Whitney, John O (1996) *The Economics of Trust Liberating Profits and Restoring Corporate Vitality.* Cambridge, MA: MIT Press

> Mistrust, argues John O Whitney, foments meddling corporate bureaucracies that police even the most trivial transactions—squelching innovation and dragging down revenues with crippling administrative overhead It discourages sales from talking to marketing, marketing to manufacturing, or manufacturing to design (or any of them talking to customers or suppliers) Mistrust provokes harassed managers to endlessly massage their budget and forecast numbers, and their superiors to doubt the results they submit

CHAPTER

Problems with Managing Multiproduct Organizations

6

Managing multiproduct, high-technology companies and organizations is particularly challenging. In addition to problems identified earlier, the complexity of the organization creates conflicts of interests, as explained in this chapter. Dealing with these conflicts has a direct impact on management's ability to control successfully the cost and delivery schedules of goods and services that constitute the business of the company Therefore, understanding the problems and mastering approaches for solving them is critically important for managers of multiproduct organizations

In a single-product organization, all resources of the company are dedicated to only one product There is no competition for time or attention of a person, a machine, or any other resource when the product needs them If, however, the company runs a large number of projects in parallel using limited resources, frequent conflicts of interest arise when more than one product requires the same resource at the same time If the nature of the work allows precise scheduling of the time each project task will get service from a resource, then managers can overcome some of the conflicts by careful planning The problem becomes much more difficult to manage when times of arrival of project tasks are uncertain The complexity grows even further when the duration of performing a task is also unreliably predictable

As most managers of high-technology companies sooner or later must face the problems of managing multiproduct organizations, the following material should be part of any textbook dealing with management of high technology Unfortunately, this has not been the case We therefore explain the problem in detail To do this, we shall need some definitions from the theory of project management We describe a "matrix" organization and explain why it represents quite accurately the work flow in a complex, multiproduct organization Then we examine the queues of tasks waiting for a resource to be available for service and quantify the extra time and cost associated with waiting in line Finally, we develop and propose methodology to minimize the cost to the company resulting from such delays.

Many successful high-technology companies originated as "start-up" companies—businesses that are usually created around one idea, which, if developed successfully, results in one marketable product The organization in this case is simple and all its resources are fully dedicated to the success of "the product" as it goes through the cycles of development, manufacturing, and marketing Usually, the people involved in the process are few in number, highly motivated, and fully informed of the situation in each stage of the operation

After a successful start-up, a company will often develop a whole line of products addressing the needs of different segments of the same market The line of products is often derivative of the basic product appropriately sized and featured to compete successfully with similar products on the market However, most successful companies go beyond this stage and in their mature phase find it necessary to develop products for other markets as part of their core business Expanding the core business of a high-technology company should not be confused with diversification in general The latter was very popular, especially among mature companies, in the 1970s and the beginning of the 1980s. Companies like ITT, to cite just one example, bought car rental businesses (Avis) and hotels, and invested in many other loosely related enterprises Most of them learned that this type of diversification failed to deliver the hoped-for results After that, many firms sold their acquisitions and concentrated on their core business.

On the other hand, a growing high-technology company usually can enlarge the scope of its core business by product diversification The need for rational diversification to decrease the impact of market fluctuations is well understood by competent management (Harriot and Pemberton, 1995) A high-technology company depending on a single product or on a single market is eventually doomed to fail, no matter how innovative and successful the product Over time, a better and more competitive product will appear on the market and thus reduce the company's market share and profit margins to a degree that makes the company no longer profitable Having a line of products rather than a single one reduces the risk of failure to a certain degree and extends the time the company stays competitive in its specific market However, real long-term stability is normally achieved only when a company reaches the stage of a multiproduct, multimarket organization.

A well-managed multiproduct, multimarket company is much better prepared than a single-product firm to cope with market fluctuations There are always situations in which one of its products is losing market share because of competition, or one of its product lines is depressed by decreased demand in its specific market. Unfortunately, however, a much higher degree of management skills is required to direct competently a complex multiproduct organization. In this chapter we examine important current problems existing in many companies that have grown from single-product to multiproduct complex organizations

THE COMPLEXITY OF A MULTIPRODUCT
HIGH-TECHNOLOGY ORGANIZATION

The simplest industrial organization to manage is the one manufacturing a single and mature product For example, Gordon and Company in London has distilled and marketed Gordon's Gin since 1769 Although manufacturing technology may have changed through the centuries, the product has basically remained the same In such organizations, all steps of the manufacturing process are strictly defined Because there is little change, communication within the organization is simple, the people involved know perfectly what they are expected to do, and as long as the taste of the customers does not change, the management can hardly go wrong

A higher degree of complexity is associated with management in mass-production, traditional industries, such as those producing the automobile, the machine, and similar products Here, most often, a family of products is manufactured The models do change every few years but large quantities of each product are manufactured repeatedly for long periods of time The research and development phase of each product, as long and costly as it may be, is generally amortized by the large quantity production line The cost of innovation is a relatively small fraction of the total product cost The products manufactured are mature, the manufacturing process is repetitive, and the large quantities justify dedicating resources to each product line In such companies, management uncertainties are normally external to the product itself. They may have to do with market demand fluctuations, supply of purchased parts and materials, and other similar external factors As long as strict process control (PC) and total quality management (TQM) are established, each step in the process can be precisely timed and just-in-time (JIT) methods can be applied with great success.

A much higher degree of management complexity is found in the high-technology organizations dealing with innovative products As discussed in previous chapters, the innovative process contains a large amount of uncertainty associated with the research and development phase of the product The more innovative the product, the greater will be the risk and uncertainty accompanying the development of its hardware and software components Start and finish dates for the successful completion of individual tasks in the product's development are merely estimates that almost always differ, sometimes significantly, from the actual, real-life results The need to meet due dates often leads a department to introduce immature products into manufacturing This, in turn, results in defects, requires rework, and disrupts the entire planning sequence Of course, the external uncertainties, like market fluctuations and on-time availability of purchased parts and materials, are just as worrisome as in the case of the traditional industries

However, as long as the company is engaged in the development, production, and marketing of a single product line, management's task is somewhat simplified by the accumulated experience in the company's field of specialization.

The highest degree of management complexity is found in organizations that engage in the research, development, manufacturing, and marketing of diversified high-technology products A typical example is found in the electronics industry Companies like Phillips, Thompson, and G E C in Europe or Hughes, Westinghouse, and GE in the United States are true multiproduct, high-technology companies Not only is the overall company diversified, but each of its divisions is often a multiproduct organization itself, developing and marketing a relatively large spectrum of innovative products Naturally, in such big companies, there are also divisions engaged in lower-tech and straightforward manufacturing of mature products. This kind of diversification stretches the scope of management's attention It requires management's attention to be divided among a variety of product lines and professional disciplines, and among different markets

Often, production quantities are small, especially if a company deals with large, high-value systems like satellite communications, radar systems, or traffic control systems In the multiproduct systems development environment, a more appropriate term is sometimes *project* rather than *product* Because a large system is often quite unique, it is handled in the company as a project that has to be delivered to a specific customer. Project management is a branch of management science that has a well-developed methodology and literature (see for example, Archibald, 1992, Davis and Peterson, 1975; Harriot and Pemberton, 1995, Meredith and Mantel, 1989, Moder, Phillips, and Davis, 1983, Shtub, Bard, and Globerson, 1994) We examine here some of the accepted ideas from the theory of project management

Useful Definitions from Project Management Theory

The selected definitions are explained briefly here The reader is also encouraged to refer to the references cited earlier or to other related literature for more detail

Project

A project may be viewed or defined in several different ways (see Shtub et al , 1994): as "the entire process required to produce a new product, new system or other specific result" (Archibald, 1992, p 3), or as defined by General Electric, "a narrowly defined activity which is planned for a finite duration with a specific goal to be achieved" (p 5) Other definitions state that project management occurs when management gives emphasis and special attention to the conduct of nonrepetitive activities for the purpose of meeting a single set of goals All definitions stress project management as dealing with a one-time effort to achieve a focused objective

In high technology, projects are undertaken for the purpose of concentrating management attention during research and development, manufacturing, and marketing of innovative products Each product is assigned a project management team, responsible for all technical and financial aspects, with the goal of ensuring the business success of the product

Professional Group

A professional group is an organizational unit concentrating human and capital resources that are specialized and dedicated to a specific professional activity For example, mechanical engineering, electronic circuit design, and printed circuits manufacturing are all illustrations of organizational units designed to perform a professional function The professional group is permanent in nature Unlike the project organization, here the same specialists perform similar professional tasks for a number of projects This structure enables them to accumulate expertise and experience, which in turn elevates the professional level of the group

Matrix Organization

A matrix organization is a hybrid structure intended to provide a balance between the needs of projects and the need for efficient use of resources Many of the tasks in projects are not repetitive, therefore, to allocate exclusively to one project all

	Professional Group 1	Professional Group 2	Professional Group 3		Professional Group "i"
Project 1					
Project 2					
Project 3					
Project "j"					

FIGURE 6 1 Matrix Structure of a Multiproject Organization

the resources necessary for its execution is usually cost prohibitive Among the most important of all resources is professional know-how This knowledge is found in the professional groups or departments of the company In the matrix organization, duplication of functional units is eliminated by assigning specific resources of each professional unit to each project This usage is illustrated in Figure 6 1

Work Breakdown Structure (WBS) and Work Packages (WPs)

The work breakdown structure (WBS) is a schematic presentation of the disaggregation-integration process by which the project manager plans to execute the project (Shtub et al , 1994) In the U.S Military Standards MIL-STD-881A, one can find the following definition for WBS "A work break-down structure is a product oriented family tree composed of hardware, services and data which result from project engineering efforts during the development and production of a product, and which completely defines the project " The work content of a project is divided into work packages (WPs) that can be assigned to professional groups in the company, outsourced, subcontracted, or executed by the project team

THE QUEUING PENALTY IN MULTIPRODUCT HIGH-TECHNOLOGY ORGANIZATIONS

Most multiproduct high-technology companies are organized in a more or less matrix structure of projects and professional groups The overall responsibility for the project/product development, manufacturing, and delivery is normally assigned to a project manager The actual development and manufacturing work is usually done within permanent professional departments that specialize in the disciplines necessary for the execution of the tasks (or WPs) the project needs The project manager is helped by a project organization of an appropriate size The project organization does the planning, divides the project into a well-defined work breakdown structure, and subcontracts the work packages to the appropriate professional departments within the company or to outside contractors

In some companies, all the development work is done in the professional groups and the role of the project organization is limited to the planning and control of the

project Other companies give more weight to the project and allocate some professional resources, other than management, planning, and control, to the project organization. In such a case, some of the actual development of specific work packages is done
within the project

The advantages and disadvantages of each approach have been widely discussed
in the literature (see Katz and Allen, 1985, Meredith and Mantel, 1989, Shtub et al,
1994) In most cases however, a combination of the two approaches is specifically tailored to fit the needs of particular projects and balance the workload between professional groups and projects. In some companies, this combination may vary from project
to project

Whatever the emphasis chosen by management, in most multiproject, high-technology companies one thing remains common: At any given time, a large number of
projects generate a huge number of work packages that arrive for service by the professional groups at randomly varying times For example, consider a medium-size electronics company with an annual turnover of $250 million, the company is engaged in
communications, radar, and computer embedded systems The typical number of concurrent projects in any given time exceeds 200 If each project is divided into some 100
work packages, the total number generated is around 20,000 Those work packages are
distributed among some 20 to 30 professional groups The uncertain arrival and departure times of this extensive flow of work packages create a queuing problem that we
need to analyze, understand, and resolve

Look at a simplified example of a single project In this case, the project consists
of the design and fabrication of a communication system Typically, its work breakdown structure looks like the one shown in Figure 6 2

In a system as large as the one shown on Figure 6 2, work can be started at the
same time on only a few of the work packages Most of the work packages in a project

FIGURE 6 2 Project Work Breakdown Structure (WBS)

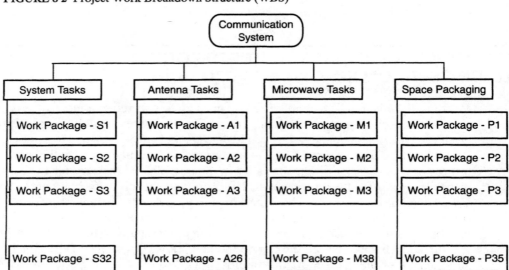

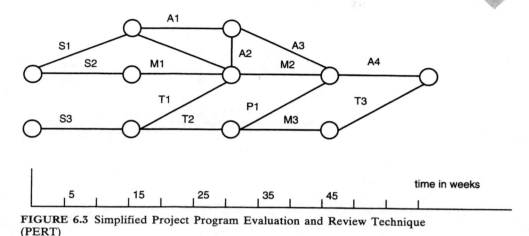

FIGURE 6.3 Simplified Project Program Evaluation and Review Technique (PERT)

Note: A = antenna task
S = system task
M = manufacturing task
T = test tasks
P = production task

follow a network type of time sequence, meaning that work on a specific work package cannot begin before the previous one has been completed For example, the design of a subsystem must be finished before its manufacturing can begin Testing cannot start before the manufacturing of the system's hardware and software components has been accomplished Therefore, it is useful to describe the logical sequence of events in some sort of a network diagram

One of the classical network techniques is the PERT—Program Evaluation and Review Technique (see Moder et al , 1983) An example in a much simplified form is shown on Figure 6.3.

The longest path in the network is defined as the critical path (CP) because it determines the minimum time necessary to finish the project Any work package on this path is defined as critical, as delay of its execution delays the whole project (For more reading on planning techniques, see Davis and Peterson, 1975, Kurtulus and Narula, 1985, Moder et al , 1983)

Note that the letters and numbers on the diagram in Figure 6 3 express the *estimated* time duration of each of the work packages In our example, S1 is the estimated time needed by the system's group to prepare the antenna system's general specification, A1 is the estimated time needed by the antenna group to design the antenna system, A2 is the estimated time needed to prepare the specification of the antenna feed, which the antenna group orders from the microwave group, and so on. Each of these estimates can be seen, in probability terms, as a random variable with a mean value equal to the estimated time and with some not-so-well-defined distribution For example, the probability density function of S1 may look like that shown in Figure 6 4.

Although true statistics that define the probability density of those estimates do not exist in the pure mathematical sense, some very useful results can be learned from

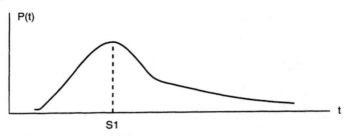

FIGURE 6 4 Probability Density Function of S1

Note: S1 = the duration of system task 1

    t = time

    P(t) = the probability of finishing system task 1 at time t

well-known statistical models These can help explain an often ill-understood but extremely important factor for so many project delays and cost overruns· the *queuing factor*

For the sake of keeping the text palatable to managers with no special taste for mathematical models, we illustrate the queuing phenomenon with a simplified graphic example The mathematical model, in an elementary form, yet totally sufficient for our purposes, is given in Appendix 6 A

To keep the same terminology as in the mathematical model, we use here the same scenario and terms that appear in Appendix 6 A In any case, we are interested only in understanding the key factors that determine the behavior of work flow through a matrix organization of projects and professional groups This understanding will allow us to define in a later section a rational policy for minimizing the negative effects of the queuing structure in this work flow.

The simple but revealing scenario that demonstrates the queuing phenomenon is the one that examines the work flow through a single server service station A customer arriving at this station is served immediately if the server is free If the server is busy, the customer joins the queue When the server finishes serving a customer, this customer leaves the service station and the next customer in line, if one is waiting, enters service

Suppose the customers arrive in a perfectly synchronized and deterministic way, that is, each customer arrives at the service station exactly at the moment service has been completed for the previous customer Clearly, there are no customers waiting in line and the server is always busy No time is wasted by the customers or by the server (see Figure 6 5a) This case illustrates the perfect efficiency that is the goal with a just-in-time (JIT) method

Now suppose customers arrive, as they usually do, without prior coordination, that is, they arrive at the service station at random Although arrival times vary randomly, the average arrival rate is λ arrivals per unit of time Similarly, the duration of service each customer gets varies randomly with an average service rate of μ customers served per unit of time This case is shown graphically in the example in Figure 6 5b

Time Units	1	2	3	4	5	6	7	8	9	10	11	12	13	14	15	16	17	18	19	20	21	22	23	24	25	26	27	Waiting Time
Arrival	c1																											0
Service	*		*	*																								
Arrival				c2																								0
Service				*		*	*																					
Arrival							c3																					0
Service							*		*	*																		
Arrival										c4																		0
Service										*		*	*															
Arrival													c5															0
Service													*		*	*												
Arrival																c6												0
Service																*		*	*									
Arrival																			c7									0
Service																			*		*	*						
Arrival																						c8						0
Service																						*		*	*			
Queue Length	0	0	0	0	0	0	0	0	0	0	0	0	0	0	0	0	0	0	0	0	0	0	0	0	0	0	0	

FIGURE 6 5a Synchronized Arrivals

c = customer

* = service time

Note that the average rate of arrival and the average rate of service in Figure 6 5a and Figure 6 5b are exactly the same The only reason for the difference in behavior between the two cases is the introduction of uncertainty in the time of arrival of customers at the service station All other parameters, including the service times, have been kept fixed for the sake of simplicity

From Figure 6 5b, we can immediately see the different behavior of the flow of customers through the service station caused by nothing but the randomness of their arrival times In this case, many customers spend a significant time waiting in line while at other times the server is often idle and waiting for work

Figure 6 5b illustrates qualitatively the forming of queues in the simple example of a single-server service station This queuing phenomenon is inevitably present in all multiproject research and development organizations, where customers are replaced by project work packages and "service stations" are replaced by company professional

```
Time      1 2 3 4 5 6 7 8 9 1 1 1 1 1 1 1 1 1 1 2 2 2 2 2 2 2 2
Units                       0 1 2 3 4 5 6 7 8 9 0 1 2 3 4 5 6 7
                                                                      Waiting
                                                                      Time
Arrival   c                                                              0
          1
Service   *   *   *
Arrival     c                                                            2
            2
Service   o o   *   *   *
Arrival       c                                                          4
              3
Service   o o o o   *   *   *
Arrival         c                                                        5
                4
Service   o o o o o   *   *   *   IDLE                                    0
Arrival                             c
                                    5
Service                             *   *   *
Arrival                             c                                    2
                                    6
Service                             o o   *   *   *
Arrival                               c                                  2
                                      7
Service                               o o   *   *   *
Arrival                                 c                                2
                                        8
Service                                 o o   *   *   *

Queue     0 1 2 1 2 2 1 1 1 0 0 0 0 0 0 0 1 1 0 1 1 0 1 1 0 0 0
Length
```

FIGURE 6 5b Realistic Arrivals

c = customer
* = service time
o = working time
IDLE = time worker is idle

groups Before returning to the more complex real world, we still need a few more quantitative expressions for the most important factors that determine the queuing phenomenon To get those, we can refer to the mathematical model described in Appendix 6.A, from which we take the following important quantities

L = The number of customers at the service station

W = The average time a customer spends at the station

Lq = The average number of customers waiting in the queue

Wq = The average time a customer spends waiting in queue

Po = The probability of finding the server idle

Examining the mathematical expressions for the above quantities, we see that they all depend on the ratio λ/μ—that is, the ratio between the average arrival rate and the average service rate. We can name this ratio the *loading factor* (LF) the higher the ratio, the bigger will be the workload on the server at the service station Rewriting just two of the expressions in Appendix 6 A helps us get a sense of the number of customers waiting in the station and the probability of finding the server idle.

$$L = LF/(1 - LF)$$

and

$$Po = 1 - LF$$

where the loading factor $LF = \lambda/\mu$.

Observe two important conditions: First, the arrival rate λ has to be smaller than the service rate μ Second, the bigger the loading factor, the larger will be the number of customers at the station, the longer will be the waiting lines and the waiting time All these values tend to grow to infinity if the loading factor approaches 1 On the other hand, if the loading factor is smaller than 1, the server must remain idle for periods of time that increase as the loading factor decreases

To illustrate this phenomenon with a numeric example, suppose the mean arrival rate is 1 every 10 minutes and the mean service rate is 1 every 8 minutes The number of customers at the station is $L = 4$, and the average amount of time a customer will stay in the station is $W = 40$ minutes In this case, the probability of finding the server idle is $Po = 20$ percent If we want on average only one customer in the station, the service rate must grow to $\mu = 2\lambda$ But then, the probability of finding the server idle grows to 50 percent

A number of important conclusions can be drawn from this simple example These conclusions are perfectly pertinent to the flow of work packages described earlier in a multiproject, high-technology organization

1. As long as arrival and service times of work packages are uncertain, there is no practical way to avoid the queuing of these packages in the various professional groups (service stations) This phenomenon must be understood and accounted for

2. Even if the service rate is significantly higher than the arrival rate of the work packages in a professional group, the average time a work package spends in the group is much longer than the estimated time needed to actually work on the package because most of the time is spent waiting in line

3. Attempts to decrease the queue length below a reasonable value will inevitably lead to increasing the idle time in the professional groups, which will now be loaded much below their capacity

To summarize, because of the stochastic nature of the time of arrivals and of the time it takes to service a work package in a multiproject, innovative environment, either work packages wait for service or the servers wait for work This queuing phenomenon of having work packages waiting in line and resources idle induces a penalty that must be accounted for

Basically, this penalty consists of three components

1. *The cost of waiting in line* (expenses the company accumulates while work packages are waiting for service)

2. *The cost of underutilization of available capacity* (service waiting for work)

3. *The cost of delayed projects* (often a contractual penalty that the company must pay for late delivery of a project)

After having examined the queuing phenomenon, we are ready, at this stage, to define in more quantitative terms the queuing penalty that inevitably exists in multi-project, high-tech organizations. This penalty is the added cost the company has to absorb as a result of the waiting phenomenon Next we examine each of its components, starting with the cost of waiting in line This will allow us later in the chapter to devise appropriate methods for minimizing the penalty

The Cost of Waiting in Line

When a critical work package waits in line a unit of time—say one day—the entire project is delayed by one day That means that the team of people working exclusively for this project is either idle during this period or is doing inefficient work If the cost for this inefficiency is x dollars per day, and the critical work package waits in line n days, the cost of waiting for this package is

$$w = x*n$$

In most projects, even those of modest complexity, more than one critical work package quite often happens to wait in line To account for all costs accumulated by one project (a) because of its critical work packages waiting in line, we must sum up the costs added to the project for each delayed critical package

$$W(a) = w1 + w2 + w3 + \ .$$

Finally, in a multiproject company that runs a large number of projects at the same time, the total penalty for all projects having critical work packages waiting in line will be

$$W = W(a) + W(b) + W(c) + .$$

where a, b, c, and so on are the names of the different projects running in parallel in the company during a given period of time, usually an accounting (financial) year

Note that this penalty is internal to the company, as opposed to penalties the company has to pay to external entities and that are discussed later To clarify further the cost of waiting in line, we have a numeric example (Case 6 1)

This simple example gives a realistic illustration of the significant order of magnitude the cost for waiting in line may have in a mid-size, high-technology company In reality, large projects have much higher (per day) costs for waiting in line than small projects. For the sake of simplicity, we took average numbers in the example in Case 6 1 However, in devising the methods for minimizing the cost to the company, managers must account for these differences, as is discussed later in the chapter

The Cost of Underutilization of Capacity

Each professional group in a high-technology company has a certain capacity to carry on work that requires its particular specialization This capacity is most efficiently used when all work is done on work packages for projects paid for by customers However, because of the queuing phenomenon, packages are often delayed, causing inefficient use of available resources Clearly, each professional group has a certain fixed cost for each unit of capacity This cost usually includes the wages of the employees in the group

---

CASE 6.1

Cost of Waiting in Line: Illustrative Example

The number of projects running in parallel in a high-technology company during a given financial year was 30

The average number of critical working packages (WPs) delayed per project in this period was 5

On average, the number of days a critical work package had to wait in line during this period was 12

The average cost per day suffered by idle project teams while waiting for critical work packages was 10 employees * 8 hours/day * $80/hour = $6,400/day

Therefore

The average cost per project for waiting in line was
$6,400/day * 12 days* 5 times = $384,000

The total cost added to the company by all the projects running in parallel during the year was $384,000/project * 30 projects, or

The cost for waiting in line = $11,520,000

---

and the amortization of the capital investment made in the group for machines, test equipment, or any other fixed asset

When the workload of a professional group drops below its capacity, the cost of inefficient use of this resource is borne by the company In most accepted cost accounting practices, there is no way to charge such costs directly to projects that may be causing the problem These hidden costs are no less real. If the cost of unit capacity in professional group "aa" is $c(aa)$, and if during an accounting period, $m(a)$ units of capacity are idle, then the cost of underutilization of capacity in group "a" is

$$u(aa) = c(aa) * m(aa)$$

To obtain the total cost to the company, sum the costs of underutilization of capacity in all professional groups in this company:

$$U = u(aa) + u(bb) + u(cc) + \quad .$$

A good first approximation for the cost of unit capacity in a given professional group is the hourly rate the company charges for work done by this group If the group is staffed by highly paid professionals, or if the company has made a significant capital investment in this group, usually this situation is reflected in its hourly rate Also, a good approximation for a unit of wasted capacity is an hour of idle time in the group To clarify further the cost of underutilization of capacity, look at a numeric example (Case 6.2)

The Cost of Delayed Projects

The cost of delayed projects is in addition to the cost of waiting in line It contains some tangible as well as some less tangible but real costs to the company for projects not finished on time Such costs may contain penalties to be paid for late deliveries, for lost

---

CASE 6.2

Cost of Underutilization of Capacity: Illustrative Example

The number of professional groups in a high-technology company is 20

The average hourly cost in 6 of the groups is *high* and amounts to $200
The average hourly cost in 6 of the groups is *moderate* and amounts to $80
The average hourly cost in 8 of the groups is *low* and amounts to $20

During the last financial year, approximately 600 work hours were wasted, on average, in each of the high-cost professional groups, because of periodic lack of adequate workload The numbers for the moderate-cost and low-cost professional groups were 500 and 700, respectively

Therefore,

The cost for underutilization of capacity in the *high*-cost professional groups was $200 * 600 * 6 = $720,000

The cost for underutilization of capacity in the *moderate*-cost professional groups was $80 * 500 * 6 = $240,000

The cost for underutilization of capacity in the *low*-cost professional groups was $20 * 700 * 12 = $128,000.

For the company, *the cost of underutilization of capacity* = $1,168,000

---

market opportunities, for lost reputation, and so on For each project, this cost is a function of the difference between the actual delivery date and the planned or promised delivery date. If the cost for one day of delay in the delivery of project "a" is $c(a)$, and the difference between the actual and promised delivery date is $y(a)$, the cost for late delivery of the project is

$$d(a) = c(a) * y(a)$$

In a multiproject company that runs a large number of projects at the same time, the total cost of delayed projects will be

$$D = d(a) + d(b) + d(c) +$$

This situation is illustrated in Case 6.3

Finally, the queuing penalty in a multiproject, high-technology company can be expressed as the sum of three factors the cost of waiting in line, the cost of underutilization of professional capacity, and the cost of delays

$$QP = W + U + D$$

CASE 6.3

Cost of Delayed Projects: Illustrative Example

In a high-technology company running 30 projects in parallel, the number of projects delivered after the promised date last financial year was 12

The contractual penalty for one of the projects was 0 1 percent of the contract value of $30 million for each day of delay, with a ceiling of $500,000 This project was late 45 days and would have cost the company a direct penalty of $30,000/day * 45 days = $1,350,000 Thanks to the ceiling clause in the contract, the direct penalty was limited to $500,000

Another project worth $10 million missed the due date for the end of the year holiday season The products were sold at a discount rate of 20 percent, causing the company a loss of $2,000,000

The average penalty and lost opportunity cost for the remaining 10 projects amounted to approximately $150,000 per project, giving a yearly cost of 10 * $150,000 = $1,500,000

For the total company, the *cost of delayed projects* = $4,000,000

Using the numbers in the examples, the high-technology company described suffered in one accounting year this queuing penalty of

$$QP = \$11,520,000 + \$1,168,000 + \$4,000,000 = \$16,688,000$$

A number of conclusions can be drawn:

- **The queuing penalty illustrated is an expression of the cost a company bears because of the queuing phenomenon only. We have assumed that the cost for the actual work on any work package is the originally estimated one. We see later that random departures from this assumption cannot induce a significant error.**

- **The queuing penalty is shown to be the most important cause for delays and cost overruns in multiproject/product, high-technology organizations with substantial research and development content. Contrary to the accepted thinking that the cost and delivery of an R&D project are hard to predict because of the inherent uncertainty of the duration (and cost) of the individual work packages, the examples show that this kind of thinking is doubtful, if not completely wrong.**

To demonstrate this statement, we should examine the probability that the actual delivery time in a large research and development project executed alone, without the interference of other projects, differs substantially from the planned one In Appendix 6 A, we examine this probability using the well-known statistical law of large numbers Simply stated, as the completion time for each critical work package is estimated independently, it is equally likely that some packages will take longer to complete than es-

timated whereas others will be completed before their estimated completion time
Thus, the two types of errors in the estimation should offset each other and average out
to zero as the number of work packages becomes large

A similar argument can be made regarding the difference between the predicted
and the actual project cost. Hence, the dominant factor for frequent project delays and
cost overruns must be the queuing factor introduced earlier (for proof, see Appendix
6 A) These observations lead to key conclusions

- **The actual delivery time of a project can be computed as the sum of the times its critical work packages spend (mostly waiting) in the professional groups. This is substantially different from the way one computes the estimated delivery time as the sum of the times critical work packages require to be worked on in the professional groups.**

- **Similarly, the actual cost of a project is the sum of its estimated cost and the project cost for waiting in line.**

METHODS FOR REDUCING THE QUEUING PENALTY

The queuing penalty in a multiproject, innovative high-technology organization cannot
be completely avoided because of the queuing structure imposed by the random arrivals of the work packages However, once this phenomenon is well understood, managers should look for logical approaches to reduce this penalty to a minimum To examine such approaches, we look more closely at each of the components of the queuing
penalty defined in the previous section

Methods for Reducing the Delay Penalty

Obviously, the only way to minimize the delay penalty is by keeping as many projects
as possible on schedule However, as keeping all the projects in a multiproject organization on schedule is practically impossible, *priority should be given to the projects with
the highest delay penalty*. Because of the importance of some less tangible penalties,
such as lost reputation, lost market opportunities, and so on, management judgment is
important in assigning those priorities Such penalties, in a final account, may weigh
heavier than the tangible penalty clauses written in the project contract

To achieve this objective, the first necessary condition is to establish a formal list
of projects that must receive special management attention Top management should
ask for frequent status reports on such projects and take appropriate action if significant deviation from planning is detected

Methods for Reducing the Underutilization Penalty

A logical policy to follow in reducing the underutilization penalty is to make sure that
professional groups with high capacity cost are seldom idle. As shown earlier, the probability of having idle capacity is a function of the loading factor λ/μ Therefore, a high-
cost professional group should have a relatively high loading factor This condition inevitably increases the queue length, however, so the management must be particularly
careful and assign different priorities for different work packages that load this group

There are basically two types of work packages those that lie on the critical path of a project and those that have sufficient slack time A rational and well-informed management should therefore set an order of priorities as follows

- First priority should be given to critical work packages belonging to high-value projects
- Second priority should be given to critical work packages of lower-value projects.
- Third priority should be given to work packages of high-value projects that have a short slack time but risk becoming critical if they wait too long in line
- Fourth priority should be given to near-critical work packages of lower-value projects, and so on

In the next section, we examine some information systems techniques that are necessary for managers of the company to have a clear picture of what is in the queue at any time Without such information, there is no way they can apply any rational priority policy

For professional groups with low capacity costs, having frequent idle times may be justified in view of the time saved by work packages not having to wait in line for service in such groups. When priorities do not have to be controlled, as all WPs are served quickly in such groups, substantial management cost can also be saved Most important, such low-cost groups should never be allowed to become a chronic bottleneck To understand the last statement fully, examine again the third component of the queuing penalty: the waiting-in-line penalty

Methods for Reducing the Waiting Line Penalty

The cost for waiting in line is a product function of two factors the project's fixed cost and the time critical work packages spend waiting in line

Methods for Reducing the Fixed Cost of the Project

The project's fixed cost is the cost of all resources—people, equipment, space, and so on—exclusively devoted to the project over long periods of time Usually, such periods are measured in years and are comparable with the life length of the project

One extreme method for reducing the fixed project's cost is to keep the project organization as small as possible—perhaps one project manager assisted by a minimal staff and no additional resources devoted exclusively to the project In this case, all work for the project will be subcontracted or done by the professional groups The project's fixed costs are thus reduced to a minimum, so even if critical work packages spend a long time waiting in line, the product function that determines the cost remains small

This approach will help also keep the underutilization penalty u of the professional groups small, as it allows an increase in their loading factor without significant increase of the waiting-in-line penalty Therefore, a "lean" project organization helps to reduce two of the three components of the queuing penalty w and u

The problem is with the third component of the queuing penalty—namely, d If projects accumulate delays on their critical work packages, the entire project is delayed Therefore, substantial tangible and less tangible penalties may be imposed on the company To prevent unacceptable increase of the delay penalty, the company must be in full control of the priorities assigned to the different types of work packages, as explained earlier To achieve this level of control, a company needs a well-educated management assisted by an adequate information system The function of the data system is to give real-time information on the status of all work packages and their priorities in the company

In practice, managers in most multiproduct companies understand this phenomenon poorly, as a result, management often takes a diametrically opposed approach. Many companies increase the size of the project organization and allocate to it more and more resources so as to give the project manager a feeling of being in better control of the project Unfortunately, this approach creates a duplication of the capacity already existing in the professional groups—in turn increasing the underutilization penalty The company suffers the extra costs, but under accepted accounting principles, these extra costs are seldom attributed to the projects Of course, under such conditions, it is natural that more and more project managers ask for dedicated resources This response and its consequences are discussed later in the chapter

Methods for Reducing the Time Spent Waiting in Line

One extreme method to reduce $w(a)$ is to assign exclusively to Project "a" all the resources it needs to ensure that no work package of this project is delayed by waiting in line In this case, the project's fixed costs will be very high, but because the time that critical packages spend in queues will approach 0, the product function will also approach 0

In reality, however, in a high-tech, multiproduct organization, the need for specialists in a wide spectrum of professional disciplines is almost always present; therefore, this approach requires the creation of a miniprofessional group structure at the project organization level This parallel professional group structure will inevitably decrease the loading factor in the professional groups at the company The loading factor in the project's miniprofessional groups will be small by definition, as those groups were created in the first place to serve only one project Obviously, the result is a large increase of the underutilization penalty for the entire company

Fortunately, for a number of reasons, the creation of a parallel professional group structure is so difficult and expensive that the use of this extreme method is relatively rare In addition to the high cost, finding sufficient competent experts in the same professional field to staff this kind of parallel professional group structure is practically impossible. What happens most often in real life is some type of compromise in which only very important projects receive dedicated professional resources that duplicate the professional group structure to a degree These compromises are rarely satisfactory, but they create a sense of comfort by allowing the company management to hold the project manager more accountable for keeping his project on time and on cost

For prestigious projects, in which being on time is much more important than the cost, a strong project-oriented organization placing most of the necessary resources under the project manager's control is totally appropriate. Some important projects—more often governmental than private—are organized in this way During World War II, the famous Manhattan Project, whose goal was to develop the atomic bomb as quickly as possible, was managed successfully in this pattern Later, when President Kennedy set the challenge to put the first man on the moon before the Soviets did, the Apollo Project was managed the same way with great success

Our interest, however, is to concentrate on the methods to improve management in multiproduct/project commercial organizations Therefore, we have these recommendations

THE RECOMMENDED APPROACH

First, note that it is more appropriate to speak of a recommended *approach* than a recommended *method* Most high-technology companies differ in many ways—size, culture, technology, markets—and the optimum method is most likely different for different companies. All high-technology, multiproduct, innovative companies, however, have a common problem of reducing the queuing penalty, so it is important and appropriate to suggest a common approach for solving this problem We suggest these steps:

1. Explain the queuing problem and make its consequences clear to all levels of management in the organization, from the company management, project managers, and the managers of the professional groups down to the floor managers

2. Analyze in detail the implications of applying the methods described in this chapter in your specific company's environment

3. Be sure the company's information system for tracking data can provide immediate information on the status of all work packages, either in process or waiting in line for the professional groups If the company does not have such a tracking system, see that one is created

4. Once the tracking system is established, reduce the resources in the project organizations to a logical minimum If possible, the project organization should be reduced to the project manager and a small staff The apparent loss of control should be compensated by the added visibility provided by the tracking system and by total management commitment to follow the rules, the logic, and the priorities as established

This approach, appropriately adapted and applied to the specific needs of each multiproduct, high-technology organization, should be effective in reducing the queuing penalty It will help keep all high-value projects on schedule and within cost while keeping the remaining projects under positive control

QUEUE CONTROL INFORMATION SYSTEM

Having real-time information on the status of a project's work packages is essential for efficient project management However, most information systems fail to give management a real-time picture of the dynamic queuing structure of the workload in the company's professional groups Seeing how an information system evolved and works in a real company is instructive

An information system was designed and implemented in a middle-size, multi-project, high-technology company involved in the design, manufacturing, and marketing of communication, radar, and computerized systems At first, its chief function was to replace manual recording of "orders" (WPs) arriving at the various professional

FIGURE 6 6 Printed Circuit Layout Design
91–05–05

Arrival date	Project	Work package number	Priority	Status	Estimated work hours	Planned delivery date	Work start date
90–06–25	AE-RX	PC-5	5	WAIT	50	90–09–20	
90–07–09	AB-TX	PC-9	4	WAIT	150	90–09–10	
91–04–02	BB-PS	PC-5	3	WORK*	100	91–05–06	91–04–30
91–04–02	BB-PS	PC-6	3	WORK*	150	91–05–15	91–04–30
91–04–06	KF-TX	PC-1	2	WAIT	200	91–06–28	
91–04–06	WY-ATN	PC-3	2	WORK*	200	91–07–06	91–05–01
91–04–06	WY-ATN	PC-4	2	WORK*	250	91–08–10	91–05–01
91–04–06	WY-ATN	PC-6	3	WAIT	250	91–08–20	
91–04–08	DA-TX	PC-1	4	WAIT	100	91–08–10	
91–04–08	DA-TX	PC-2	4	WAIT	50	91–08–10	
91–04–08	DA-TX	PC-3	4	WAIT	30	91–08–10	
91–04–08	DA-TX	PC-4	4	WAIT	50	91–05–01	
91–04–15	EF-PS	PC-1	1	WORK*	50	91–05–01	91–04–20
91–04–15	EF-PS	PC-2	1	WORK*	30	91–05–01	91–04–20
91–04–18	EE-SA	PC-1	4	WAIT	30	91–05–18	
91–04–20	EC-SP	PC-1	3	WAIT	100	91–06–20	
91–04–20	EC-SP	PC-2	3	WAIT	150	91–06–30	
91–04–20	EC-SP	PC-3	3	WAIT	200	91–07–10	
91–04–20	EC-SP	PC-4	3	WAIT	150	91–07–01	
91–04–23	KK-DP	PC-5	4	WAIT	100	91–07–01	
91–04–23	KK-DP	PC-6	4	WAIT	80	91–07–05	
91–04–23	KK-DP	PC-7	4	WAIT	70	91–07–25	
91–04–27	KF-TX	PC-3	2	WAIT	50	91–06–01	
91–04–27	KF-TX	PC-4	2	WAIT	100	91–06–01	
91–05–02	DA-RX	PC-1	1	WAIT	150	91–06–05	
91–05–02	DA-RX	PC-2	2	WAIT	100	90–06–15	
91–05–02	DA-RX	PC-3	2	WAIT	200	90–06–30	
91–05–03	WY-SP	PC-1	1	WAIT	120	90–06–01	
91–05–03	WY-SP	PC-2	1	WAIT	140	90–06–01	
91–05–03	WY-SP	PC-3	2	WAIT	50	90–06–01	
91–05–03	WY-SP	PC-4	2	WAIT	200	90–06–20	
91–05–03	WY-SP	PC-5	2	WAIT	100	90–06–20	
91–05–04	EF-DP	PC-1	3	WAIT	150	90–09–01	
91–05–04	EF-DP	PC-2	3	WAIT	140	90–09–01	
91–05–04	EF-DP	PC-3	3	WAIT	200	90–09–05	
91–05–04	EF-DP	PC-4	3	WAIT	250	90–09–05	
91–05–04	EF-DP	PC-5	3	WAIT	100	90–09–05	
91–05–04	EF-DP	PC-6	3	WAIT	200	90–09–01	
91–05–04	DA-RX	PC-4	1	WAIT	100	90–06–01	
91–05–04	DA-RX	PC-5	1	WAIT	150	90–06–01	
91–05–04	DA-RX	PC-6	1	WAIT	100	90–06–01	
91–05–04	AD-SP	PC-1	2	WAIT	200	90–09–10	
91–05–04	AD-SP	PC-2	2	WAIT	250	90–09–10	
91–05–04	AD-SP	PC-3	2	WAIT	150	90–09–10	
91–05–04	AD-SP	PC-4	2	WAIT	200	90–09–10	

*Work packages being processed at the time of the report's printing

groups The records included the date of arrival, the name of the project requesting the work, the estimated amount of working hours to be spent on the work package, the promised due date, and the actual delivery date Initially, the system was used to measure throughput from each professional group

After the records were computerized, a number of new possibilities for sorting data became available First, sorting all work packages according to their arrival date became easy After the run-in period, a dynamic queuing structure developed enabling control of the throughput in a rational way Figure 6.6 shows one of the outputs of the system In this example, the status of the work packages in the printed circuits design group is logged according to their arrival time

A number of interesting and valuable conclusions can be drawn from looking at Figure 6 6 First, note that two work packages with relatively low priority have been neglected in the queue for months! Actually, when this system was initially implemented, the first computer runs exposed work packages forgotten for more than a year Somebody in the appropriate project organization would have eventually discovered that these WPs were needed for the following week, at which point the work package with the long slack time would originally all of a sudden have become critical and most urgently required Obviously, the minimum time required for the delivery of any work package is the net time needed to work on it Because this time is usually longer than whatever slack time is left of the forgotten package, most of its processing time translates directly into project delay time.

Over time, the phenomenon of forgotten work packages will gradually disappear Responsibility for not neglecting these packages in the queue will be transferred from the project organization to the professional group The professional group can now be held responsible for surveying daily the status of all WPs submitted to it and for applying the priority rules established by company management

Additional sorting of the same data base can be done easily For example, managers can establish a meaningful statistic for the average time work packages wait in line, by priority, and review this result periodically against company policy The average actual time spent to work on different types of WPs is another useful statistic that can be used by managers to improve future estimates for similar work packages

Another very important feature of the queue control information system is its transparency Although daily inputs of the data are entered by professional groups, the outputs appropriately sorted are available in real time on every computer display in the company For example, if the output on Figure 6 4 is sorted by project name, all project managers can have a daily look at the status of their work packages in every professional group Among other reasons, this transparency is very important because it can ensure the necessary check and balance between the interests of the project managers and those of the professional group managers

SUMMARY

Successful high-technology companies usually grow from start-up, simple organizations to multiproject, complex organizations The motivation for this diversification is the need to achieve a sufficient degree of business stability. Companies that do not grow usually die out or are bought by bigger, diversified, and therefore more stable companies

Managing a diversified, high-technology innovative company is particularly complex and difficult Unlike low-tech production or mass manufacturing of strictly mature, high-technology products, the work process in the innovative high-technology multiproject company is inherently stochastic This is because of the uncertainties associated with the duration of the development cycle of each work package, inducing randomness of the start and finish times of subsequent packages Therefore, attempts to manage the queuing process by deterministic tools will fail

The uncertain arrival and departure times of the work packages imply a queuing structure of the workload in the various professional groups Concepts from queuing theory and stochastic processes were shown to be extremely useful for in-depth understanding of the delays and frequent cost overruns of projects executed simultaneously in a multiproduct organization

To quantify the waiting phenomenon, the term *queuing penalty* was introduced Analyzing its nature, we found that there is no practical way to avoid this penalty completely However, it can be minimized, we examined several methods for doing this and noted their applicability for different situations

A necessary condition for rational management of the queuing process is to have access to real-time information Such data should include the status of all work packages, those waiting in line as well as those being worked on in the professional groups An appropriate information system for this tracking was described Finally, we recommended a method for reducing the queuing penalty to a minimum.

For Further Reflection

1 As the management of a diversified, high-technology innovative company is particularly complex, can it be divided into a number of independent, smaller, and more manageable organizations? Explain all the advantages and disadvantages of such a move

2 Why are queues and waiting lines created in a multiproject, innovative, high-technology organization? Can they be avoided? Can we apply JIT techniques, in their narrow sense, to decrease or avoid the penalty imposed by waiting lines in such organizations?

3 Give your opinion for or against a strong project organization with ample resources allocated to the project manager in a multiproject company Is such an approach justified? If yes, why?

4 Of all factors responsible for the delays and cost overruns witnessed in so many innovative projects run by multiproject companies, what is the most important factor and why?

5 Outline the methods for controlling the process of work flow through a multiproject company What are effective methods for controlling the time? For controlling the cost? What is the optimum approach for controlling both?

6 What are the essential characteristics of an information system suitable for monitoring the flow of work in a multiproject organization?

References and Further Reading

Archibald, R D (1992) *Managing High Technology Programs and Projects A Complete, Practical and Proven Approach to Managing Large-scale Projects* New York: John Wiley

Davis, E W , and J H. Peterson (1975) "A Comparison of Heuristic and Optimum Solutions in Resource-Constrained Project Scheduling " *Management Science*, April, p 41

Harriot, Peter, and Carol Pemberton (1995) *Competitive Advantage through Diversity* London: Sage

Jain, R K , and Triandis, H C (1990) *Management of R&D Organizations* New York John Wiley

Katz, R , and Allen, T J , (1985) "Project Performance and the Locus of Influence in the R&D Matrix " *Academy of Management Journal* 28:67–87

Kurtulus, I , and S C Narula (1985) "Multi-Project Scheduling: Analysis of Project Performance " *IEEE Transactions on Engineering Management*, March

Meredith, Jack R , and Samuel J Mantel, Jr (1989) *Project Management A Managerial Approach* New York: John Wiley

Moder, J J , C R Phillips, and E W Davis (1983) *Project Management with CPM, PERT and Precedence Diagramming* 3rd ed New York: Van Nostrand Reinhold

Nobeoka, Kentaro, and Michael A Cusumano (1994) *Multi-Project Management Inter-Project Interdependency and Organizational Coordination in New Product Development*, Working Paper Cambridge, MA: Sloan School of Management

> This study explores the influence of interproject interdependencies on organizational coordination requirements A questionnaire survey of 256 component engineers in U S and Japanese firms provides evidence that the organizational coordination required to manage component design—with and without interproject interdependencies—differs significantly. For example, in projects with no dependencies on other projects, both intrafunctional coordination and cross-functional coordination have a strong impact on performance in component design The paper concludes, much in line with the approach presented in this chapter, that, to manage interproject interdependencies effectively, firms need a new type of organization aimed at achieving both cross-functional coordination and intrafunctional coordination simultaneously through the active coordination of multiple projects

Ross, Sheldon (1972) *Introduction to Probability Models* New York, NY: Academic Press Inc

Shih, W (1974) "A New Application of Incremental Analysis in Resource Allocation " *Operational Research Quarterly*, December

> The author makes an attempt to arrive at an optimal solution for the problem of resource allocation In this and the next article, (Shih, 1977), optimum allocation of limited resources is analyzed The models developed are relevant to the problems discussed in this chapter They have theoretical merit but seem difficult to apply in the real industrial environment

Shih, W (1977) "A Branch and Bound Procedure for Class of Discrete Resource Allocation Problems with Several Constraints " *Operational Research Quarterly*, June

Shtub, A , J Bard and S Globerson (1994) *Project Management Engineering, Technology and Implementation.* Upper Saddle River, NJ: Prentice Hall

This is a comprehensive and up-to-date text addressing most aspects of project management The book is intended to serve as a reference for the practitioner and for students at both late undergraduate and graduate levels The reader can find most relevant definitions and many illustrative examples covering the subject of project management

APPENDIX 6 A

A Queuing Theory Mathematical Model

THE SINGLE-SERVER EXPONENTIAL QUEUING MODEL

In chapter 6, the queuing phenomenon associated with work flow in a multiproject, innovative, high-technology company was described Useful, quantitative information regarding this phenomenon can be learned from queuing models in probability theory

One such mathematical model describes the formation of waiting lines in front of a service station when customer arrival times are stochastic Analysis of such a model shows that if customers arrive at a service station at random, rather than in well-defined intervals of time, a queue will inevitably form at certain moments whereas the service station will be idle during other periods (Sheldon, 1972) In this mathematical model, the probability density function is defined to be of a Poisson type with a mean value of $1/\lambda$, meaning that on average, the customers' rate of arrival is λ arrivals per unit of time Assuming that the service station has only one single server and that this server is free, the customer is served immediately If the server is busy, the customer joins the queue When the server finishes serving a customer, this customer leaves the service station and the next customer in line, if any are waiting, enters service The successive service times are also assumed to be independent exponential random variables having a mean $1/\mu$, meaning that the average service rate is μ customers served per unit of time

Applying probability theory to the above mathematical model leads to the following results:

$$L = \frac{\lambda/\mu}{1 - \lambda/\mu} \qquad W = \frac{1}{\mu - \lambda} \qquad L_q = \frac{\lambda}{\mu - \lambda}$$

$$W_q = \frac{\lambda}{\mu - \lambda} \qquad P_0 = 1 - \lambda/\mu \quad \text{for } \mu \geq \lambda$$

where

L = the average number of customers in the service station

W = the average amount of time a customer spends in the station

L_q = the average number of customers waiting in line (length of queue)

W_q = the average amount of time a customer spends waiting in line

P_0 = the probability of finding the server idle.

We can make two observations. First, the arrival rate λ has to be smaller than the service rate μ Second, the number of customers in the station depends on the ratio λ/μ, which is defined as the *loading factor* The bigger the loading factor, the larger will be the number of customers in the station, the longer will be the waiting lines and the waiting time All these values tend to grow to infinity as the loading factor approaches 1 On the other hand, if the loading factor is smaller than 1, the server must remain idle for periods of time, which increase as the loading factor decreases

THE QUEUING PENALTY

The model just described, which is probably the simplest in queuing theory, is nevertheless quite revealing Though simple, it is adequate to define in more quantitative terms the queuing penalty that inevitably exists in multiproject, high-technology organizations. This penalty is the added cost the company must absorb as a result of the queuing phenomenon Next, examine each of its components, starting with the cost of waiting in line

The Cost of Waiting in Line

If

$C_{F,j}$ = the fixed cost per unit of time for project "j,"

and

$W_{q,j}$ = the time spent waiting in line by work packages critical to project "j"

then the waiting-in-line component of the queuing penalty is

$$P_{W,j} = \prod_k C_{F,j} \, W_{q,j,k}$$

where

$P_{W,j}$ = the added cost to project "j" for waiting in line

For the multiproject company we are interested in the total cost of all projects caused by the waiting factor, or

$$C_W = \sum_j P_{W,j}$$

where

C_W = the total company penalty for projects waiting in line

The Cost of Underutilization of Capacity

If

C_i = the cost of unit capacity in professional group "i,"

N_i = the number units idle in professional group "i,"

$Pr \, N_i, t$ = the probability of N units being idle at a given time, then the component representing underutilization of capacity in the queuing penalty is

$$C_{u,j} = \Phi \, C_i, N_i, Pr \, N_i, t$$

where

$C_{u,j}$ = the cost of underutilization of available capacity in group "i"

Here again we are interested in the cost to the company of the total wasted capacity caused by the queuing phenomenon in all the professional groups, or

$$C_u = \sum_i C_{u,i}$$

where

C_u = the total company penalty for underutilization of available capacity

The Cost of Delayed Projects

If

$T_{a,j}$ = the actual delivery time of project "j"

and

$T_{p,j}$ = the planned (promised) delivery time of project "j,"

then the delayed project's component of the queuing penalty is

$$C_{d,j} = \Psi \, (T_{a,j} - T_{p,j}) \text{ for } T_{a,j} \geq T_{p,j}$$

where

$C_{d,j}$ = the cost of all penalties caused to the company by the late delivery of project "j"

As before, to find the total cost to the company for all projects delayed, we must make the following summation

$$C_D = \sum_j C_{d,j}$$

where

C_D = the cost to the company for delayed projects

Finally, the overall queuing penalty in a multiproject, high-technology company can be expressed as the sum of the three factors the cost of waiting in line, the cost of underutilization of professional capacity, and the cost of delays

$$C_Q = C_W + C_U + C_D$$

THE DOMINANT ROLE OF THE QUEUING PENALTY

The queuing penalty is probably the most important cause for delays and cost overruns in multiproject/product, high-technology organizations with substantial research and development content Contrary to the accepted thinking that the cost and delivery of an R&D project are hard to predict because of the inherent uncertainty of the duration (and cost) of the individual work packages, we can easily show that this kind of thinking is doubtful if not completely wrong To demonstrate this statement, we should examine the probability that the actual delivery time in a large R&D project executed alone, without the interference of other projects, differs substantially from the planned one

The estimated project delivery time is the sum of the estimated times the critical work packages spend in the professional groups This can be expressed as

$$T_P = \sum_i \sum_k \bar{\tau}_k$$

where

T_p = the estimated project completion time

$\bar{\tau}_k$ = the estimated time a critical work package k spends in professional group "i "

As $\bar{\tau}_k$ can be seen as a mean value of a random variable, from the law of large numbers in probability theory, it follows that when k is large, the sum Tp must converge in probability to the actual completion time Ta That is,

$$\lim Pr\,[Tp \neq Ta] \to 0 \text{ for } k \to \infty$$

Simply stated, as the completion time for each critical work package is estimated independently, it is equally likely that some work packages will take longer to complete than estimated whereas others will be completed before their estimated completion time Thus, the two types of errors in the estimation should offset each other and average out to 0 as the number of work packages grows

A similar argument can be made regarding the difference between the predicted and the actual cost of the project Hence, the dominant factor for frequent project delays and cost overruns must be the queuing factor, which was introduced in this chapter

CHAPTER

Marketing of High Technology, People, Strategies, and Timing

Marketing of high technology requires all the skills necessary to market any product, but in addition, it poses specific problems that require appropriate solutions One of the problems is the high technoscientific content of most high-technology products This is especially so with large systems and with institutional products—as defined in chapter 2 In this case, the high level of sophistication of the institutional customer poses an additional challenge Another difference, compared to low technology, is the fast pace of technology change, which has direct implications on marketing In this chapter, we examine approaches that have been applied and proven effective in marketing of high technology. Readers interested in general marketing management are referred to Kotler, 1983, and Newell, 1997.

Marketing of high technology is much like a war There are no real enemies in this war, but there is a fierce competition on the battlefield No one is physically injured, but many companies die or fade away in the confrontation. High-technology marketing is no place for amateurs

Marketing of high-technology products is a profession—probably one of the most challenging professions today It is demanding and requires people of high intellect Initiative, imagination, dedication, and perseverance are only a few of the prerequisites necessary for those who aspire to succeed in this most competitive and dynamic market

Managers of a high-technology company should be extremely selective when choosing its marketing staff. In chapter 2, we discussed the critical importance of innovative people for the future of a high-technology company. Other chapters have stressed the challenge of finding creative researchers, inventors, and innovators The marketing organization of a high-technology company demands equal attention A company's business success depends as much on the quality of the people engaged in marketing as it does on the quality of the products it offers to the market Therefore, staffing the organization with the best marketing personnel deserves to be a priority of the company's management.

In this chapter we first define the qualifications required of a successful high-technology marketer and outline a way to acquire people with these characteristics Next, we compare the methodology used in conducting a war to the one necessary for winning the battle of competition in high-technology markets Establishing a company strategy, building an intelligence network, and developing winning tactics are subjects we examine and illustrate with real-world examples Finally, approaches for conducting the battle successfully are described for two types of high-technology marketing the competition for large, institutional high-technology systems, and the competition for market share in the general high-technology market

THE QUALIFICATIONS OF A SUCCESSFUL HIGH-TECHNOLOGY MARKETER

Recruiting high-technology marketers is not a simple matter. Gone are the days when high-technology companies solved personnel problems with engineers who did not do well enough to succeed in research and development or manufacturing by "promoting" them to marketing. Hiring business school graduates with no high-technology orientation is not particularly useful either, unless they are recycled through the organization The purpose of this recycling is to familiarize the recruits with the technological aspects of the high-technology business in which the company is engaged In addition to general skills and techniques (Tracy, 1995), a successful marketing executive in the high-technology business usually possesses most, if not all, of the qualities listed here

Imagination and Creativity.   People engaged in high-technology marketing are often faced with unexpected situations Occasionally, they must address large audiences of customers alone and be able to respond on the spot to difficult questions The ability to handle such situations is an important prerequisite, and a company should demand it before agreeing to entrust marketers with the responsibility of representing the firm to its customers.

Good Communicating Ability.   Marketers must be able to present their case clearly and defend it effectively, both to the customer and to the managers inside the company They should inspire confidence, be sensitive to the customer's needs and requirements, and translate them effectively to the technical personnel of the company

Strong Engineering Background.   People in marketing must be knowledgeable and up-to-date with the latest technological developments in the relevant professional field They do not necessarily need to have "know-how," but they should definitely be of the "know-why" type (see chapter 2)

Reliability.   High-technology marketers must not only inspire confidence but must be truly reliable Reliability is important both externally and internally Any promise made to the customer must be fulfilled—if possible, even beyond the customer's expectations No short-term gains are worth commitments that cannot be kept On the other hand, any status reports, market assessments, and recommendations made by marketers to the company must reflect objective reality rather than wishful thinking.

Enthusiasm, Devotion, and Perseverance.   Marketers must be enthusiastic about marketing their company's products They must be devoted to the mission and prepared to work unusual hours to get the task done Faced with situations in which all indicators say a business deal is going to the competition, perseverance and the will to fight to the end have more than once turned things around and brought victory to a determined marketer

Recruiting and staffing the marketing organization of a high-technology company with first-class marketers is a necessary but not sufficient condition for success The marketing team must be guided by a well-defined business strategy

ESTABLISHING A STRATEGY

Every company, big or small, must define and establish its own strategy. A vision of where it wants to be in five to ten years and what it wants to achieve in defined periods of time are the preliminary questions management must examine first (Urban and Hauser, 1993, Wright, Kroll, and Parnell, 1996) It must then give clear and explicit answers to these questions If the company is a start-up, establishing mid- and long-term objectives may not need to be a formal process Whatever the process is, though, it must involve the key people, at least in some informal discussions The essential point is to have a debate and allow free expression of all relevant views Only then can there be agreement on a strategy that everybody understands and follows If the company is large, establishing a strategy is more formal

In the case of a large company, management should appoint a small team of executives to develop and propose a strategy to the board of management This team normally includes the vice president of marketing and people involved in business development If necessary, the team may use some outside help from professional consultants, but the best solution is to arrive at an internally generated strategy At a minimum, strive to achieve a widely accepted agreement on strategy with which all key personnel will identify and will strongly support.

It is legitimate and sometimes necessary to change a strategy when circumstances change substantially, but this should not happen too often Once established, a strategy can be reviewed and modified if necessary, but only after having been given a real chance to succeed In most cases, this will require a minimum trial of two to three years

The procedure for establishing a strategy is essentially the same whether conducted formally or informally It requires an analysis of the current situation of the company and of future projections This includes identifying the company's strong and weak points and analyzing market possibilities of present and future product lines The process should answer some key questions, such as whether it is better to be a leader or a follower in this professional field, whether the company should concentrate on the local market or operate globally, and so on

Analysis of the Company's Strong and Weak Points

The first step in the analysis is to establish, as explicitly as possible, the current status of the company This involves a thorough review of all the advantages (strong points) the company has and all the drawbacks (weak points) needing improvement as compared to the competition in corresponding market segments. Some of these points may be objective and difficult to change Others depend more on altering the company's actions. The important thing is to address all such issues and arrange the strong and weak points in decreasing order of importance—that is, putting the most important first

All relevant factors must be included in this analysis financial, economic, geopolitical, and technological aspects Also included should be market trends, product line performance, know-how availability, human resources, key individuals' aspirations, reactions from the competition, and other factors To illustrate the outcome of such an analysis, we can examine the results of an actual case (Case 7.1), which can be considered typical

---

CASE 7.1

An Israeli High-Technology Company Example

The company in question was a mid-size, high-technology company that operated with four business units It was generating approximately a 7 percent net profit on $150 million in annual sales At this point, management decided to review the company's strategy to determine whether some changes might be necessary to prolong and extend the success they were enjoying As a result of the analysis, the following strong and weak points were revealed

1 Strong Points

  a Creative and Innovative Work Force
- The company's products are among the best in their respective professional fields
- The cost and time to introduce a new product is highly competitive

  b Product Diversification
- The four business units, each responsible for a line of products, have given the company a good level of stability Highly profitable product lines are compensating for difficulties and even losses in other branches experiencing periods of slow-down

  c Good Financial Position
- The company has been profitable every quarter in the last five years Sales grew from $70 million to $150 million during this period
- The company has a sound cash flow and a very good debt-to-equity ratio

  d Good Market Position
- Despite very strong competition, the company has marketed its products successfully. The forecast suggests that except for the product lines of one of the business units, the market will continue to demand all products of the three remaining divisions The company has established a good reputation and enjoys a largely satisfied customer base

2 Weak Points

  a Geopolitical Situations
- The company is located in a small country The local market is limited, and cannot possibly support on a continuing basis the extensive research and development effort necessary to maintain the company's lead in product innovation

and performance Certain political restrictions severely limit the exportability of some government-controlled product lines

b Growth Prospects
- Despite its good market position, the company seems unlikely to maintain its current rate of growth based on its present product lines Eighty percent of the company's orders are below the $10 million mark A few orders are in the $10 to $30 million range Orders of greater magnitude are exceptional One of the four business units is facing a declining demand for its goods and services The future of the other three seems good but uncertain

c Key Personnel Aspirations
- Most of the company pride and the employees' strong morale derive from the company's position on the front line of technology Despite its currently sound financial status, the company seems unlikely to be able to continue the necessary research and development effort by itself If, as a result, the company starts lagging behind, it risks losing some of its best and most creative people

After debating these points, the management of the company arrived at the following conclusions regarding necessary changes in its strategy

1. Add Large Systems to the Company's Product Lines
- To enable continuous growth, the company decided to try to use the synergy embedded in its four business units. Using the joint experience in all its divisions, it will attempt to offer large, complex systems to the market. A goal was set to secure at least one order of $50 million a year, or larger It was assumed that this, together with the current level of smaller orders in the $180 million-a-year range, should create an attainable goal for increasing combined sales to reach the $200 million-a-year level in three years or less

2 Seek to Establish Joint Ventures with Top International Companies
- To decrease the geopolitical disadvantages as much as possible, the company decided to make a concentrated effort to find synergy through association with respected international companies The goal is to establish at least one such joint venture or strategic alliance for each business unit in the coming two years

3 Diversify Research and Development Funding Resources
- To ensure sufficient funding for its research and development efforts, the company decided to use its good record for success in developing new, innovative products This record, together with its sound financial position, would help it attract venture R&D capital and make more use of available R&D credits

4 Redirect One of the Business Units
- The business unit with declining market demand was directed to identify a growing market niche, best fitting the expertise and technology available in the division, and move into this more promising business area

Once formulated and accepted, the new strategy described in Case 7 1 was put into practice Some three years after its acceptance, the company reached $200 million in annual sales; not long after meeting that goal it was well on the way toward the $300 million-a-year mark

Leader or Follower: Which Is Better?

An important strategic question the management of a company must ask early in the company's life concerns leading or following the market. As usual, there are advantages and disadvantages to both approaches Success and failure are associated with each of them The basic advantages and drawbacks of the two possible strategies need to be explored thoroughly

Market Leader

A market leader is a company that regularly introduces top-of-the-line products in its field of activity A market leader develops and introduces innovative products well before a defined market demand for them has emerged By acting as a pioneer, the leader creates the market for innovative products (Treacy and Wiersema, 1995).

The advantages of being a leader are obvious. The company benefits from the reputation of being on the front line of performance and technology Leading the market often means that the company is the first to open a window of market opportunities This helps the leader enjoy generous returns during the period of no (or low) competition

However, being a leader is also associated with accepting much higher levels of market uncertainty (see chapter 2) The investment necessary to create a market is usually much higher than the one necessary to operate comfortably in an existing market A useful example for learning about the advantages and disadvantages of being a market leader is the example of Sony (Case 7 2)

CASE 7.2

The Sony Example

Sony is a company that for years has followed the strategy of being a market leader, a course that has led to both success and failure Sony was one of the pioneers to introduce the videocassette recorder (VCR) for home use It grasped the enormous market potential of successful miniaturization and cost reduction of video recording machines, previously developed by RCA and Ampex in the United States for television studios By making the VCR practical for home use, Sony initiated the creation of a multibillion dollar market The company was generously rewarded from this success However, Sony opted for the Betamax standard in the early years of the VCR market development. This standard was quickly overtaken by the technically superior VHS standard developed by JVC and other competitors, causing Sony to fight a losing battle and finally to adopt the winning VHS standard (Cusumano, Mylonadis, and Rosenbloom, 1992)

Subsequently, Sony developed an even better video recording standard the Hi8, but by then, the window of opportunity for the home VCR market was already closed The VHS was so widely accepted that it was practically impossible to convince millions of VHS users to throw away their investment and switch to Hi8 Sony, however, found another niche for its Hi8 standard and implemented it in a quite successful line of camcorders

---

The example in Case 7 2 shows the magnitude of rewards available to companies ready to take risks and be a pioneers with new technology in uncertain markets It also demonstrates the limits of the window of opportunity for a company seeking to promote state-of-the-art, novel products

Market Follower

A market follower is a company that emulates and often improves on products successfully introduced to the high-tech market by the market leaders Obviously, a follower has the advantage of building its strategy on the safe ground of proven market success forged by the leader The follower thus avoids by a large degree the market uncertainties the leader has to accept However, the follower must face competition from the very first moment its products are introduced to the market The profit margins of the follower are, therefore, more limited The one way to widen them is to ensure a substantially lower production cost together with a superior quality

The market follower must compete on price To capture a share of the market, its products must get to the market with a substantially lower price tag. The customer would be reluctant to switch from the leader, who normally benefits from a well-established reputation, to a less-known company offering an equivalent product, unless the price was substantially more attractive Once customers are attracted by the lower price, they must be convinced also that the quality of the product is not inferior and may be even superior to that of the leader

Plenty of companies have been successful followers The number that have made fortunes by introducing IBM-compatible computer "clones" and accessories is too long to mention Perhaps most of the success story of the "new dragons" (Taiwan, South Korea, and to a lesser degree, Singapore) has been built on the "follow the market leader" strategy Such strategy is easier to implement in low labor cost countries because of the importance of competing on price However, with an appropriate "twist" of original thinking, companies in the West have also shown success using the market follower's strategy As an illustration, look at Packard Bell (Case 7.3)

Local or International Player?

Another important strategic question that management must ask itself early in the high-tech company's life concerns territory: Where is the major market for the company's products to be found? Basically, there are two possible strategies: either to concentrate the major effort in the local market, or to design and designate the company's products for the world market As usual, there are advantages and disadvantages in both approaches

Concentrating on the Local Market

The local market has a number of advantages compared to the world market It is close geographically and culturally to the company There are no language problems and the company may benefit from some protective shields against foreign competition, such as import duties, quotas, and other devices designed to limit the import of similar products.

The Packard Bell Example

The U S -based Packard Bell company was able to capture a remarkable share of the personal computer market by offering the right mix of performance for a price customers were ready to pay Although the company's products do not lead in technological innovation, original marketing and distribution methods, together with a highly developed ability to predict customers' taste accurately, have played an important part in the company's success On 17 October 1994, *Newsweek* wrote. "Packard Bell is introducing the Spectria   Catering to the home market in design as well as function, it comes with a variety of pop-off colored panels—the better to go with your home's decor "

If the local market is large enough to satisfy the company's aspirations, it might logically concentrate most if not all its marketing efforts at home By doing so, the company will not have to spend the effort and money associated with creating an international marketing and product support organization However, as the world becomes more and more one open market, the company must still follow global trends If not, it may lag in technology and in innovation to the point of becoming obsolete in a short time.

Competing in the World Market

If the local market is too small to satisfy the business potential of a high-technology company, an almost inevitable decision is for it to adopt an international attitude and strategy Such strategy requires management, in the development of each new product, to consider not just the local needs and requirements but the global needs and trends as well Operating as a global player requires from the company a special effort and organization to be successful This subject is treated in detail in chapter 8

Defining the Company's Strategy

After examining the company's strong and weak points as well as its potential in the local and in the international markets, and after debating the leader-follower question, the company's management should formulate its policy for the coming few years The definitions must be clear, simple, and quantitative They should allow the success of the strategy to be checked and evaluated at well-defined points of time

The answer to the question of whether to be a market leader or follower depends largely on the results of the strong–weak points analysis, the company's culture, and the aspirations of its key personnel. In Case 7 1, the company had a market leader attitude It was clear that receding to a follower position would have caused many of the company's most creative people to leave its employ Therefore, to preserve the company's spirit and culture, the management in this case had to find ways to continue acting as a leader In general, however, a change in strategy is justified only after a thorough analysis of the causes that impose it It is imperative, then, to have a healthy debate at appropriate management levels where the need for the strategy change will be explained and where adequate support for the new plan will be ensured

---

COLLECTING INTELLIGENCE

Having reliable and timely intelligence is as important for a high-technology company as for any army Companies can hardly expect to win the highly competitive war for high-technology markets consistently by guessing in the dark Therefore, successful high-technology companies have to devote management attention and adequate resources to a competent and efficient market intelligence service

Agents, Representatives, and Other Information Sources

Different methods are available to companies in organizing their intelligence gathering Usually, in the marketing division there are information centers or organizations that scan and search publications The name of this needed source for information gathering doesn't matter The essential is that the task of such groups is to collect, organize, and distribute anything relevant to the company's business to the right people in a timely manner In today's world of information, a small staff of competent people familiar with computerized database searches can provide a bonanza of highly valuable market intelligence Using e-mail, this intelligence can then be disseminated to the interested people in real time

As with gathering technological information, the main difficulty in making the most practical use of market intelligence is not the availability of information but the ability of the users to formulate clearly and effectively what they need Even today, management must often impose discipline and coerce the marketing people to make effective use of information that is readily available in open databases The new generation of marketing people, however, are expected to be sufficiently computer literate to perform such searches themselves, enjoying the full benefits of immediate access to essential information

To widen the circle of people collecting intelligence and to enhance the personal awareness of the key people in the company, I established this requirement in my company: Each project manager, group leader, and product line manager will be personally responsible for having on file the most recent information on the most "dangerous" competitive products Although this task might be considered the responsibility of the market intelligence group, I found that the more effective way was to assign it directly to the business managers First, as technical experts, these managers knew much better how to read and evaluate competitors' performances Second, by making them personally responsible for having the latest information, we made sure that they would be the first to read it Of course, no one prevented these managers from using the market intelligence group or any other source for collecting their information Any time we needed an update on our position vis-à-vis the competition, I would drop into the appropriate manager's office and ask for an on-the-spot briefing

Agents and representatives are another important source of information Their role is particularly significant when a company operates globally Almost any high-technology company that markets its products and services in worldwide markets must establish a network of local agents and representatives This is discussed further in the next chapter. However, at this point, assuming that such a network exists, it should provide the company with information about any significant developments in the respective countries Timely information about market opportunities, market trends, customer needs and desires, customer satisfaction or complaints about the company's products, and the products' competitive stand versus the competition represents only a partial list of the kinds of valuable information an agent should provide the company he serves and represents

Whereas representatives may be company employees dispatched to serve in a foreign country for a given period of time, local agents are permanent residents of the country of their assignment These local agents not only speak the language of their country but are also deeply involved in its local culture and society As such, they can best sense the country's real spirit and its people's mentality Hence, local agents are usually a better source for indigenous information than company representatives The latter should direct and coordinate the work of the agents but can hardly replace them

To make the best use of its agents as an intelligence source, the company has to make clear that information gathering is a part of their task. Many high-technology agents rightly understand their role as primarily one of promoting the company's products It is therefore understandable that they care only about the commercial aspects of the business without paying too much attention to information that could be useful to the company The local agents don't have to behave like "undercover agents" in the service of military intelligence, but requesting that they give their attention to and report on information that is judged important by the company is totally legitimate Once sensitized to and convinced of the need to perform this intelligence gathering function, local agents normally do the job quite well. In fact, they often even enjoy this assignment, which makes them much more aware of the total environment and thus, more effective with their business dealings

Learning Competitor's Strategies

In addition to collecting information on competitor's products and closely following their moves in local and foreign markets, companies also need to learn and thoroughly understand the strategy of their market adversaries. First, management must analyze the competitor's strong and weak points, much as they did for their own company They need to ask such questions as this What is the competitor's financial strength? How critical is it for that business to win a specific competition? What happens to the firm if it wins? What happens if it loses? These are relevant questions that have to be answered as objectively as possible In case of doubt, the worst-case answer should be assumed

Second, managers should learn from the long-term behavior of the competitor Analyze and understand the trends Where the competitor was, where it is, and where it is going are among the pertinent questions that must be asked and answered as accurately as possible

---

CASE 7.4

Example of Aborted Cooperation between Competitors

The top management of two high-technology companies engaged in the design and manufacturing of defense electronics products made the decision to cooperate rather than compete against each other in a foreign market By so doing and by making a unique, more competitive proposal against the international competition, these managements were convinced that their combined chance to win the contract was significantly improved However, the project leader of one of the companies was strongly persuaded that he could win the international competition alone, and by doing so gain a local advantage against the second company His drive to beat his local competitor was so strong that he and his team undermined the cooperation He created so many obstacles to a joint venture that his management finally had to give up on the idea

---

Third, managers should analyze carefully the personal aspirations of the competitor's major player—the person leading and directing the moves made by the competitor This is normally the person assigned by the competitor with the responsibility of winning the contract, or the individual employee who is the real driving force behind the competitor's effort To make this point completely clear, we purposely emphasize the competitor's major player and not necessarily the competitor's top management We have seen many examples in high-technology companies where strong personalities holding key positions were able to abort top management decisions and even reverse company strategies A typical example illustrating the need to watch the behavior of key players appears in Case 7 4, a case of aborted cooperation between two defense contractors

Because of the enormous weight that specialists have in the high-technology industry, they often become the key players Whoever fails to take this phenomenon into account can easily be misled by positions that may be declared by management, but that cannot be successfully implemented in the field Some characterize such situations by the witticism, "The company is not responsible for decisions made by the management "

Although understanding the competitor's strategy is a complex task, its importance can hardly be overstated Some companies will go as far as "stealing" senior executives from a competitor company They do this by offering these executives attractive advantages, mainly for the purpose of gaining insight on the competitor's planning and strategy Such a practice, however, may prove to be a double-edged sword and act in some later day as a boomerang As fierce as the competition may be, maintaining professional ethics has always been a better long-term policy. To illustrate the kind of knotty problems that may develop between companies allegedly engaged in such practices, look at the dispute between General Motors (GM) and Volkswagen (VW) (Case 7 5)

CASE 7.5

The Example of General Motors (GM) versus Volkswagen (VW)

In April 1993, General Motors filed its first legal complaint against Volkswagen in Germany General Motors demanded compensation and interest for industrial secrets it alleged that VW gained when GM's former purchasing chief, Jose Ignacio Lopez, and seven other managers defected to the German automaker General Motors claimed that the managers took secret documents with them, causing a loss of several hundred million marks to its Opel subsidiary In April 1996, a civil lawsuit was filed by General Motors, this time in Detroit Volkswagen, its chairman Mr. Piech, and Mr Lopez denied that any industrial spying had taken place

In May 1996, Volkswagen filed a defamation suit, demanding 10 billion Deutsche marks ($6 6 billion) for allegations that GM officials made at U S and German news conferences after the filing of the Detroit suit A spokesman for VW's management board, Mr Kocks, said at the occasion that the U S automaker defamed it and its chairman "Now we can force GM to either prove their point or drop it completely "

Information and Misinformation

Collecting information is important, but disseminating it effectively is even more essential Most high-tech companies publish information in different forms advertising material, commercial brochures, publication in professional journals, conference speeches, and so forth. The major purpose of this action is, obviously, to build and maintain the image of the company and advertise its products to potential customers

The importance of publishing and advertising is well understood and does not need further elaboration An understandable but often overlooked point is that most of what a company prints and publishes will be available to and used by the competition also

In most high-tech companies engaged in innovative work, there is a natural desire among the scientists and researchers to publish their achievements This is a positive drive and should be encouraged, provided that market-oriented specialists do appropriate "sanitizing" of those parts of the publications that should be kept confidential to the company However, it is also important not to go to extremes Barring all publications on sensitive matters is an easy solution but not a very smart one In the long run, it is bound to hurt the company A truly professional approach calls for finding the right compromise Publish what strengthens the company's image and market position, and ban sensitive information that does not have to be disclosed or that may harm the company if put into the hands of the competition. Every company should find an appropriate way for deciding what and what not to publish There must be a specific individual who holds personal responsibility for performing this function professionally

---

CASE 7.6

Example Showing Use of Misinformation

To illustrate, here is a real-life example: Our company was bidding in an important competition for a government contract in a foreign country At a certain point, we had strong reason to believe that important features of our proposal, which we knew to be attractive and unique, had been leaked to one of our major competitors As a result, we found in the next phase of the competition that our competitor, helped by a third company not originally in the competition, was offering similar features, hence, substantially reducing our advantages We knew that in the final phase before the decision, the customer required a live demonstration of the critical system's performances, so we purposely let everyone believe we were having serious problems in reaching two of the system's important parameters This increased the self-confidence of the competition Being sure to win, the competitor tried to improve his margins by asking substantial prices for some open points in his "best and final" proposal By the time the competitor learned that we actually did not have a problem with the critical parameters, it was too late for him to change his bid We won the contract

---

Surprise has been a decisive factor in many battles To surprise the competition is something many high-technology companies have attempted to do In addition to working quietly on some revolutionary new product or process, another method is to disseminate purposely misleading information.

Misinformation has been used by many high-technology companies in crucially important competitions (Kawasaki, 1995). Naturally, no company likes to publicize or even acknowledge using the method Usually companies are very careful, and rightly so, to make sure that whatever is published by them is accurate and reliable However, if management has serious reason to believe that parts of such information are being used by the competition to improve its position, the company can legitimately feed the competitor misinformation (see Case 7 6)

The management of a high-technology company must be aware that a professional competitor may use misinformation as part of his competitive strategy Therefore, any significant information that may have a decisive impact on the competition must be cross-checked and verified by as many independent sources as possible

DEVELOPING WINNING TACTICS

Having established a strategy and set in place the intelligence infrastructure, a company still has to prepare a specific set of tactics adapted to any particular competitive situation This requires a clear definition of the objectives, an analysis of relevant intelligence, the creation of an image, and the establishment of a pricing policy

Defining Objectives

A company's management should define the goals and objectives the company wants to achieve by participating in a competition. These goals should be clearly transmitted to the key people responsible for winning the competition Different goals justify different investments in effort and money Not all competitions are equally important, therefore, they should be treated accordingly Often, companies engaged in competitions become so carried away in their effort to win that the resources they spend become disproportional to the stakes they can possibly hope to realize This topic is examined further in the chapter when we discuss battles a company cannot afford to lose versus battles worth losing

Sometimes, a company competes to penetrate a new market, or to win a new customer and thus enlarge its customer base. Either is different from increasing its market share in a well-established market Other objectives could be to increase turnover, which might be different from increasing profit, or to provide meaningful workload for a group of specialists who are about to finish their last project and have no customer-funded next assignment. Some of the objectives might be of vital importance to the company; others might be strategically important, just important, or nice to have Each of these cases requires different tactics

The goals and objectives need not be mutually exclusive Very often managers face a combination of two or more complementary objectives Yet, it is important to define what the first objective is and what the next objectives are The appropriate tactics may be completely different for varying priorities of the same set of objectives.

Analyzing Intelligence

Once objectives are clearly defined, all pertinent information that may influence the outcome of the competition must be carefully analyzed First, establish as precisely as possible what the decision criteria of the customers are These criteria should be arranged in descending order of importance If possible, try to quantify the weight the customer attaches to each decision parameter In many real-life cases, a clear distinction must be made between the true objectives of the customer and the officially announced ones

Next, strive to obtain as clear a picture as possible of the rules peculiar to the specific competition In some cases there are well-defined, formal rules In others, the rules are informal and vaguely expressed Yet, there is always one person or a small group of people who are the true decision makers This decision maker must be accurately identified, and all formal and informal objectives must be verified by the key people responsible for winning the competition A real-world example involving objectives appears in Case 7 7

Once the "rules" of competition have been established, a thorough comparison of "our" proposal versus the competitors' proposals can be carried out, taking into account the customer's true criteria After establishing the competitive advantages and disadvantages of the various proposals, the next step is to estimate the degrees of freedom the competition has for improving on its disadvantages In a competition, it is always safer to assume that a professional competitor will make logical moves to improve

---

CASE 7.7

An Example of Understanding True Objectives

After the disintegration of the Soviet bloc, one of the newly formed central European democracies was interested in modernizing its lagging rural telephone network The European Bank for Reconstruction and Development (EBRD), which was financing a substantial part of the project, recommended to the local authorities that they invite a number of competent contractors to bid on the design and implementation of the project.

The competition was conducted according to the rules prevailing for such competitions in the West. The customer issued a specification and a list of requirements, including a nonimperative but desirable completion date. This very ambitious completion date imposed the need to work in parallel on a number of sites, thus increasing the cost of the project Most of the contractors chose to offer a more realistic time schedule.

However, a nondeclared yet vitally important objective of the local authorities was to win the coming elections. Any proposal that did not promise inauguration of the new facility well before election day was considered inferior and automatically discarded from the competition under all kinds of pretexts

---

his position Collecting specific intelligence on such moves then becomes a priority When analyzing the possibilities available to the competition, managers should also take into account the other company's limitations If, for example, the major competitor has shown some financial weakness in recent quarterly reporting, and if there is evidence that the board has criticized management for too many nonprofit ventures, a plausible deduction is that such a competitor will not be ready to accept high levels of risk

Normally, most competitions go through several stages At each stage, the competitors provide information to the customers Every competitor will most probably try to get as much intelligence as possible with regard to what the other companies are doing and on how their competitive position has changed as a result of such action Often, the customer will voluntarily tell you that you have to improve your proposal In most cases, such suggestions (hints) are reliable. However, because the customer has a clear interest in improving even the best proposal, the company should be careful when assessing such information

In some cases, the customer may issue a well-defined request for proposal for some high-tech system. This is typically the case with large government contracts In such situations, the desired system performances are usually specified Starting from this specification, an analysis of the technologies and the know-how available to the competitors may be quite useful If your competition lacks some critical technology, and if the number of sources for such technologies is limited, it might be advantageous to quickly come to an agreement with companies holding such technologies in order to bar the road of your competition. At the same time, such agreement should improve the competitiveness of your company's proposal

It is hard to enumerate all possible situations that require intelligence analysis The examples we have used describe some typical situations The essential principle is never to establish a set of tactics before all the available information and ad hoc intelligence has been carefully analyzed, and critical factors have been checked and cross-checked

Establishing an Image and Reputation

An important part of any tactic concerns the image a company wants to portray Based on intelligence analysis, this image must be made to conform with the expectations of the target customers If the main consideration of the most important customers is performance, the company must establish its image as a market leader (see chapter 9, the case of Loral). If reliability and after-sales service are the most important parameters for customers, the company must convincingly portray its established reputation for reliability and service. In each case, the image must fit the customers' needs and expectations

However, in high technology, as in any long-term business, no image can replace substance If a company wants to become a major player in the general aviation avionics market, a good beginning is to establish a network of competent after-sales service organizations in as many airports as possible Availability of service and spare parts is a major consideration for any aircraft owner who wants to avoid being grounded because of a missing part or lack of service

Although everybody knows that it is "better to be young, healthy, and rich," in high technology, a company can seldom be all things at one time The image a company wants to portray should therefore not only match the expectations of its most important customer base but should also be supported in reality by a reputation earned in the field

A company that has established a reputation for being a first-class but rather expensive supplier may be appealing to exclusive customers However, if the company considers moving into some less exclusive market niche, it might consider establishing a separate subsidiary with a different name The latter should portray the appropriate image for its own products, which might be totally different from the mother company's image

Establishing a reputation is important in all businesses In high technology, however, the importance is even greater because not all the qualities of an innovative product are immediately known or broadly understood If the customer has confidence in the firm offering the product, his decision is greatly simplified

Establishing a Winning Price

Price is always one of the basic decision parameters Although in high technology performance is often more important than price, price still remains a fundamental consideration Therefore, one of the most important tactical decisions a company has to make in a competition is to establish the *winning price* it has to offer in order to prevail

Here, we define *winning price* as that price that just tilts the customer's decision in favor of the winning company Any price lower than that would, of course, also favor that company, but at the same time, it would deplete the profit margin the company would expect to realize from winning the contract. The winning price is not necessarily the lowest price In the process of establishing its winning price, a company has to take into account all other parameters with their respective weight as they would be viewed by the customer Then, the company should adjust its price, with full consideration of that of the competition, so as to turn the final decision in its own favor

In most cases, the company will be able to establish only an estimate of the winning price Even with the best intelligence, a company may seldom have sufficient knowledge of exactly what the competitors are proposing Therefore, there is usually an uncertainty gap whose size depends on the amount and reliability of information available This gap should be made as narrow as possible

There is no relation whatever between the winning price as defined here, and what it costs the company to deliver under the contract The simplistic method of calculating your own company's cost and then adding to it a fixed profit margin is a sure way to lose in the sophisticated high-technology marketplace A company operating this way is bound to lose twice First, it may lose an opportunity to penetrate an important market, for which paying an "entrance fee" is well worth the cost Second, it may lose the opportunity to realize all the profit potential available because it underestimates its own market advantages in the face of a weak competition

The pricing policy of a high-technology company must reflect long-term profit strategy Tactically, a totally justified move could be to accept no profit at all, or even a sensible loss, if the loss can be seen as a justifiable investment with good potential return for the future This is often the case when one of the company's objectives is to penetrate an important market If the company is sure of the values and quality of its products, the most reasonable policy might be to pay the price for establishing a foothold in an important market This policy was widely applied by Japanese industry in the 1960s when this industry had not yet established a good reputation for quality and reliability

In some institutional high-technology competitions—for example, the private or government purchase of a new generation voice and data communication system—the customer may run the competition in phases Such phases are typically composed of a request for information phase, a request for proposal phase, and a request for best and final proposal phase In such cases, companies are requested to provide price information in each phase of the competition

A company with a well-established reputation in the specific field and which also has reliable information that it will not be excluded from competition at early stages for bidding too high has all the reasons to bid high at the beginning By bidding high, the company establishes a reference level which, if leaked to the competition, does not drive the prices too low from the very beginning. This strategy can also help the customer to prepare a reasonable budget for the acquisition and improves the chances of the project's realization

At the final stage, when more and more intelligence about the relative position of the competitors becomes available, the company that wants to win the project must bid the winning price If this price has been correctly estimated, the company has a much more realistic chance to win

Management of a competent, high-technology company should ask at all stages of the competition, "What is the current winning price?" At the beginning, the estimated winning price may vary in a relatively wide range With the accumulation and analysis of appropriate intelligence, this range should be reduced The cost to the company is of course an important parameter for management in its decision of whether or not to bid If the estimated cost is higher than the winning price, the only reasonable action for management to undertake is to seek to reduce its costs If a company consistently finds its costs higher than the winning prices after a number of competitions, and if there is no way to reduce its costs below the winning prices, the company should consider closing this line of business

In summary, the notion of *winning price* plays a critically important role during a competition. It should be used methodically by management as a measure of the company's competitive standing It should be adjusted according to the latest information available and offered to the customer at the decision point

Establishing Correct Timing

The well-known rule that prevailed in the Old West was "the fastest gun wins." Competition in high technology may resemble in many ways the gunfights of the Old West— but not in this respect In the high-technology fight, the one who wins is usually the one who shoots last Shooting first in a high-technology competition usually divulges information that enables the other side to correct its fire Acting fast can be effective only if the company is sure to win by a knockout Usually this is not the case with customers who wish to take their time, compare, and thoroughly evaluate all offers they receive from various competitors In most practical cases, a high-technology company can significantly improve its competitive position if it can manage to shoot last

Having observed the outcome of many competitions in which our company participated, I found a high degree of correlation between the number of times we were the last company to make a presentation to the customer and the number of times we won the contract I found that one underlying reason for this was the clear advantage we gained by being the "last shooter" because of the greater amount of information we were able to gather After the customer has spoken to every other competitor, he has an almost uncontrollable urge to criticize the proposal of the last company he visits or talks to The customer would very often point out all the weaknesses that company's proposal had in comparison to other competitors If the company is well prepared to improve its weak points skillfully by clarifying "misunderstandings" with the customer, and if the customer likes the last company's proposal after correction of the criticisms, the last company has a much greater chance to turn the decision in its favor

In a multiphase competition, the number of companies showing interest in the first phase is usually quite large The customer normally selects a few of the best companies to reduce the list of competitors to a more manageable number As the competition progresses, only a short list of competitors should remain in the final phases so that the customer can evaluate and compare their proposals in greater depth At "the best and final" proposal phase, usually just the two leading companies are invited to submit final proposals

The goal for each phase should be to pass on to the next one Therefore, the right timing to disclose all advantages and propose a winning price is at the best and final phase A full and early disclosure of all attractive features may give the competition sufficient opportunity to improve their proposals accordingly Having some good surprises for the customer at the moment of decision is always a good tactic, provided that doing so does not unduly weaken the negotiating position along the way.

Another critical timing question occurs in selecting the right moment for the first introduction to the market of a novel, innovative product In general, all high-technology companies try to make best use of the window of market opportunity To face minimum competition for the longest possible period of time, the logical moment to announce the new product is the moment the company is totally prepared to launch the product That means it has a completely "debugged" product and a well-running production line capable of meeting the projected demand An earlier announcement of the product could be a mistake, as it may give the competition time to come up with a response

Some high-technology products are so innovative, however, that the market needs extra time for promotion before a strong demand can be built In such cases, it might be wise to plan and prepare for two models of the innovative product The first would serve as the introductory model with the purpose of building the market The second, dotted with superior characteristics, should be the company's planned response to anticipated competition Such a tactic acts on the expectation that the time necessary for promoting the first model may be used by others to produce a competitive product, thus reducing the window of opportunity for the originating company Having an improved model can then provide the introducing company the means to regain momentum and recapture any lost market share

In summary, timing is a very important tactical consideration in high technology The company that comes forcefully at the opportune moment is most often the winner. Early product disclosure is usually counterproductive, but of course, late may be too late Here again, the best guidance a company can follow is to make a careful analysis and use all the available market intelligence it can get

Battles a Company Cannot Afford to Lose

One of the most important distinctions a company must learn to make is the distinction between all possible competitions it might seek to win and the few that are strategically important—and sometimes even vital for the company's future A strategically important competition is one that not only brings the business on the winning contract but also opens an entire market with the promise for many follow-on contracts Losing a strategic battle to the competition can mean not only losing the contract but can also mean eventually being forced out of this type of business

A high-technology company engaging in a strategically important competition must mobilize all its resources to win A first and very important step is to establish a "war cabinet" or a competition team: a body of competent senior people who are totally dedicated to winning the battle The chief commanding officer appointed to direct this body should be either the president of the company or a top-level executive reporting directly to the president and having powers to act in the president's behalf In view of the long-term implications of winning or losing a strategic competition, the top management must be totally committed to the success of the operation

The war cabinet should be provided with full and current intelligence reports It should participate in establishing a set of tactics and decide appropriate timing for every move All feedback coming from the customer or from other sources should quickly be made available to the cabinet members through preestablished communication channels The information flow, the protocols of the tactical decisions of this group, and all other data related to the competition must be handled as *company confidential* information.

One of the worst mistakes management can make during a strategically important competition is to listen to the "good news" and ignore even the smallest causes for concern Although we all prefer to hear good news, in critical situations the "bad news" reports are those that should get the highest priority and attention Agents, representatives, and all company personnel who come in contact with the customer should be specifically instructed to listen and report with the highest priority on any negative development There is always ample time to savor good news, but if a negative development is overlooked or not handled promptly, there soon may not be enough time to take corrective action

The war cabinet should strive to maintain as accurate an estimate as possible on the winning price during all the phases of a vital competition The director of the specific business unit may be the one responsible for submitting the final bid to the customer In competitions of strategic importance, however, the president or the chief executive officer must assume full responsibility for the proposal with all the consequences of winning or losing the contract

If a company mobilizes itself and acts as described in this chapter, its probability for winning the battle is greatly improved If the competition wins despite all efforts made by the company, this should result only because of some fundamental superiority the competition possesses and not because of mistakes, omissions, or neglect by the company's management If indeed the competition is superior, the company should conduct a critical review of its future in this line of business

Battles Worth Losing

In war games, in chess tournaments, and similarly in business, losing is sometimes advantageous, whether the loss is a project that goes to the competition, a chess piece sacrificed to the opponent, or a battle lost in order to win the war! War history is full of examples of this kind Some go as far back as to ancient Greece and Rome. Remember the famous victory of Pyrrhus in his battle at Heraclea? Pyrrhus won the battle but at such a cost in lives that finally he had to retreat, losing the war against the Romans This event gave birth to the term, *a Pyrrhic victory*

In more recent times, Tolstoi, in his nineteenth-century epic *War and Peace*, describes the battle of Borodino, the last victory won by Napoleon in his drive toward Moscow The Russian General Koutouzov sacrificed Moscow by losing the battle of Borodino (which he knew he couldn't win). Napoleon on the other hand lost one-quarter of his army in winning this battle, and after conquering Moscow, he had no choice but to organize his retreat (and that, Koutouzov also had rightly anticipated)

In some high-technology competitions, as in war, the better move is occasionally to let the competitor win If the battle is not of strategic importance to your company

---

CASE 7.8

An Example of Making the Competition Bleed

Some years ago, our company was engaged in a competitive war with another high-technology company in the very specialized field of signal intelligence Both companies had roughly the same technological level and engaged in bitter battles for every contract By following the strategy described earlier, we made sure that every contract won by the competitor would lead to a substantial financial cost for that firm After a while, the competitor lacked sufficient resources to invest in adequate research and development in this specific field When our company won a strategically important competition, it became obvious to some of the best specialists the competitor had that their company could not continue to invest in this field effectively We gladly employed those specialists who soon wanted to join our company and increase their chances for remaining in their chosen field This loss further weakened the competitor to the point that the firm's activities in this area faded away and disappeared from the map of competition

---

and if you can make the competitor pay a dear price for victory, it might be to your best long-term advantage to lose one such competition This is especially true in the case of long-term wars fought between two companies engaged in the same line of business Every company has finite and limited resources; if the contract won by the competition is going to require it to invest a substantial amount of its resources in order to deliver, this situation will inevitably weaken it for near-future competitions By concentrating effort on winning battles of strategic importance and by letting the competitor win occasional costly victories, a competent management can greatly increase its chances to win the overall war of competition (see Case 7 8)

By making a clear distinction between battles a company must win and battles worth losing, and by following appropriate tactics, a high-technology company can substantially improve its strategic position and win the war of competition

---

THE BATTLE

The management of a company must establish a strategy and develop a set of appropriate tactics for competing successfully in the sophisticated high-technology markets Only when this is accomplished can the company management assume the moral right to engage the company's resources in the battle As explained in previous chapters, there are two different types of high-technology business, each requiring a slightly different competitive approach The first to be discussed here is the business of large, institutional high-technology projects, like air traffic control installations, regional communication systems, some major defense contracts, and so on. The second type is the consumer business, with products ranging from software packages and computer work stations to innovative pharmaceutical products This type of business is concerned with winning a share in markets that have a large number of customers With these companies, the unit product price is moderate or even low, but the quantities sold are so large that the total contract value may still be quite important

The Battle for Large, High-Technology Projects

Competition for large, high-technology projects is characterized by the existence of a well-defined customer Typically, this type of competition goes through a number of stages First, the customer issues a request for information based on a roughly defined statement of need Based on the responses received, the customer prepares a set of specifications and a request for proposal. These are then sent to companies judged competent to satisfy the specifications if they should receive the bid The companies are invited to submit their proposals by a specified date From the submitted proposals, the customer usually selects the two or three best ones and invites the chosen companies for negotiations After all the technical and contractual issues are clarified during the negotiations, the finalists are often required to submit their "best and final" proposals

Following such a procedure, the customer is able to learn a lot from the different competitors These negotiations allow him to assess comparative advantages and disadvantages of the competitors and to improve both the content and the price of his acquisition The first significant move every competitor must make is to submit an adequate proposal to the customer

Preparing a Winning Proposal

Preparing a winning proposal requires true professionalism Many books and articles have been especially dedicated to the subject One of the best methodologies and techniques has been developed and described by H Silver (1989) and is available in various forms such as short specialized courses and video presentations The reader who has to work on such proposals is strongly advised to refer to one of the specialized publications on the subject In this section, we summarize the essentials and make some comments based on lessons we learned during numerous real proposal preparations and the way customers responded to them

Probably the most important step after assigning formal responsibility for preparing the proposal to a capable individual is to outline formally in writing all essential messages (the themes) the company wants to convey to the customer These explicit messages should be in the hands of the preparer before he or she begins actually to write the proposal Remember that the purpose of a proposal is to make sure that these messages are clearly transmitted to and understood by the customer The customer should also find in the proposal proofs that the statements made by the company are reliable and correct First, however, the company must establish for itself the list of messages, which if accepted by the customer, will make the proposal a winning one Among the messages a company may want to convey in its proposal are these:

> *Utility of the Proposed Solution* why and how the proposed system is going to meet all the customer's requirements.
>
> *Unique and Innovative Features* what makes this proposal better for the customer than any other solution

Growth Potential: how easy it is to upgrade the proposed solution, if in the future additions or upgrades become necessary

Reliability of the Proposal: what experience the company has in similar fields and why the customer can rely on the reputation and the proven record of the company

No or Low Risks: assurance that the risks, if any, are acceptable—especially important for customers who are strongly risk aversive

Cost Effectiveness of the Proposal: the full cost to the customer; the cost of a complex system is usually composed of the acquisition cost, the maintenance and logistic support cost, personnel training costs, and so on The proposal should show why the system proposed has an attractive total life cycle cost

These six points certainly do not constitute an exhaustive list of all the important messages a company should emphasize in its proposal, but they convey the concept, which is to make certain that such a list is established before the proposal is written Having the list available is the surest way to see that the proposal presents forcefully all the identified messages with all the arguments necessary to support them

Another important point to remember is that the most important people receiving the proposal seldom have the time to read it thoroughly Therefore, an executive summary should be prepared and attached to the detailed proposal All the important messages mentioned earlier must appear in the executive summary Elaboration of these messages and full descriptions that flesh out and prove the validity of all statements made in the executive summary will be referenced so they can easily be found in the main proposal

If for some reason the required format of the proposal does not allow for an executive summary, the same content can be enclosed in the first 20 or so pages of the main proposal It is advisable to have these pages ready in advance, much before the rest of the proposal is completed This will allow an in-depth discussion of the proposal by the management, the "war cabinet" or the "blue team–red teams" (see chapter 3) while there is still time to introduce corrections or contribute ideas to the main proposal

Although this approach to preparing a winning proposal is logical and straightforward, I have witnessed too many cases in which these simple rules were not applied Instead, the team responsible for writing the proposal too often dives deeply into technical details describing the various subsystems and system building blocks The team members are gleefully busy drawing block diagrams and detailed drawings Only at the last minute do they start worrying about whether the customer will be able to extract the essentials out of their proposal, which might by now be some 800 pages long

Proposals are seldom ready much before the submission date Usually, teams work overtime to meet the proposal deadline When management asks to have a preview of the proposal prior to submission, it is often snowed by hundreds of draft proposal pages This leaves management with little choice but to rely on a verbal interpretation and summary given by the proposal manager in a last minute briefing Such situations allow for very limited management contribution to the quality of the proposal

The customer's response to this type of proposal is often disappointing to the company and to the team of people who have worked hard to prepare what turned out to be an ineffective proposal There is no guarantee that writing a proposal according to the rules and procedures described in the beginning of this section will always result in winning the contract However, one can be sure that if a competition is lost, it will not be by mistake or by a misunderstanding of the advantages the company has in comparison to what is offered by the competition

The last important point with respect to the preparation of an effective proposal is to remind the team writing the proposal that eventually it may end up in the hands of the competition Therefore, there is no need to include material that may serve as a handbook of how to solve sensitive technical issues Technical explanations should be detailed only to that level needed to convince the customer that the company has the solution Often, engineers and scientists, rightfully proud of their achievements, will go overboard with unnecessary details If such information leaks to the competition, it may deprive the company of important competitive advantages

Use of Real-Time Intelligence

Throughout this chapter, we have emphasized the importance of establishing an effective information gathering network Before "the battle," the information gathered was an essential element in establishing the company's strategy and tactics During the active competition phase, the timeliness of intelligence becomes critically important Real-time intelligence is usually defined as appropriate information arriving to the right person in time for him or her to act on it productively Intelligence that arrives too late to be used by the company to change its course—even when the information to be used is detailed and accurate—is not real-time information because it is not available at the time the company needs it

For real-time intelligence to be effective, the company must open direct access to the person who has the power and authority to act on the information Many companies establish stringent hierarchies that can delay or distort the information before it gets to the authorized person Suppose the only person with authority to act on this type of report is the president of the company If a low-level employee obtains important intelligence, it often trickles through channels until it reaches the top of the hierarchy By then, so much time has elapsed that the information cannot be used as the basis for taking effective action One way of overcoming this difficulty is to establish parallel reporting so the information goes directly to all levels concerned In a company with the right team spirit and mutual trust of the people in the hierarchy, such an arrangement should not cause too many problems

The most critical real-time information usually comes directly from customers It is vital, therefore, to maintain an ongoing dialogue with the customer during all phases of the competition. Managers should be particularly sensitive to messages of concern or dissatisfaction expressed by customers Even if the customers are making some of these remarks because of misunderstandings or even mistakes, they should be encouraged to express their thoughts rather than be ignored or told they are wrong. I have seen inexperienced engineers arguing with a customer to show that he had made a mistake I have yet to see a customer who likes to be proven incompetent or stupid One has to remember the old saying. "The customer is not always right but he is always the customer "

There are, of course, other possible sources for real-time intelligence In some large-scale competitions, there might be political implications that require close monitoring of the state of mind of people influencing the decision Last is information about every critical move made by the competition A company that wants to be serious about winning the competitive battles in high-technology markets must make sure that the channels are open to receive and act on all pertinent information in real time

Gaining Support Positions

Any general knows quite well that storming an enemy's stronghold without preparing adequate support positions will most likely lead to a disaster. Similarly, in the high-technology business, expecting to win tough competitions without preparing a strong support base for your proposal is very unwise These support positions must be in place well before the moment of decision. Although the final choice may be made by a small number of people or even by a single person, the decision process usually involves much larger groups of people who have a legitimate say on competitions for a large, multimillion-dollar high-technology system Therefore, in many cases, a positive decision cannot be made final until an adequate level of consensus has been reached with everyone involved

Many of the features of a proposed system are often new and innovative; therefore, they are not always easily understood by everyone who may have a say in the competition Preparing and submitting a professionally written proposal does not provide sufficient explanation. Long before the submission of the proposal, the company must develop and explain its case to all interested parties Given the different, sometimes even diverging, interests of the people in question, the company must prepare a set of tailor-made presentations Each presentation has to explain the forthcoming proposal and do this by emphasizing the factors of special importance to the individual or group being addressed For example, some parties are strongly concerned about ecological aspects, others by the advance of technology or the creation of employment opportunities, and so on

Making the effort to gain strong, broad-based support for the company's approach often must be done by the same people who occupied more than full time in writing the proposal They may also be busy responding to continuous questions and inquiries coming from the customer The increased demands on their time must be taken into account Usually, with advance planning, such conflicts can be resolved The problem is much harder to deal with if management requests that presentations be prepared at the last minute.

In a number of cases, gaining support for the company involves more than presenting its approach to interested parties Often, in the high-technology business, the customer's decision is strongly influenced by his or her perception of the people the company plans to assign to the project if it wins the contract If the company has a first-class team, it needs to introduce these "stars" to the customer. Personal contact between key people on the team, with a record of impressive achievements, and representatives of the customer has often helped create a high level of confidence and generated support for the company's proposal. Gaining support positions will greatly enhance the ability of the company to make an effective lobby and influence the final decision, as discussed in the next section

Follow-Up, Lobbying, and Influencing the Decision

In addition to preparing a winning proposal, using intelligence effectively, and cultivating support, the company must develop a formal procedure to assure that every action receives adequate follow-up The effectiveness of the action must be analyzed and supplementary steps taken if this is appropriate An effective way of ensuring continuity is to assign a specific individual the responsibility of reporting on follow-up actions Usually, even the most effective actions, meetings, or presentations leave some open points or unresolved questions Occasionally, some issues may need time to surface and be explicitly raised by the customer If the company does not have an organized follow-up procedure, competitors may exploit this omission and profit from the situation

Also during the decision period, the company must actively lobby. The lobby is most effective after the company has presented its case The lobby usually consists of one-on-one meetings between an individual who will be influential in the decision making and a competent representative of the company. In these meetings the lobbyist seeks to obtain active support for the company's proposal and a commitment from the individual to exercise influence in favor of the company's proposal Sometimes, a company representative can organize a coordinated action by a number of such influential individuals For this to happen, in addition to the one-on-one lobby, someone in company management must coordinate the action of those key individuals who should then talk to the decision makers in an effort to influence the decision.

Influencing the final decision requires a total concentration on the decision makers to ensure that nothing is left to chance Lobbyists must be certain that every message the company wants to convey, directly or indirectly, has been received and well understood Remember that the decision on large, high-technology programs is seldom an instant event It is a process In this process, one of the competitors may have an outstanding advantage until the last moment and still lose the competition if some new consideration emerges unexpectedly Therefore, nothing is final until the contract is actually signed and sealed Until that point, no professional company should abandon hope or leave the battlefield

On the other hand, if a contract has been awarded to a competitor, it is usually counterproductive to fight the customer's decision, even if the company losing the contract is badly disappointed Real-life experience has shown that the probability of reversing a customer's decision is extremely slim. However, the probability is very high that the customer can be antagonized to the point of never considering the company for any future business. Therefore, as no company can reasonably hope to win in every competition, every firm should be prepared to lose gracefully, as in sports Many times, a gracious attitude has been rewarded by customers who seek to compensate a respectful company for its professional effort to deliver a "good fight." This compensation can come by awarding it some portion of the business or by assigning it some other contract.

The Battle for Market Share in the General High-Technology Market

The general high-technology market is characterized by products offered to a large number of customers at moderate or even low prices Because of the quantities sold, the entire scope of business is often larger than some of the large, high-technology projects discussed in the previous section Examples of products in the general high-technology markets are personal computers (PCs), computerized workstations, multimedia machines—which include PC, TV, stereo sound, telephone, fax—and all the software packages offered for them Other examples are various new chemical or biochemical products, new synthetic materials, or high-technology innovations that have broad applications

After establishing a strategy and developing the appropriate set of tactics, a company competing in this market should choose the most appropriate penetration positions. Then it should concentrate on winning these positions and establishing a satisfied customer base Thereafter, the company should strive to fortify its position and expand, enlarge its market share, and diversify its customer base (For supplementary reading, see Cusumano and Selby, 1995, and Cusumano, Mylonadis, and Rosenbloom, 1992)

Choosing the Penetration Position

As in any battle, it is wise to choose the positions with minimum resistance for first market penetration However, once a company penetrates a market already occupied by well-established competitors, all elements of surprise are lost The competition has all the opportunity to examine, learn, and analyze any advantages and disadvantages the new competitor brings The competition will then most probably prepare its defenses accordingly Therefore, choosing the penetration position has strategic importance Normally, if an innovative product is well accepted in a strategic market, the frontiers are opened for further expansion A successful penetration should at least make it difficult for the competition to dig in and stop further advances

One of the classical penetrating positions has been, and still is, the local market The local market has many advantages First, it is close to the company in every sense physically, mentally, and sometimes politically as it can be well protected from outside competition by an array of tariffs and barriers. The local market should allow a company to fully debug and test a novel product without jeopardizing its reputation abroad The lessons learned during introduction of the product may not be as expensive as those a company must bear when learning in a foreign market

If the local market is large enough to satisfy the company's aspirations, an appropriate choice might be a niche in this market If the local market is too small, the company may wish to divide its effort and fight on two fronts: the local market, and some foreign market In any case, because the initial success is always important, the company must choose the areas for market penetration with care. Among the factors that companies need to consider in choosing the specific penetration sector are these·

1. The need or demand in this market sector for the type of novel product offered by the company

2. The buying power of potential customers in this market segment

3. The degree of resistance or opposition against use of such products that may be present or generated by cultural, ecological, or other local considerations

4. The degree of competition existing from local or foreign companies already established in this market sector

5. The strength and the weakness of the existing competition

6. The adequacy of using this market sector as a test ground for determining the satisfaction of customers with the novel product and for receiving their feedback for product improvements

After a careful analysis of these factors and other relevant considerations, the company should choose the theater in which it will concentrate its market penetration efforts

Concentration of Effort to Establish a Customer Base

To be successful in winning a foothold in a new market, the company must invest concentration of effort, strong will, and total dedication If the company disperses its efforts in too many directions, it may be unable to obtain a decisive local advantage and thereby establish itself in the new market

The concentration of effort involves dedicating top people and adequate resources to ensure the success of the operation The person appointed by management to lead the market penetration effort should coordinate the work of local agents and representatives He or she must have all the real-time intelligence necessary to direct the company in making the right moves, and possess sufficient authority to commit additional resources wherever necessary.

Usually, the first step of the operation involves a well-organized advertising campaign The advertising agency should be closely guided by the company The company should carefully select the essential messages the advertising agency must convey to the customers in an effective way Sometimes a good advertiser may propose not just the form but also the content of messages, if the agency has previous experience and intimate knowledge of the local culture, this may indeed be an effective approach However, these messages must always be reviewed and approved by the company to avoid causing damage to the company's image in other markets An example of the importance of this rule is the advertising campaign launched in mid-1994 by the Italian company Benetton (Case 7 9)

During or before the advertising campaign, the company must define and establish the way its product will be distributed and sold in the new market Usually, this requires coming to agreement with one or more well-established local distributors Sometimes, however, the better local distributors are bound by exclusive contracts with the competition In this case, the company will need to find alternatives or establish a distribution network on its own. In any case, before actually beginning sales of the new product, a very important step is to thoroughly train vendors about all the different features the product offers This training should focus on its advantages as opposed to the competition If the use of the new product is not totally obvious, the vendors should also be trained and required to run public demonstrations on the operation of the product

Training of vendors, as well as all other first steps for introducing the new product to the market, must be done by some of the best product specialists the company

---

CASE 7.9

Advertising, or Bad Advertising: The Benetton Example

Under the headline, "The United Colors of Benetton," some very colorful pictures of different parts of the world appeared Among others, there were pictures showing the misery of the people in Biafra, a man's arm tattooed with the words "HIV Positive," and so on The pictures were definitely effective in attracting public attention, but for the consumers of some very important markets, this type of advertising was too shocking For example, Benetton's advertisements prompted protests in France, Italy, Germany, Britain, and the United States The public was so disturbed by these pictures that the company's sales plunged by significant percentage points.

---

has The literature accompanying the new product should be tested by a representative sample of "friendly" customers or by future vendors Such future vendors, under the supervision of the company specialist, should try independently to execute the operating instructions and solve problems using the product's manuals Some high-technology, innovative products require a certain level of knowledge for the customer to make the best use of them and fully appreciate their advantages compared to the competition Because the first line of product support is usually given by the vendors, an important sales strategy is to train them to a sufficient level of competence with the new product

The next critical step is to make sure there is an effective mechanism for handling feedback from customers regarding their satisfaction with the product Any criticism should be considered seriously No effort should be spared to remedy problems as quickly as possible, and before the bad rumors—which the competition has an interest in amplifying—have had a chance to spread Unchecked rumors could not only jeopardize the future of the product but also damage the reputation of the company

The mission of penetrating a new market can be considered as successfully accomplished only after a significant percentage of market share has been conquered and after strong evidence has been collected that most of the customers are totally satisfied and ready to recommend the product to other potential customers The establishment of a satisfied and happy customer base is a prerequisite for expanding the success to other markets

Fortifying Conquered Positions and Expanding to New Markets

Before moving into new markets, a successful company must take care to fortify its achievements in the market segments already conquered Practically speaking, this means that the products of the company continue to receive strong after-sales support and that the existing customer base is routinely informed of all new product improvements and updates

Some companies keep track of their market share in the particular market in which they are engaged and take corrective action only when they detect a losing trend in market share. Other companies, in addition to tracking their market share, also keep periodic "switching reports " These are summaries of how many customers have switched from a competitor product to theirs, and vice versa As long as the balance in the switching report is strongly favorable, all the company needs to do is to analyze the few cases in which their customers have switched to the competitors The results of the analysis should show whether there may be trends in customer disappointment

If the trend is moving in the wrong direction, much more energetic action is required from the company if it is to stay in this market Such action may involve investing additional resources in research and development, strengthening the marketing force, modifying the advertising approach, or taking other appropriate measures that will remedy the problem

Assuming that the company has successfully penetrated a certain market, it must move on, as quickly as company resources allow, to extend the success into additional markets The quicker the company moves, the less time is left for the competition to get organized Also, the earlier a product is introduced in a high-technology market, the longer it can benefit from the open window of opportunity (see chapter 4)

Moving quickly also requires careful planning First, managers must decide what the next targets will be The markets that are natural extensions of the first success are obviously the immediate ones to be explored For example, if the first successful penetration has been in a German-speaking country, extending the success to other Ger-

---

CASE 7.10

Example of Learning from Past Mistakes

In its efforts to penetrate a Central European country's market, a small high-technology company reached an agreement with an important distributor of similar equipment One of the clauses of this agreement prohibited direct contacts between the high-technology company and what the distributor called "my customers "

Despite training on the product given to the distributor's vendors, a number of unexpected problems soon arose with different customers The vendors did their best to handle the problems but kept the original designer unaware of the situation The customers were disappointed and the distributor decided to announce to the company that he would like to withdraw from the distribution agreement because of the expressed dissatisfaction with the product Only in the last minute, after the parties thoroughly discussed the problems, did he decide to give the agreement another chance

This time, the engineers of the company were allowed to join the vendors in instructing the customers. The early problems were quickly resolved and the product enjoyed an excellent market success to the full satisfaction of the customers, the distributor, and the high-technology company In expanding this success to other markets, the company never again agreed to grant any distributor exclusive rights to talk to the customers.

man-speaking countries should be relatively easy, given the cultural similarity, the availability of proven documentation in the same language, and the relatively short geographical distance between these countries.

Strategically, however, it might be more important to use the initial success to move quickly into some larger market before strong competition has been established there In this totally new market, the company has to repeat the steps that won the initial success This will now be on a much larger scale, but with the advantage that the company will not have to repeat the same mistakes All lessons learned to conquer the initial market position should be applied to develop the new, larger market Case 7 10 on page 181 illustrates one of the mistakes a company should never repeat

By making the necessary efforts to fortify and expand its marketing positions, a high-technology company can greatly stabilize and improve its business future Therefore, devoting time and resources to market expansion should be considered by management an important element of the battle tactics for winning market share in the competitive high-technology marketplace

---

SUMMARY

In this chapter, a comparison was made between the methods used to plan, prepare, and conduct a war and those necessary to win the fierce competition in marketing high-technology products. The parallel between planning and executing a military operation and capturing and holding a market share, or winning a contract for a large system, was made obvious

First, we devoted attention to the important issue of choosing the right people—those who are capable of dealing successfully in high-technology marketing Only those who have the basic characteristics and an adequate level of training can become fully competent and professional high-technology marketers There is no place for amateurs or for compromise in the qualifications required of the people who engage in this very demanding and challenging profession

Next, we examined the ways a high-technology company should establish a winning strategy The process, either formal or informal, always involves a market projection, an analysis of the company's strong and weak points compared to existing or potential competition, and a thorough, in-house debate among all the key personnel of the company Important issues such as being a market leader or a market follower as well as the choice between operating mainly in the local market or becoming an international player were shown to be part of the process involved in establishing the company's strategy

Then, the issue of collecting and analyzing intelligence was discussed Methods for building a network of reliable and timely sources of information were described The important topic of how to learn and analyze the strategies used by competitors as well as how to use information and misinformation in a high-technology competition were outlined and illustrated with examples.

Further, we examined how to develop a set of winning tactics. We debated the question of how to define tactical objectives, how to analyze available intelligence and how to establish a company image and reputation The idea of *winning price* was introduced, defined, and illustrated with some examples showing how to use it effectively in a competition Not all competitions have the same importance for a high-technology company, some are vitally important and therefore justify all efforts to win whereas others may be worth losing—especially if by doing so the company gains important long-term advantages We discussed ways to distinguish between the two and the appropriate tactics to apply in both situations

Finally, we explored how to conduct the battle to win the competition in high-technology markets A distinction was made between the methods applicable to battles for obtaining contracts for large-scale projects and those appropriate for battles to increase a company's share in the general high-technology market In both cases, managers need to apply to the "battle" the conclusions drawn from all the results of the preliminary work done by the company in establishing its strategy, collecting intelligence, and developing a winning tactic

To conclude, high standards of professional marketing excellence were shown to be as important for the success of a high-technology company as is excellence in technology, product development, and innovation The methodology described in this chapter is applicable in both local and foreign markets Because high-technology companies are becoming more and more dependent on global markets, the next chapter is devoted to the special issues relevant to companies that have decided to become successful international players

For Further Reflection

1 Describe the similarities and differences between conducting military operations and marketing high-technology products Is such a parallel relevant? What are the major lessons to be learned from such a parallel?

2 Outline and explain the major prerequisites required for a person applying for the position of high-technology marketer What qualifications are necessary to become a successful marketing executive in the high-technology business?

3 Give an example of the methodology applied to establish a company's strategy, using some practical situations from your experience Describe the present status of a company and, with the help of the relevant methodology, suggest a winning strategy for the firm

4 Describe the advantages and drawbacks of being a market leader in the high-technology business Do the same for the strategy of being a market follower

5 What are some of the most important methods available to high-technology companies to establish a network of intelligence gathering sources? What is the difference between "real-time" information and general information?

6 Comment on making professional use of information and misinformation in high-technology competitions When and how are these two kinds of information applicable?

7. Comment on the difference between a customer's official criteria for selecting a winning contractor and the real criteria Why is there often a difference? How does one go about learning what the real criteria are?

8 Define the notion of *winning price* How should a company make best use of this element of the bidding process? Explain the role of *correct timing* What should a company be aware of in establishing correct timing?

9. Are all competitions worth participating in also worth winning? How can a company make best use of losing a competition?

10. What are the major differences between competing for a large, high-technology project and competing for a share in the general high-technology market? Describe the methodology applicable in both cases

References and Further Reading

Cusumano, Michael A , and Richard W Selby (1995) "Microsoft's Competitive Principles: Pioneer and Orchestrate Evolving Mass Markets," Working Paper 129 Cambridge, MA: Sloan School of Management
> The undisputed success of Microsoft to establish itself as a world leader in the software industry has attracted the attention of many researchers In this paper, Cusumano and Selby examine the competitive strategy of the company and arrive at the following conclusions: To compete in a growing variety of related segments in the software industry, Microsoft follows a strategy that is described as "pioneer and orchestrate evolving mass markets " The authors break down discussion of this strategy into five principles: (1) Enter evolving mass markets early or stimulate new markets with "good" products that set industry standards (2) Incrementally improve new products and periodically make old products obsolete (3) Push volume sales and exclusive contracts to ensure that company products become and remain industry standards (4) Take advantage of being the standards provider with new products and product linkages (5) Integrate, extend, and simplify products to reach new mass markets

Cusumano, Michael A , Yiorgos Mylonadis, and Richard S Rosenbloom (1992) "Strategic Maneuvering and Mass-Market Dynamics: The Triumph of VHS over Beta," Working Paper 40 Cambridge, MA: Sloan School of Management
> This article deals with the diffusion and standardization rivalry between two similar but incompatible formats for home videocassette recorders (VCRs): the Betamax, introduced in 1975 by the Sony Corporation, and the VHS (Video Home System), introduced in 1976 by the Victor Company of Japan (Japan Victor or JVC) Despite being first to the home market, the Beta format fell behind the VHS in market share during 1978 and declined thereafter By the end of the 1980s, Sony and its partners had ceased producing Beta models This study analyzes the history of this rivalry and examines its context—a mass consumer market with a dynamic standardization process subject to "bandwagon" effects that took years to unfold and that were largely shaped by the strategic maneuvering of the VHS producers

Johnson, R. M (1974) "Trade-Off Analysis of Consumer Values " *Journal of Marketing Research* 11: 121–128

Kawasaki, Guy (1995) *How to Drive Your Competition Crazy* New York: Hyperion Press
> In his book, Kawasaki, former "software evangelist" for Apple Computer, reveals himself as a master at coming up with tactics sure to annoy competitors He explains how to devise moves—from running a disinformation campaign to using packaging as a weapon—to disrupt the market and gain an advantage

Kotler, P. (1983). *Marketing Management Analysis, Planning and Control* Englewood Cliffs, NJ: Prentice Hall

Moore, W L (1982). "Concept Testing " *Journal of Business Research* 10: 279–294

Newell, Frederick (1997) *The New Rules of Marketing. How to Use One-to-One Relationship Marketing to Be the Leader in Your Industry* New York: McGraw-Hill

Shocker, A. D , and Srinivasan, V (1979) "Multiattribute Approaches for Product Concept Evaluation " *Journal of Marketing Research* 16: 159–180

Silk, A J , and Urban, G L (1978) "Pre-Test Market Evaluation of New Packaged Goods " *Journal of Marketing Research* 15 (May): 23

Silver, H (1989) *Technical Marketing and Proposal Preparation* Torrance, CA: HSA Publications

Tracy, Brian (1995) *Advanced Selling Strategies* New York: Simon & Schuster.
> The author shows how salespeople can become highly paid, top performers In over 400 pages, he offers detailed tips and techniques for every phase of the sales process, from prospecting to closing You'll learn everything from how to dress to how to deal with objections A comprehensive, easy-to-read resource for every salesperson

Treacy, Michael, and Fred Wiersema (1995) *The Discipline of Market Leaders* New York: Addison-Wesley.
> The best companies have chosen one of three "value disciplines"—operational excellence, product leadership, or customer intimacy. The great examples in this book—Airborne Express, Intel, Home Depot, AT&T Universal Card, Price/Costco, and others—bring the concepts to life

Urban, Glen L., and John R Hauser (1993) *Design and Marketing of New Products* 2d ed Englewood Cliffs, NJ: Prentice Hall
> Technology, the economy, changes in consumer behavior—these are just a few of the factors impacting new product development In this text, authors Glen L. Urban and John R Hauser present a thorough yet practical how-to exploration of each step in the strategy, opportunity identification, design, testing, launch, and profit-management stages of new-product development and marketing

Wright, Peter Memphis, Mark J Kroll, and Tyler John Parnell (1996) *Strategic Management Concepts and Cases* 3rd ed Upper Saddle River, NJ: Prentice Hall
> This text integrates recent academic theory with current business practices in strategic management Liberally illustrating concepts with examples from some of today's most progressive global organizations, it features a diverse selection of applications-oriented and thought-provoking cases This book draws insight from all business disciplines as well as disciplines from the social sciences that have contributed to the study of strategic management

CHAPTER

8

The Global High-Technology Market

As the twenty-first century draws near, one of the most notorious trends we see in the world economy is globalization (see Shepard, 1994, Yip, 1996) Instant communication, high-speed travel, the Internet (Martin Jr , 1996), and most important, the liberalization of trade have all contributed to making the world a "global village " In an article in *Newsweek* (July 1, 1996), M Hirsh writes, "In the last five years, driven by [free] trade, the world's wealth has leaped 50 percent, by $10 trillion" (p 42) Indeed, thanks to GATT (the General Agreement on Tariffs and Trade) and efforts by governments toward deregulation and breaking old monopolies, the world has become a much more open marketplace Open competition has largely benefited consumers No one can deny today that competition from Toyota, Honda, and others forced the U.S auto industry to make substantially better cars than it did two decades ago The globalization of trade opens vast opportunities, especially for high-technology companies

For years Silicon Valley has been the synonym for success in high technology This symbol for entrepreneurship and innovation used to be a purely American phenomenon The relative availability of venture capital and the reasonable ease with which it could be raised by way of appropriate stock exchanges, like NASDAQ, gave birth to American companies like Intel and Apple In Europe, British, French, German, and other entrepreneurs are trying hard to follow the U S lead One of the most striking success stories, however, comes from Israel. If there was a need to prove that innovation and high technology have no frontiers and that even a small economy can join the global high-technology market, Israel has provided that demonstration In an article published by *Newsweek* (April 8, 1996), Mark Dennis and Michael Hirsh write

> Today Israel possesses what many analysts believe to be the greatest concentration of high-tech start-ups anywhere outside California's Silicon Valley   Company founders are typically engineers and scientists who trace their inspiration back to stints with elite Israeli army units or defense-related research projects   The analogy is tempting. Silicon Valley, for all its free-market ethos today, was weaned on U S government de-

fense contracts In fact, however, Israel's sector is likely to prove less a rival to the valley than a powerful satellite of it.   Already 72 Israeli firms are listed on U S exchanges—mostly New York's NASDAQ–more than from any other foreign country except Canada Almost all are high-tech   In some product niches Israel's firms   have even surpassed their Silicon Valley counterparts   In wireless communications, in encryption and compression schemes for moving video data over cable lines, the Israelis often make the best stuff . Rather than competing, Israeli companies seek cooperation with U S companies   Ubique, an Israeli maker of 3-D graphics for the World Wide Web, was purchased by America Online   and this week, *Newsweek* has learned, yet another Israeli defense-spawned start-up, Checkpoint, plans to announce a lucrative tie-up with America's MCI for its much sought-after "fire wall," or network security software (Dennis and Hirsh, 1996, p 36) *

The Israeli example is by no means unique Countries as small as Singapore and as large as India are all joining the global high-technology market They all bring their share of innovation and their contribution to the global high-technology village A high-technology company choosing to become a global player must organize for a long-term international presence (Dominick, 1996) In this chapter, we examine the different options available for achieving this goal

Some companies prefer to market their products using their own organizations whereas others establish strategic alliances and joint ventures with partners (Coy et al , 1994) Often, a company's marketing strategy includes both direct marketing for its products in some territories and joint ventures in others. We examine and analyze the advantages and disadvantages of these approaches for high technology and try to point out which is appropriate at what time and under what conditions

Finally, we bring some of the most recent conceptual thinking with regard to marketing high technology Essentially, the most effective strategy is the simple principle of serving best the customer's needs As basic as this sounds, the managements of many companies have long acted as though the company's interest came first and the customer's second Such short-term vision is more and more being replaced by a more long-term view that sees the customers as the company's real asset

To conclude the chapter, we examine another modern approach that has been gaining acceptance in recent years It emphasizes the marketing of products by competing in value added to the customer as opposed to competing on price or performance (Hanan and Karp, 1991) We show that such an approach can be very effective as a way to preserve the company's competitive edge, given the right circumstances

ESTABLISHING AN INTERNATIONAL MARKETING OFFICES ORGANIZATION

Any high-technology company wishing to play a serious role in the international market must have a solid structure of marketing representative offices in key geographical locations There are four reasons for this

1. The way business is done differs from country to country, even if one deals with exactly the same products (Debackere and Rappa, 1992; and Sasin, 1990)

2. Local aspirations, local culture, and local politics play a key role in the success or failure of a business venture

3. There is no good alternative for a thorough understanding of local factors except to have competent representatives who have lived for a number of years in the country

4. Competent representatives with intimate knowledge of their company on one hand and of the "secrets" of the local market on the other are probably the best possible detectors of any business opportunity relevant to the company These representatives also should know how to open local doors

The major function of the representative offices and of the regional headquarters worldwide is to promote and coordinate the business of the company in their respective areas of responsibility In some cases, these representatives do the actual sales and after-sales service for the company's products and have full responsibility for the company's business in their territory In others, sales are done by the mother company and the local representative's functions are essentially restricted to marketing and promoting the company's products and services. The representative office is also responsible for coordinating the network of local agents and assistants as well as identifying candidates to serve as local agents

In establishing the international marketing organization, two key questions normally arise· Where should the company locate the limited number of representative offices it can afford to open? How should it select the people who will represent the company abroad?

Very few companies can afford to have representative offices in every country of interest in the world, therefore, they must carefully select the locations to maximize the business generated for the company In its choices, the company must consider these factors:

1. The assessment of potential business volume a certain market can generate for the company

2. The possibility of using one office to cover a whole region in which the markets have similar characteristics and geographic proximity

3. The fiscal and bureaucratic process involved with establishing a representative office Some countries have liberal laws encouraging foreign companies to establish business or commercial representation Others have more stringent laws and impose high taxes and restrictions on such activities

4. The annual cost for operating a representative office in a given country compared to a valid alternative Such cost takes into account the expense of payroll, office overhead, communications, travel, and so on

5. The availability of adequate infrastructure: banks; health, education, and cultural facilities for the families of the representatives; airports, railways, and other convenient connections

These five factors do not represent an exhaustive list of all elements a company may need to consider in its choice of where to locate its representative offices, but it does cover the most essential ones The next serious concern is the choice of candidates who will most efficiently represent the company abroad.

For many companies, sending representatives abroad has been and still is a sensitive issue. Often, such an assignment is given to less-than-competent people for reasons that have little to do with the qualifications for the mission. Sometimes it is convenient to send abroad an influential person in the company because he frequently criticizes management's policy In some extreme cases, people are sent abroad just because nobody wants them around Considering the numerous mistakes made by so many high-tech companies in their choice of delegates to marketing missions abroad, we need to examine the real qualifications necessary for an effective representative

1. The candidate must be a mature and independent thinker, capable of correctly analyzing complex situations He or she, acting alone, must be able to synthesize solutions to challenging problems so as to remove obstacles from the company's way

2. The candidate should speak the local language or be able to learn it quickly enough to sense and absorb the local culture and mentality as soon as possible The candidate should also be an effective communicator and possess the qualities required of any marketing executive as described in the previous chapter.

3. The person selected must be trusted by the top management of the company and respected by all levels of the company's management This is necessary because he or she may have to activate any department in the company to handle an important problem immediately if and when it arises.

4. In such a candidate, the skills needed by any marketing representative—namely being a brilliant soloist rather than just a good chorus singer—are magnified because this person must operate effectively in a foreign environment

Another essential point in the establishment of an effective international marketing organization is the way this organization integrates into the structure of the overall company (see Ghoshal and Westrey, 1992; Dominick, 1996) Truly internationally oriented companies usually set up a number of regional headquarters or subsidiaries, with each having representative offices in key cities or countries in the region of their responsibility A typical example is an American high-technology company that has European headquarters in Brussels and representative offices in Paris, London, Frankfurt, Milan, Moscow, and Madrid The same company might have another regional headquarters established for Southeast Asia—located in Singapore with representative offices in Indonesia, Malaysia, and so on Concentrating management in regional headquarters can make sense because of the mutual relationship that often exists between countries in the same region However, managers must also be aware of historical animosities and competitions that sometimes exist between neighboring countries This is typically so in Europe, even within the European Community, where beneath the surface, centuries-old rivalries still persist

ESTABLISHING A NETWORK OF LOCAL AGENTS AND ASSISTANTS

Even if a company could afford the cost of establishing a representative office in every city and important business center, it would still need local agents and assistants whose role is substantially different from that of the company's representatives Being permanent citizens of the country in which they are assigned to act for the company, the agents and assistants are obviously fluent in the local language, familiar with the culture of the country, and able to understand the habits and mentality of its people They are not company employees strictly speaking, but they work for the company on a special contract that defines the relationship, rights, and mutual obligations between the company and its agent The agent's role may be to act on behalf of the company in a territory in which the company does not have a representative office In other words, the agent functions on behalf of the company but does not represent it

A good local agent should be very well connected to influential people in the territory He or she should be able to provide the company with reliable and timely information about its competitive position and be able to lobby effectively for the firm

The way a company compensates an agent is explicitly written in the agency agreement There are two basic methods for such compensation, in some cases, a combination of the two may be used The first method—commission only—is based on actual business success Here, the agent receives an agreed-on percentage of the business turnover realized by the company in the territory defined in the contract The second method consists of paying the agent a monthly fee (retainer) and an agreed-on success fee for each contract the company wins in the territory A company should have a very good reason to choose the second method Usually, most companies prefer to remunerate the agent only after they have actually received payment from the customer as a result of the business secured with the agent's assistance In the second method, the company must compensate the agent regardless of whether business results from his or her efforts.

The first and most important step in establishing a network of local agents is to find the agency or individual who will best serve the interests of the company Sometimes a company may need more than one agent in a territory to handle different products. In any case, what really counts is the specific ability of the agent to promote business in a well-defined category. If a high-technology company is interested in promoting two different products that target two different sets of customers in the same territory, the best course may be to work with two different agents The objective would be to have each agent very knowledgeable of one line of business A difficulty with this strategy is that having more than one agent in the same territory can easily generate confusion and sometimes even intrigues between the agents When a new business opportunity arises, each of the agents tries to convince the company that only he can bring success In such a case, the company must define very clearly the borders of representation and responsibility of each of the agents. Otherwise, real conflict may arise between the agents, and this will surely lead to the company's losing the business to the competition

Choosing the right agent in a foreign country is not a simple matter Sometimes even such usually reliable criteria as past performance are not good predictors of future success An agent may have been successful working in the past with influential people who have now been moved from their positions There is no assurance that the agent will be able to achieve the same results with the new set of decision makers

Another pitfall a company must guard against is hiring a pretender or bluffer Business agents have a strongly developed flair for sensing the propitious moment when a company is in an excellent position to win a contract We have seen cases in which such individuals approached the visiting team of a potentially winning company, soliciting appointment as the company's agent These people cite their excellent connections with the customer, and if the company does not check their credentials carefully, it may indeed hire them The company may win the contract but finds out too late that the agent made no real contribution to that outcome Unfortunately, the company by then has no choice but to pay the bluffer the agreed-on success fee or commission

From personal experience, I have learned how wrong it is to appoint agents under pressure of time just when a business opportunity emerges The approach I have adopted and which has proved most satisfactory is to avoid hasty appointments at the last moment Instead, we undertook the methodical creation of a network of local agents, covering all potential territories of interest This approach allows sufficient time to check and cross-check each candidate There is opportunity for analysis and interviews, and for consulting potential customers, something that can hardly be done in the middle of an ongoing competition

Also, I have always found it more reasonable to pay agents a generous commission for winning a contract rather than a retainer and a small success fee In the first case, the agents receive nothing if the contract goes to the competition or is not awarded at all In the second, the agents collect the monthly retainer even when they generate no business for the company In the first case, agents are totally motivated to helping the company win the contract In the second, especially if the chances for winning are slim, the motivation is to see the competition last as long as possible, regardless that continuing the battle is very expensive to the company Smart agents (you only pick smart ones) always have a story to tell the company, and in most cases, the company has no way to check it Therefore, the better course is to tell the agent from the beginning, "Our company is interested in the final result. We are ready to listen to every bit of information that helps us win the contract and we will accept all reasonable recommendations made by you in order to win But if we lose, you lose You lose all the time, the effort, and the money you invested in the competition exactly as we are going to lose ours Don't expect any compensation from the company " I have found that this attitude and setting of the rules from the beginning are fair and create the right motivation on both sides

The cost to the company for having an agent, as long as no contracts are signed, is much lower than maintaining a representative office in a given place It is thus a good policy to develop a network of agents everywhere the company has reasonable business potential If business develops in a certain market, the commissions paid to local agents may exceed what it would have cost to establish and maintain a company representative there However, the commission is paid only after the business has been secured Also, there is no assurance that a company representative could have won the contracts without the help of a local agent

To summarize, the roles of company representatives and local agents can be seen as complementary The first are faithful company employees They should recruit the most suitable local agents for the company, guide them, and supervise their work The local agents and local assistants should cover all areas on the map where there is a business potential for the company They should, on their own account, do much of the daily promotion of and lobby for the company's products They should provide their intelligence and advice to the company in all its activities in the territory assigned to them

ESTABLISHING STRATEGIC ALLIANCES AND JOINT VENTURES

As the twenty-first century comes nearer, the world is becoming more and more a global marketplace where no company can operate and prosper without considering the interests and aspirations of the many different countries that constitute its market In the industrialized world, one of the most sensitive socioeconomic and political issues is the problem of unemployment In the United Kingdom, France, Germany, and other members of the European Community, the number of unemployed people in 1994 exceeded 10 percent of the active population, threatening to rock the political system Unemployment was and remains a sensitive issue in the United States as well. This is despite the progress made by the American economy in creating new job opportunities from 1992 to 1997.

When a foreign company attempts to penetrate the market in the industrialized world, it naturally generates fierce opposition from local business. Such attempts have often mobilized joint efforts of the local company's management, organized labor, and politicians to push back the foreign intruder Therefore, one of the approaches to use in overcoming or avoiding such problems is to create a joint venture between the foreign company and a well-established, local high-technology industry This case is discussed later in the chapter under "Industrial Cooperation in the Industrialized Nations "

Developing countries aspiring to catch up with the richer and more prosperous industrialized nations have a strong desire for foreign investment and technology transfer They want to bridge the gap between their traditional, low-technology economy and the brighter perspectives offered by high technology Today, countries like Taiwan, Singapore, and South Korea are examples of successes in achieving such objectives in record time Countries like Indonesia, Malaysia, Thailand, Chile, Brazil, and others are following close behind Many such countries welcome competent, foreign, high-technology companies willing to bring technology, experience, and know-how to their less developed industry In "Technology Transfer to Less Industrialized Nations," we deal with joint ventures whose main purpose is to answer this need

Sometimes, a strategic alliance may be more appropriate than a joint venture or an acquisition A strategic alliance does not establish a contractually binding joint venture or a legal entity Rather, it defines a long-term cooperation between two companies in pursuing a common goal The decision to acquire an existing company, to establish a joint venture, or to establish a strategic alliance is never simple Some reports suggest that a strategic alliance is sometime preferable even in the company's own country An interesting illustration of the choice dilemma appears in Case 8 1

A high-technology company that has decided to be an international player in the global market must adapt its policy to specific conditions in each country It should

---

CASE 8.1

Strategic Alliance versus Acquisition:
The AT&T-Lotus Example

In 1991, AT&T acquired NCR for $7 5 billion The NCR acquisition never produced the "synergy" AT&T had sought But AT&T seems to have learned that—in the computer industry, at least—it is not necessary to swallow the competition just to have a piece of the action This time AT&T has tried a different approach Early in 1994, it signed a marketing and development agreement to make Lotus's widely used Lotus Notes software available to business on AT&T's public networks While the Lotus venture did not get much press attention, it marked what promises to be the next focal point for the entire company: bringing the power of desktop software to the public telephone and data network for all sizes of business to use (*International Herald Tribune*, December 22, 1994, p 11)

---

master all the tools for cooperation discussed to this point and use them as appropriate We next examine the approaches suitable for industrialized nations and describe those that are applicable to less-developed countries

---

INDUSTRIAL COOPERATION IN THE INDUSTRIALIZED NATIONS

An industrialized nation is by definition a country with a long-established industrial base A normal expectation, therefore, is that a foreign high-technology company wishing to penetrate such a market would face strong resistance from indigenous competition Even if products offered by the foreign company are clearly superior to the local production, both in performance and price, penetrating the wall of tariffs, standards, and other obstacles specifically designed to protect the local manufacturers is often extremely difficult Even with all the progress made in the GATT (General Agreement on Tariffs and Trade), many nations still find ingenious ways to protect their local interests, driven by the fear of even higher, politically unacceptable levels of unemployment

One effective way to overcome these problems is to seek industrial cooperation with an appropriate local partner who also can profit from such a collaboration The ideal local partner should have a strong interest in the success of the joint venture and sufficient local influence and lobby power to overcome all remaining resistance and opposition from other interested parties

The form and structure of the industrial cooperation may vary The first approach applied by many multinational companies was to establish fully owned subsidiaries in foreign countries By appointing local managers and creating local jobs, companies like IBM, Ford, Philips, Brown-Bowery, and Matsushita have been quite successful in operating as local companies in many markets in the world This form of industrial participation in a foreign country is typical when the company feels strong enough technologically, economically, and politically to enter the foreign market on its own In such a case, the company maintains full control over its foreign subsidiary and has substantially more influence on its business decisions than it would in a strategic alliance with a similarly powerful local company

In the last decade, however, more and more joint ventures or strategic alliances between two or more strong industrial players have appeared, each bringing some important contribution to the cooperation For example, recent reports claim that Bell Atlantic and Pacific Telesis of the United States have allied with Olivetti to lead a cellular phone joint contract in Italy, that Philips, the Dutch electronics giant, has established a design center with Motorola to make videocircuits for a multimedia CD-ROM player in the United States, these are just two of many As more competent and competitive industrial players appear around the world, industrial cooperation seems to move from relatively simple participation to the more complex form of strategic alliances and joint ventures This form requires participants to have a much better understanding of each other's strong points and weaknesses in order to identify and establish a solid common interest even among competitors (For studies on related topics see Jap, 1995, and Katz, Rebentisch, and Allen, 1995)

TECHNOLOGY TRANSFER
TO LESS-INDUSTRIALIZED NATIONS

The term *technology transfer* is used to describe a variety of situations in high technology For example, in the 1970s, the adaptation of space innovations for commercial use was widely debated (Chakrabarti and Rubenstein, 1976) Early in the 1990s, the "hot issue" was conversion of defense-related research for nonmilitary use (Gansler, 1995) All these activities were labeled transfer of technology Here we are interested in another kind of technology transfer: the one that helps create international joint ventures and strategic alliances (Katz et al., 1995, Rebentisch and Ferretti, 1993).

In the process of transforming their industrial base, less-developed nations are usually very interested in gaining modern high technology, together with money, marketing, and management experience After the disintegration of the Soviet bloc and the bankruptcy of the communist system, practically all countries that had previously operated under planned economies decided to become market economies In doing so, they soon found that they had to rebuild their industrial structure from scratch Even countries with past significant technological achievements, like Russia and China, realized that to compete in world markets, they all desperately needed the same essential elements: *M*oney, *M*anagement, *M*arkets, and *T*echnology (or in short, M3T) In this regard their needs were much the same as those of the less-developed countries

To satisfy the need for these elements in less-industrialized nations and at the same time build a customer base with sufficient buying power for modern high-technology products, many high-technology companies today accept a long-term investment policy in their business approach toward these countries They establish either fully owned subsidiaries or joint ventures with local partners Initially, they provide these subsidiaries or joint ventures with technology. At first, the major part of the production goes to the more traditional markets, with only a fraction needed to satisfy the emerging local market Later, in addition to importing technology, a successful joint venture is expected to develop some original high-technology products, it is also expected to extend its sales in the local market as this market develops and grows in needs and in buying power.

This strategy differs substantially from the one used most in the 1960s a search for cheap labor At that time, companies looking for cheap labor would transfer labor-intensive, mostly assembly work to countries of the Third World During this period, a large portion of the U S. semiconductor industry established manufacturing and assembly subsidiaries in the Far East. However, little or no research and development work was assigned to these subsidiaries After the introduction of automation in the manufacturing and assembly process, most companies found it preferable to bring those tasks back home

Today, most high-technology companies that have established or are in the process of establishing foreign subsidiaries or joint ventures seek to achieve a long-term presence in the local market Therefore, they tend to build a more balanced local structure with all the organizational elements of a stable, high-technology company—that is, research and development, manufacturing, marketing, product support, and so on The joint venture distributes the products of the mother company in the local market but at the same time develops and markets its own products, which are often better adapted to local market needs Naturally, some of these products are also distributed by the mother company in other markets The multinational firm established in this way provides product support in all its markets for the total spectrum of the company's products An example of such a joint venture is the one established recently by the German car manufacturer Volkswagen with the Czech company Skoda The Czech firm benefits from the money, management, markets, and technology support given by the German company, but it continues to develop and manufacture its own models Also, each organization provides marketing and after-sales support for the products of the other

---

SERVING THE CUSTOMERS' NEEDS BEST

As world markets become more and more global and open to competition, some of the marketing methods and approaches that worked well in the past are less effective, if not obsolete, today Several of these methods are discussed in the next section

Optimizing Long-Term Business versus Short-Term Gains

The conflict between long-term business objectives and short-term gains is not unique to high technology However, a number of high-tech companies still harbor management attitudes that hide a strong preference for short-term gains This approach appears in many different guises, such as "serving the best the interest of our shareholders" or "putting the company's interests first." These expressions sound very positive and convincing at first, but they often hide something much more important—not explicitly stated yet well understood by people in the company. "This year's bottom line is more important than long-term customer satisfaction," or "The company comes first, the customers come after," or even, "It is our duty to defend the company's interest against customers' claims."

These attitudes are—or were—more current in the United States than in Europe or in the Far East One reason for this is apparent in the way success of executives is measured and rewarded in the United States as opposed to Europe or Japan Because many high-technology companies in the United States are public, the end-of-the-year balance sheets determine to a large extent the value of the company's shares on the stock market This naturally puts pressure on company executives to show growth year after year, or even quarter after quarter, in the company's revenues and net earnings Sometimes this effect is amplified by incentives the executives receive as end-of-the-year bonuses or premiums, all linked to the short-term profit and loss statement Not surprisingly, long-term investment in customer satisfaction, which may pay off only after several years, is sacrificed

In Europe, by contrast, most of the shares of companies, even of big public companies, are held by banks, insurance companies, or other financial institutions These institutions are motivated to appoint professionals to the board of directors who know how to look for the long-term interest of the owners Because there is no contradiction between the long-term interests of the company and its customers' satisfaction, this kind of problem is less pronounced—though not entirely absent—in Europe

Today, more and more companies realize that their best interests are better served when their management takes a long-term view of the needs of the company and emphasizes the "customer first" approach Practically, this calls for implementing policies like these

1. The company should listen more carefully to the needs of the customer Many high-technology products can be specifically adapted to slightly different needs by software or other adaptations. The famous words attributed to Henry Ford—"You can buy any color of car you like as long as it is black"—can today serve only as a bad example or as an illustration of what has changed in the way companies compete for business from Ford's time to today

2. Any customer's complaint should be seriously treated and analyzed If the customer is right, the company should bear all expenses related to fixing the problem, even if the small print on written guarantees says otherwise Also, the company should use complaints as feedback and ask itself whether similar problems are likely to be experienced by other customers If so, the customer friendly approach is to warn the potentially affected users and offer to modify the product at no cost to them

Sometimes the customer is not totally right, but right or wrong, a complaining customer is an unhappy customer When there are good reasons to refuse total responsibility and acceptance of all the expenses, the least the company should do is find a way to comfort the customer The less the company participates in the expenses, the more forthcoming its personnel should be in trying to make the customer happy The customer should receive a clear explanation of the company's point of view so as to be convinced that the company's position is justified In addition, the company should find some effective way to compensate the customer on the spot or in the future Case 8 2 illustrates this situation The facts in this example are real, but at the request of one of the companies, the names have been changed

By acting in the best interest of its customer, Hitex displayed the responsible behavior of a supplier helping a customer in need. Rejecting the temptation to "punish"

Handling Customer Complaints
in High Technology: Example

A high-technology company (called here Hitex) builds computer-integrated manufacturing machines (CIM) for the textile industry Hitex had delivered and installed a new generation of such equipment in a plant of one of its international customers (called here Amfabric) Amfabric received an important order to deliver a large quantity of fabric, using a special pattern and a specified synthetic material The order was to be executed and delivered in a short time Amfabric accepted the order on the basis of their belief that the new, modern CIM just acquired would enable them to deliver the order on time Their customer made on-time delivery an explicit part of the order, as he needed the fabric for the Christmas 1995 sales season

Amfabric ordered all the materials they needed on highest priority and prepared to work two shifts daily to deliver the fabric on time Because some of the material had to be purchased abroad and was not delivered for several weeks, very little time was left to experiment with the specific material Confident in their newly installed equipment, the textile engineers programmed the process according to their best understanding of the instructions they received during their training and after studying the user's manuals.

To their total surprise and disappointment, the entire first lot of fabric showed clearly unacceptable defects Afraid they had made a mistake, the engineers tried again. Now the second lot was a total loss Immediately, they alerted the management

The manager of Amfabric was furious He called the president of Hitex without regard to the seven-hour time zone difference between Amfabric and Hitex The president of Hitex received the call at 2 A M After absorbing all the anger and accusations from Amfabric's technical director, the president of Hitex tried to learn exactly what had happened In response, he was told that his new equipment was "not worth s " and that if it could not be fixed in the next 48 hours, Amfabric would sue Hitex The manager threatened to claim all the consequential damages resulting from losing their customer's order, including any damages the customer might claim from Amfabric

The next morning, the president of Hitex convened an urgent meeting of the director of engineering, the director of marketing, and the chief instructor (just back from a six-day intensive training session he gave the technical personnel of Amfabric) After a brief discussion, the management team decided to send a group of specialists to Amfabric The chief designer, the chief instructor, and the director of engineering were all dispatched by the first available flight to investigate and solve the problem on site.

On their arrival at Amfabric, the Hitex team was presented with the problem in detail After less than two hours, they saw clearly that the process required for manufacturing the specific fabric fell outside the specifications of the new machines and that this particular model of the machine was not designed to do the kind of job Amfabric thought it could do Referring to the documentation of the machines and the exchange of letters between the two companies, Hitex's team was able to show the following:

1 There are specific instructions to avoid programming the machine the way Amfabric did

2 During the negotiations, Hitex had proposed a more expensive model, capable of handling, among others, the type of process needed for this particular job But Amfabric had persisted in their selection of the cheaper, less capable model

At the end of the fact-finding meeting, the textile engineers from Amfabric were faced with undisputable evidence that they had misunderstood what the new machines could and could not do

At this stage, the team of Hitex specialists could have returned home claiming victory and asking Amfabric to apologize for all the insults, inconvenience, and expenses caused to their company By acting this way, Hitex would have obtained the satisfaction of proving their point and would have avoided any further expense to their company However, they would have left a very unhappy customer. Amfabric had certainly misunderstood the specifications and the limitations of the newly purchased machines, and they were now on the verge of an economic disaster because of their inability to deliver the very important special order Instead, after a telephone consultation with their president, Hitex's team made the following proposal to Amfabric

1 An exchange of letters will take place immediately Amfabric will acknowledge that they have no claims on Hitex with respect to the equipment purchased Hitex will commit to upgrade the machines by adding the necessary modules in the coming six days (still in time for Amfabric to deliver the special order)

2 Hitex will charge Amfabric only the direct cost and expenses for the necessary modifications This will keep the price paid by Amfabric still substantially below the price of the more expensive model, which has capabilities beyond the scope of Amfabric's requirements

the customer for the aggravation caused by its own misunderstandings, and resisting the impulse to sell the customer the more expensive model of the new machine, Hitex's management chose to serve best the long-term interest of their company

Organizing the Best Team to Meet Customer Needs

The major consideration for a company in attempting to win access to global markets today is how to fulfill customers' objectives that are wide ranging Such complex objectives may include a combination of maintaining high performance and low cost, advancing the local technology, and increasing local employment. To score high on such multi-attribute competitive comparisons, a high-technology company must learn to share work with local partners in a truly meaningful way This may require giving up substantial portions of work tasks the company might otherwise do more efficiently alone.

A number of high-technology companies function by the principle, "Anything worth doing, we do ourselves " This approach consists of attempting to have within the same company all the centers of professional expertise and excellence necessary for the development and manufacture of a certain line of high-technology products. The advantages are independence, added value, better control of the total product cost, and so on Some of these, if not all, are real advantages Therefore, it is very hard to argue against those who defend the "do it all in the company" approach However, one should not overlook two important counterconsiderations:

1. Often, for the sake of independence, a company pays more by doing some of the work it could have successfully subcontracted at more competitive prices

2. Completely independent companies are not complementary, in any respect, with other companies active in the same line of products Therefore, they are not predisposed to cooperation with similar companies and suffer strongly from the "anything you can do, we can do better" syndrome

If the company's culture sets a high priority on putting the customers' interest first, any other consideration assumes secondary importance Such companies understand the need to deprive some of its departments of work they know and are qualified to perform so as to share the work with a local company—a move that often helps in winning the contract There are no short cuts in developing such a culture in a company To reach this goal, the company's management must indoctrinate the entire workforce and explain convincingly that the company's real, long-term interest is achieved by best serving the customer's needs Without such indoctrination, managers can expect strong internal resistance, union action against "exporting employment," and other similar charges, all of which can damage the company's business and the morale of its employees

It is important, therefore, to fight the total self-dependence syndrome and prevent it from becoming a real obstacle to the company's participation in joint ventures with other companies In this respect, of course, the management's task is greatly simplified if the company is not totally vertically integrated, meaning that it is not structured to perform every part of the product's development and manufacturing cycles internally Sharing work through subcontracting is always easier if this is not the type of work that is the mainstay of the company (For an interesting study relating to this issue see Fine and Whitney, 1996)

Whatever the difficulties, in today's extremely competitive environment, only companies with sufficient flexibility for adapting their policy to the needs and requirements of their customers can survive and prosper The "happy customers base" is probably the most important asset a high-technology company has It is a fragile asset that requires constant attention and care, but with the increased trend toward deregulation, even some old monopolies—such as the European telecommunication companies (British Telecom, French Telecom)—have begun to stress giving their customers the best possible service.

MARKETING VALUE

Many high-technology products have an embedded value to their potential customers—a value only partially visible before the customer becomes entirely familiar with all the capabilities of the novel equipment or system In some cases, acquiring new high-technology equipment may open much better ways for the customer to perform important functions of its current business It may even open new opportunities not previously available

One of the best and most efficient methods of marketing high-technology products is to emphasize the value to the customer of acquiring the product rather than stressing price and performance This approach requires a significantly higher degree of sophistication from the marketing force of the high-tech company, but after some training, they generally achieve results that largely compensate for the extra efforts required

Hanan and Karp (1991) identified a number of reasons that competing on value is a better approach than competing on price and performance If a company competes on price, it eventually has two unfavorable choices either it must give up market share to keep profit margins or give up profit margins to meet price competition and maintain volume that keeps costs in line In both cases, the result depletes the company's income, reducing the company's ability to invest in research and development, in modern equipment, in advertising, and in many other areas essential for its future

In certain businesses, competing on product reliability and performance is difficult In today's high-tech market, a product's performance often outpaces the customer's ability to learn how to make the best use of it These extreme performances contribute only marginally to the product's attractiveness With the impressive leap in quality and reliability companies have achieved by implementing methods such as total quality management, certain products reach levels beyond what customers consider "good enough " If the difference in performance and the difference of quality between two competing products is perceived by the customers as not significant, the classic approach followed by many customers is to revert back to merely comparing prices

Marketing value rather than just performance is an alternative approach that helps to break the trend of reverting to pure price competition To market value successfully, marketers should know how to assess the value of their products and services, how to price this value, and how best to sell it to the customer

Assessing the Value of Products and Services

To assess the value of a product or a service to a customer, the company wishing to sell its product needs to know more about each customer than in the past In particular, it has to know precisely what end result the customer expects to achieve by buying the product or the service Acquiring this information imposes an extra effort on the high-tech company to learn in greater than usual depth how each customer conducts its business, as illustrated in Case 8 3

The value to the company of acquiring the new data collection system (Case 8 3) was therefore some $2 million a year, or a 40 percent increase in pretax profit To this, one should add all the less-tangible benefits derived from the acquisition Because such systems help in keeping delivery dates as promised, there should be a higher degree of

CASE 8.3

Assessing Value, an Illustrative Example

A Swiss high-technology company was engaged in the design, manufacturing, and marketing of computerized data collection systems (CDCS) One of its customers was an industrial company that manufactured machine parts The high-technology marketer had to analyze and determine, in a quantitative way, what total benefits the machine parts manufacturer could expect from the introduction of the new CDCS The total benefits are usually a combination of the increase of revenues (resulting from increased sales) and the savings from lowering production cost that the customer may realize with the introduction of the new system

The first step was to establish how the CDCS would contribute to increasing the output of the machine parts manufacturer The answer was that the CDCS would provide better control of the bottleneck resources, improve material and work flow, and keep better priority control on the order backlog Each of these—especially the last one—could enhance the manufacturer's ability to meet commitments made to its customers

Next, the marketer developed a quantitative monetary value of the increased output that could be attributed to these improvements For example, if the annual production of the machine parts company before the introduction of the new CDCS was $50 million a year and the improved data collection could increase the output to $56 million a year, the customer's annual benefit from increased output is $6 million, or a 12 percent increase in sales

Similarly, savings resulting from a decreased number of white-collar personnel necessary to collect and process the data and savings from better inventory and work-in-progress control had to be translated into monetary figures These savings were estimated at roughly $1 4 million per year

Then, given that the company realized a 10 percent pretax profit on sales before the introduction of the CDCS, the additional sales of $6 million would yield an increase of $0 6 million in pretax profit Taking the increased profit of $0 6 million and the $1 4 million in savings, a total of $2 million a year in additional earnings was projected This would result in a significant 40 percent increase in pretax profit.

customers' satisfaction with the performance of the company At the same time, employees in the company, who have received enhanced training in operating such an advanced system, are expected to feel a higher degree of professional achievement Such training includes engineering support provided by the high-technology supplier as part of the deliverable services accompanying the sales and installation of the CDCS Considering that the cost to the customer for acquisition and installation of the CDCS was less than $0 5 million, the high-technology marketer had no difficulty selling the product

Stated more generally, the true value of a high-technology system to the customer is the added profit to the acquiring company's annual profit and loss statement, the added prestige to the company's image, and the added satisfaction of both customers and personnel All these factors translate into an improved competitive edge for the high-technology customer The customer achieves these advantages not by just acquiring the high-technology equipment but by receiving all the training and support that comes with it

Pricing the Value of Products and Services

After assessing the value of a high-technology product and associated services to the customer, the high-technology company must set a price that will be attractive, both to the customer and to the supplier To make the product attractive to the customer, high-technology marketers need some insight into the logic behind the customer's decisions At this point, it is important to distinguish between the attitudes of customers operating at different levels in the hierarchy ladder Buyers at the lower levels in an organization usually tend to compare products on price and performance, top management prefers to approach the purchase of equipment or service as it would any business investment proposal, considering its net present value, the payback period, and the relative rate of return

Pricing a proposal so as to make the net present value of the investment positive is normally not difficult, especially if the investment horizon is sufficiently long and if the cost of capital to the customer is not too high However, because there is always a degree of uncertainty associated with estimates, such as the impact of the investment on the company's increased sales and savings, the prudent course is to make relatively conservative projections In addition, marketers should run the usual sensitivity analysis, familiar to every financial manager, to convince the customer of the attractiveness of the proposal.

A further consideration, the payback period, is important to the customer because an investment that takes too many years to pay for itself loses appeal The longer the payback period, the higher is the uncertainty regarding future estimates of the benefits resulting from this investment. Therefore, the price of the proposal should be established to make the payback period look at least acceptable if not attractive

Finally, the internal rate of return of the proposal should compare favorably with both the cost of capital to the customer and with the internal rate of return of the competitors' proposals, if any If the high-technology company has no cash flow problem, it might improve its chances for winning the contract by spreading the payments over a longer period of time Alternatively, it may offer at no cost some assistance or services that otherwise would require a substantial up-front investment from the customer

Ideally, if a high-tech company can enter a dialogue with the customer as with a partner, whereby the marketer listens to the customer's needs and adjusts the proposal to best meet these needs, the probability is highest for arriving at a price proposal that is both competitive and still profitable for the high-technology supplier

Selling the Value of Products and Services

Major differences in attitudes exist at the various levels in a customer organization. For this reason, marketers have a clear interest in making their proposals to and conducting negotiations with those in the highest level of management they can reach—especially when selling the *value* of the high-tech proposal

If the negotiation is conducted with a low-level purchasing manager, this person's attitude might very well bring the discussion down to comparing all available proposals on price only Because lower-level managers usually have limited understanding of the performance of high-technology systems, their attitude is to avoid plunging too deeply into performance comparisons, assuming that all proposals have an adequate level of minimum performance. If this is the case, and if the high-technology company wants to avoid what will inevitably follow from such an attitude, marketers must try to bring the case to a higher level of decision making in the customer's organization. This, however, is easier said than done In many cases, if the negotiation process is well advanced in a low-level purchasing department, the entire company organization will stick to it, there is little chance to move to a higher stratum

The best policy is to start the process at a high level in the company Marketers must thoroughly understand the organization of the customer Most often, the purchasing department plays only an administrative role in the acquisition process Behind the request for proposals there is normally a business-oriented organization, with medium- or high-level management These individuals are capable of conducting a meaningful dialogue on how a new high-tech acquisition can best improve the competitive edge of their business They can understand and appreciate the performance advantages in a high-tech proposal They can guide marketers to add functions that are important to the customer and to subtract others that cost money but are of limited or no interest to them In this case, the customer has a keen interest in using the high-technology company's proposal in a way that increases the customer's performance, therefore becoming a natural partner to the high-technology marketer

Once a true dialogue on value is begun between a high-technology company and a customer, many ways open to bridge difficulties that normally would arise in the course of the negotiation To illustrate, consider a case in which the customer is short on budget or cash but the business is solid and trustworthy, and the acquisition of the high-technology equipment offers a much better internal rate of return than the cost of money borrowed Here, it is entirely plausible for the seller to provide a short-term loan that could be reimbursed by the customer during the payback period. After payback, the investment in the high-technology equipment will result in pure profit for the customer, by providing the loan, the high-technology company makes the sale a win-win situation

The highest level of marketing value may be achieved when the high-technology company reaches a dialogue of true partnership with its customer and when the high-technology company is totally sure of the added value of its proposal When fully confident, the high-technology company may propose to demonstrate its certainty by installing its equipment at no cost to the customer There would, of course, be an agreement on how to share the benefits from the increased sales and savings resulting from the new equipment Such a partnership has many advantages to both the customer and to the high-technology company, such as these:

- The customer can be totally certain of getting the best support and all improvements the high-technology company may introduce to update its next generation of similar equipment Considering how quickly technology changes, this is a significant advantage to the customer.

- The high-technology company can be reasonably sure of getting full compensation for the true value of its equipment and services (totally disconnected from its cost) In this way, the company may realize much better profit margins than those possible if competing on price

Selling the value of high-technology products and services on a partnership arrangement with the customer achieves the highest level of marketing value Unfortunately, this is not always attainable in practice. A high-technology company should try to reach this level, but even if the goal is only partially attained, the approach of marketing value definitely has a better probability of yielding higher returns to a company than the one attainable in a price competition To achieve this higher plane, the company should be ready to invest the intellectual effort necessary to better understand the true needs of its customers

SUMMARY

This chapter complements the discussion of important marketing issues, with emphasis on the global high-technology market First, the question of how to establish an effective international marketing organization was examined. Location of the representative offices was shown to require an analysis, and staffing these offices with the right type of people plays an important role in the success of the organization Some practical recommendations were given with respect to these topics

Next, we examined the approaches and critical points to be considered when establishing a network of local agents and assistants The peculiar nature of good local agents was covered, with some warnings about typical situations that may lead a less-experienced company to appoint the wrong type of people as local representatives The question of how best to compensate local agents was debated, with practical recommendations given

The need for establishing strategic alliances and joint ventures with foreign companies was discussed The differences in economic conditions and sociopolitical aspirations in the industrialized nations, compared to those in less-developed countries, require a different approach for creating such alliances and joint ventures In the industrialized world, there is an increasing trend toward strategic alliances between strong corporations from different countries This new trend is quite different from the creation of fully owned foreign subsidiaries, which were more popular in the 1970s and the 1980s

In less-developed countries, the creation of foreign subsidiaries or joint ventures is normally accompanied by a transfer of technology, together with financial investment and the necessary guidance in management and marketing techniques. This is the case in the former Soviet bloc countries In some of these, their technological achievements were evident, but these countries lacked the business culture and structure to function effectively in a market economy The practical way to establish cooperation with such countries is similar to the one for less-developed nations To achieve long-term success, however, such joint ventures should develop more than simple local manufacturing and assembly capabilities They should also incorporate their own research, development and engineering capabilities to ensure stability and long-term growth

As world markets become more and more global and open to competition, the ways to best serve the customer's needs are changing A successful company should always prefer ensuring long-term customer satisfaction, even if this conflicts with some short-term gains Also, the necessity to satisfy needs from the customers' perspective, such as improving local employment and other national goals, requires a more flexible approach than the one traditionally taken by some high-technology companies In particular, the willingness to share work on a project for which the company has all the competence in house was shown to play a key role in winning the customer's favor Sharing the work is often preferable even when the local company has less know-how and experience Doing so contributes to setting the right political climate for winning the contract

Finally, marketing value rather than competing on price and performance was described This approach has the potential to improve the probability of beating the competition and to increase the high-technology company's profit margins However, such strategy imposes on high-technology marketers the need to become very familiar with the way the customer conducts business if the marketers are to devise a proposal that adds real value to the customer How to assess this value was examined Then we discussed how to price the value proposal correctly and how to sell the value proposal successfully

Much of the material described in chapter 7 is also applicable in the context of the global market. Therefore, the reader should look at chapters 7 and 8 as two parts of the vitally important subject of marketing high technology

For Further Reflection

1 Describe the characteristics and qualifications required of a successful high-technology company representative abroad What should managers look for when appointing commercial agents and assistants?

2 Enumerate and explain the most important considerations in planning an international marketing network.

3 Explain the differences between an approach prone to help a high-technology company penetrate a foreign market in an industrialized country versus the one appropriate for less-developed countries.

4 Is there a basic difference between fully owned subsidiaries, joint ventures, and strategic partnerships? If yes, what is each structure best suited for?

5 Suppose your company wants to penetrate the high-technology market in a former Soviet bloc country like Poland or Hungary Outline the most important topics you would need to check and analyze before you make your recommendation Then, write a reasonable set of assumptions and outline your recommendations.

6 Comment on the "anything worth doing, we do ourselves" attitude List and explain the advantages and disadvantages of this attitude Under what type of business conditions is such an attitude justified?

7 Many high-technology companies look at transfer of technology as a big strategic mistake The most frequent argument supporting such attitudes is the danger of helping to create foreign competition that may take a significant portion of the company's future business Discuss the merits and drawbacks of such attitudes Comment on what a company should do under various circumstances

8. What are the new ideas behind the old concept of "serving the customer's needs best"? How should a company proceed to implement such ideas in practice? What needs to be sacrificed to achieve this goal?

9 What is the basic difference between marketing a product's value and the traditional marketing techniques in the high-technology industry? Are additional requirements imposed on the high-technology marketer who chooses the "marketing value" approach? Explain

10 What steps are necessary for successful implementation of the "marketing value" approach? Give a short description of the methodology applicable at each step

References and Further Reading

Chakrabarti, A. K , and Rubenstein A H. (1976, February) "Interorganizational Transfer of Technology—A Study of Adaptation of NASA Innovations " *IEEE Transactions on Engineering Management*, Volume 23, pp 27–30

Coy, P , S Mashavi, G Smith, and G McWilliams (1994, December 19) "There Is More Than One Way to Play Leapfrog " *Business Week*, pp 31–32

Debackere, Koenraad, and Michael A Rappa (1992) "Life on the Frontier: An International Comparison of Scientists in an Emerging Field," Working Paper 63 Cambridge, MA: Sloan School of Management

> This paper examines national differences in the performance of research and development activities of scientists in five major industrial countries: France, Germany, Japan, the United Kingdom, and the United States Evidence is presented from a recent survey of nearly 600 scientists working in the field of neural networks

Dennis, Mark, and Michael Hirsh (1996, April 8) "A Land of Tech and Money" *Newsweek*, p 36

Dominick, Salvatore (1996) *Managerial Economics in a Global Economy* New York: Mc-Graw-Hill.

Fine, Charles H , and Daniel E Whitney (1996) "Is the Make-Buy Decision Process a Core Competence?" Working Paper 140 Cambridge, MA: Sloan School of Management

> The authors examine the interesting issue of how to make rational make / buy decisions in the context of creating dependencies between the buyer and the supplier. They assert that most of today's products are so complex that no single company has all the necessary knowledge about either the product or the required processes to completely design and manufacture them in house. As a result, most companies are dependent on others for crucial elements of their corporate well-being Typically, however, companies have some choice as to whom they become dependent upon and for what sorts of skills and competences Examples are given in which similar companies, facing similar choices, select make/buy patterns in very different ways, resulting in very different patterns of interdependencies along companies' supply chains The authors' goal is to convince readers that the main skills companies should retain transcend those directly involving product or process, and are in fact the skills that support the very process of choosing which skills to retain

Gansler, Jacques S (1995) *Defense Conversion* Cambridge, MA: MIT Press
> Jacques Gansler is the author of two books on the defense industry He examines the need to convert this industry from an inefficient and noncompetitive part of the U S economy to an integrated, civilian/military operation According to his findings, one of the obstacles on the road to successful conversion is what he calls "the influence of old-line defense interests " Gansler discusses growing foreign involvement, lessons of prior industrial conversions, the best structure for the next century, current barriers to integration, a three-part transformation strategy, the role of technological leadership, and the critical workforce He concludes by presenting examples of restructuring, outlining 16 specific actions for achieving civil/military integration

Ghoshal, Sumantra, and D Eleanor Westney, eds. (1992) *Organization Theory and the Multinational Corporation* London: MacMillan Press

Hanan, M , and P Karp (1991) *Competing on Value* New York: AMACOM

Jap, Sandy D. (1995). "Achieving Strategic Advantages in Long-Term, Buyer-Supplier Relationships: A Longitudinal Investigation," Working Paper 138 Cambridge, MA: Sloan School of Management.
> This working paper develops and tests a "mental model" of factors that drive a buyer and supplier's decision to create interdependencies that form the bases for long-term, strategic advantages The roles of three classes of variables are examined: partner firm characteristics (goal compatibility and complementary competencies), environmental characteristics (demand for the buyer and supplier's products, level of dynamism, and degree of complexity) and interpersonal characteristics (mutual trust) between the individual representatives The author suggests a number of implications for management. Among the most interesting are the following:
> - Trust is an important factor, but not entirely necessary Trust is an important factor in the process of working closely together Some payoffs, such as the attainment of strategic advantages is facilitated earlier when trust is present Synergistic results can still be achieved, however, without a high level of trust
> - Common goals can act as substitutes for trust If there is a low level of trust between the buyer and supplier, the two can still work together and achieve synergistic results In this case, the members will look at the extent to which they share similar goals
>
> The author gives as an example the interdependencies created in 1991 between Apple and Sony Apple lacked the manufacturing capacity to produce its entire line of PowerBook notebooks. By working closely with the Sony Corporation, they were able to quickly bring a part of the PowerBook line to market, selling over 100,000 Sony-made models within a year

Katz, Ralph, Eric Rebentisch, and Thomas J Allen (1995) "A Study of Technology Transfer in a Multinational Cooperative Joint Venture," Working Paper 131 Cambridge, MA: Sloan School of Management
> This research examines the transfer of technologies over a three-year period in an international joint venture comprising three operating divisions of large multinational chemical companies located in Germany, the United States, and Japan Descriptions of the types of technologies, the methods used to transfer them, their degree of success, and the organizational, national, and cultural differences in which the international transfers took place are investigated

Martin Jr , Chuck L (1996). "The Digital Estate: Strategies for Competing, Surviving and Thriving in an Internetworked World " New York: McGraw-Hill

Mills, Mike. (1994), "Phone: AT&T, Shedding Old Habits, Positions Itself for New Market " *International Herald Tribune,* December 22, p 11

Mead, Richard (1990). *Cross-Cultural Management Communication* New York: John Wiley
Cultural differences can create tremendous problems in communication, and in today's international business world, this can have dramatic effects Author Richard Mead shows how management priorities are communicated in different cultures, examining the various communication problems facing the manager dealing with people from other cultures In particular, the author shows how managers can develop skills to recognize the differences, analyze them, and identify and apply appropriate solutions—before the differences become headaches

Rebentisch, Eric S , and Marco Ferretti (1993) "A Knowledge Asset-Based View of Technology Transfer in International Joint Ventures," Working Paper 86 Cambridge, MA: Sloan School of Management
This working paper analyzes technology transfer from the perspective of remise of knowledge asset between the parties involved in two international joint ventures studied by the authors The authors propose a knowledge asset-based model of technology transfer They define technology transfer as the transfer of embodied knowledge assets between organizations. The framework depicts the organization as a collection of embodied knowledge assets Differences between firms result from the different combinations of embodied knowledge types that are used to accomplish the same ends Four concepts describe important aspects of the transfer process: transfer scope, transfer method, knowledge architectures, and organizational adaptive ability Transfer scope describes the extent of embodied information being transferred Transfer method describes the approaches used to transfer the technology. Knowledge architectures describe types of knowledge assets the firm possesses and the relationships between them Organizational adaptive ability describes its ability to change its architectures over time. Technology transfer involves selecting the proper transfer method given the demands of the transfer scope, working within the constraints of the existing organization's architectures and its adaptive ability

Shepard, S B (1994, December 12) "21st Century Capitalism—How Nations and Industries Will Compete in the Emerging Global Economy." *Business Week*, Special Report, p 4

Yip, George S (1996) *Total Global Strategy Managing for World Wide Competitive Advantage* Upper Saddle River, NJ: Prentice Hall
This book makes a good general reading for understanding global strategy It treats important subjects like diagnosing industry globalization potential, building global market participation, designing global products and services, locating global activities, creating global marketing, making global competitive moves, building the global organization, measuring industry drivers and strategy levers, and conducting a global strategy analysis

CHAPTER

Growing in High Technology by Acquisitions

In previous chapters we have discussed different strategies and tactics for achieving success in high technology On numerous occasions, the subject of mergers and acquisitions was mentioned as a meaningful way for a company to grow, to gain access to markets, to obtain proprietary technologies, and to reach strategic objectives Mergers and acquisitions play a particularly important role during periods of restructuring and change. For example, after the end of the cold war, the need to reduce excess capacity in the U S. defense and aerospace industry caused a wave of consolidation among the larger firms Mergers and acquisitions are by no means unique to high technology For general reading on this topic, refer to the list of publications at the end of the chapter Here we emphasize those aspects that are particularly appropriate in high technology

Rather than focus on theories and texts that are readily available, we chose to devote this chapter to the real-world experience of one of the most successful masters of high-technology acquisitions: Bernard Schwartz—a founder and until recently chairman of Loral Under his leadership, Loral grew from a small defense electronics company into a $10 billion business Most of this growth was achieved through successful acquisitions in only five years, between 1990 and 1995 One can hardly find a more competent tutor than Bernard Schwartz for learning the art of growing in high technology by acquisitions Hence, most of this chapter is a direct contribution from him in the form of conversations, interviews, and his revisions of the draft text

THE ROLE OF MERGERS AND ACQUISITIONS IN HIGH TECHNOLOGY

One of the phenomena that distinguishes high technology from other industries is the large number of start-up companies that appear in this sector each year With respect to this phenomenon, Bernard Schwartz remarks

The true innovation, the true entrepreneurial spirit in high technology, and in electronics in particular, requires only a small amount of financial capital. There is no need in this business for large investments in fixed capital The capital that makes our business grow is human capital It is mobile, it is very much driven by innovation, by the entrepreneurial spirit, and by the desire to be your own boss and to get rich That has generated a very large base of small, valuable companies across a great spectrum of activities

This large fragmentation in the high-technology sector creates from time to time an outstanding opportunity for integration and consolidation, with the value of the new organization being greater than the sum of its parts As Schwartz puts it

What was needed, from my point of view, was to rationalize by bringing together many companies that can be integrated smartly in a way that creates a common cultural center Analyzing such companies usually shows that each of them has its own distinct characteristics, its own strengths and weaknesses Some are good in research and development, some have good programs, some have good markets

By combining their strengths intelligently and by fortifying their weakness, these fragments can be united into formidable new structures, stronger, more competitive, and of course, much bigger than the originals Growing by acquisitions is, therefore, a particularly suitable method for increasing the value of a high-technology company to the full benefit of its shareholders

THE DIFFERENCE BETWEEN MERGERS AND ACQUISITIONS IN HIGH TECHNOLOGY AND IN GENERAL BUSINESS

Apart from the fact that high technology produces a much larger number of start-ups than traditional industry in a given period of time, there are other important differences that necessitate a special approach for successful mergers and acquisitions in high technology One of these is the difference between the relative stability of business conditions in traditional industries and the volatility in high technology. Consider the acquisition of a more traditional industry such as machine parts manufacturing, food processing, or paper milling etc Conceivably, at least in the near term, the future business environment is not going to be too different from the one that existed in the preceding few years Therefore, in assessing the value of such acquisitions, investors usually examine the previous three- to five-year average earnings, average income, and their trends With the help of typical multipliers applicable to the specific business sector at a given time, the investor can arrive at a good approximation of the market value of such a firm rather easily

The rapid changes in technology and the frequent introduction of new and innovative products make this approach doubtful if not totally inappropriate in high technology Just think of the reliability of such an evaluation if applied to Apple Computers in 1996 Judging from Apple's performance between 1991 and 1995, the company could have been assigned a much higher value than its market valuation in 1996 Clearly, a distinctly different approach is needed in assessing the value of acquisitions in high technology Later in this chapter, we present and discuss the strategy and the methodology that brought Loral a flawless sequence of successful acquisitions

Another important difference between mergers and acquisitions in general versus those in high technology is the strong dependence of the value of the acquisition on the specific buyer In most cases, a business has a certain market value that may vary only slightly as function of the buyer, in high technology, the same company may have a totally different value for different potential buyers If a high-technology company contemplates the acquisition of another high-technology company, one of the prime considerations is the synergy to be created by the merger or acquisition In traditional industries, such considerations may also be relevant, but they are rarely dominant We examine next, in the case of Loral, the role such factors play in high-technology acquisitions

---

LORAL—A CASE OF SUCESSFUL GROWTH BY ACQUISITIONS

The Loral Story

Loral was founded in 1948 by W Lorenz and L Alpert (The name Loral combines the first syllables of their names.) With the arrival of Bernard L Schwartz in 1971 as chairman and chief executive officer, the company began to focus on defense electronics and to divest itself of its nondefense activities

Under Bernard Schwartz's leadership, the company began acquiring selected defense electronics companies as early as 1974, when it purchased Conic Conic was a small, San Diego-based company specializing in telemetry products for defense and space communications A second acquisition occurred in 1980 with the purchase of Frequency Sources With this acquisition, Loral bought the ability to design and build microwave components that would serve as building blocks for systems being developed within its other divisions A year later, Loral purchased Randtron, a company specializing in antenna systems and components In 1993, Loral enhanced its presence in the microwave area by acquiring Narda Microwave

Between 1985 and 1990, Loral extended its technological breadth with the acquisitions of Xerox's electro-optical systems, IBM's Rolm Mil-Spec computers, Goodyear's aerospace subsidiary, Fairchild Weston systems, and Honeywell's electro-optics division These acquisitions further bolstered Loral's presence in the realm of defense electronics Now Loral had added to its core business such diversified capabilities as electro-optical countermeasures, electronic imaging, combat simulation and training, shipboard and airborne radar, military computers and software, and so on With all these carefully assembled, complementary technologies, by the end of the 1980s Loral had accomplished its transformation from a "black box" supplier to a system house and a thoroughly competent prime contractor

The real opportunity for Loral to make a gigantic leap and become one of the major players in defense electronics presented itself at the beginning of the 1990s With the fall of the Berlin wall, the end of the cold war, and the ensuing pressures to decrease defense spending, many large companies were eager to sell off their defense businesses For Bernard Schwartz, who already had the vision to build a real powerhouse in defense electronics, this became a most welcome development Swimming against the current, he was able to acquire from Ford Motor Company its aerospace subsidiary Ford Aerospace complemented Loral in every business area and brought a new one: space communications. Loral gained eight new operating divisions and its annual business turnover jumped to $3 billion In August 1992, the company purchased LTV Aerospace & Defense's Missile Systems Division In doing so, Loral captured an important and strategic leadership position within the U S Army This move was followed by another strategic acquisition in 1994 To position itself as a world-class system integrator, Loral needed the competence and the experience of an organization like IBM's Federal Systems Division. This acquisition brought Loral the proficiency to integrate large and complex software and hardware systems

By the end of 1995, Loral was probably number one in defense electronics worldwide Having realized his dream much beyond most expectations, at the beginning of 1996, Bernard Schwartz decided to sell Loral to Lockheed-Martin, the undisputed world leader in the defense and aerospace business By then, the market value of Loral had reached $10 billion This last strategic move should secure Loral's future as part of the world's most powerful defense contractor organization According to Bernard Schwartz, the synergy created by adding Loral's capabilities in defense electronics to the airframe and systems expertise of Lockheed-Martin would create a formidable industrial structure Loral's reputation as a company that has grown in high technology by successful acquisitions generates wide and well-justified interest Behind this success story is the vision and strategy of a small team led by Bernard L Schwartz

The Strategy of Bernard Schwartz

Leadership

A key factor guiding Bernard Schwartz's strategy was the aspiration to achieve a leadership position in every field of Loral's activities Being a leader in defense electronics meant offering the customer the best operational performance available at a given point of time With the critical importance of electronics in the modern battlefield, the outcome of most competitions in this field were, and still are, strongly influenced by performance offered by the different competitors Therefore, being a leader in defense electronics also means having a better chance to win contracts in this demanding business Speaking about Loral's strategy, Schwartz noted

> Leadership is important I made it a goal from the very beginning that in each subsection, each segment of the activity we were trying to be in, we achieve a leadership position In [electronic] imaging, for example, we tried to develop internally and through acquisitions the commanding position in this technology so that we became one of the leading companies in the world in all the different disciplines having to do with imaging, and so on with each of the sections of Loral's defense electronics business
>
> If you look at Loral Corporation as it exists today [January 1996], in the defense market we operate in only five areas But in each of the five areas, we are either number one in the U.S market or very close to it In tactical weaponry or electronic warfare or training or Reconnaissance–C31 or in space, we are among the leaders One of the first things I looked for was a company that was a leader and that could fit in Loral's structure

Synergy

A cornerstone of Loral's acquisitions strategy was the search for synergy This search begins with a good understanding of the market trends Loral's management was especially talented in reading the road map of the future They understood exactly where Loral stood on this map and what the company needed to move in the direction the market was moving They knew the capabilities available at Loral and looked around for the additional capabilities Loral needed If an opportunity appeared for them to acquire such capabilities, the acquisition was examined not just as a financial transaction but as leverage for increasing Loral's ability to compete successfully for future business. This guiding principle was clearly stated by Schwartz

> In considering our position, one of the first rules was to look for companies that enhanced and had a business fit with our existing business base and therefore secured and reinforced our leadership position
>
> The final decision [to buy or not] was made on the basis of whether we could gain synergy by adding Loral's capabilities to the other company's capabilities—not to curtail, not to eliminate activities, but to expand our opportunities

Value to Customers

Under the leadership of Bernard Schwartz, Loral strived to position itself in areas strategically important to its customers By acquiring the best available capabilities in a mosaic of complementary technologies, Loral aimed to offer the highest value of products and services to its customers Being diversified yet well focused in defense electronics, Loral was able to support its customers' needs in a variety of areas This made Loral important to its customers, as expressed by Schwartz

> One of the first things I looked for was a company that complemented Loral's technology or had a complementary program base, so that we could become more important to the customer, and as a leader in that enterprise, be able to focus our attention and our strength

Value to Shareholders

The value each acquisition added to the shareholders' equity was always an important element of Loral's strategy Before buying Ford Aerospace in 1990, Loral's equity was estimated at $416 million. After investing $630 million in debt and equity for this acquisition, on the eve of purchasing LTV Missiles in 1992, Loral's equity jumped to $1,226 million, then to $1,307 million after the acquisition of IBM Federal Systems in 1994, to reach $1,764 million by the end of 1995, prior to the consolidation with Lockheed-Martin Adding all the financial investments made by Loral for acquisitions between 1990 and 1995, the company spent roughly $3,300 million In the same period, the market value of Loral grew from $831 million to almost $10,000 million

These figures describe better than many words the leverage power of well-planned and well-executed acquisitions To accomplish these achievements, an investor needs to have a well-defined approach, a life-tested and proven methodology, and a dedicated management, as was the case with Loral

Loral's Approach to Mergers and Acquisitions

In the pursuit of its strategic acquisition goals, Loral applied a well-defined plan I asked Bernard Schwartz to describe the critical factors that need to be examined in an acquisition opportunity According to him, Loral focused on the four major considerations discussed next

Investigate Future Potential Rather Than Past Performance

The first factor we considered was the business fit We had to be assured that [the acquisition would give us] adequate skills and adequate technologies that reinforced our strengths That was the number one consideration . In every case, our analysis of value has to do with future business, not with history And that is the difference between our method and the approach of bankers The bankers look at the five-year history and they have no sense of what the future is going to be in terms of growth and profitability In our case, we look at the programs; by reviews and analysis of the program profiles, you could see what the forward course of the company was going to be

Examine the Portfolio of Projects and Programs of the Potential Acquisition

The second [consideration] for me was program base We examined our acquisitions [by looking at] the programs the company has The military business differs from the commercial business in that we do not look for market share but for programs that have long life and the opportunity to grow and reach to other technical developments that materialize into new programs So we always examined the program base to see the vitality, the long life, the position in the cycle of maturity and how profitable they are [or could become under Loral's management].

I asked Mr. Schwartz about the possibility of using acquisitions to eliminate or reduce competition His response was quite instructive:

Eliminating a competitor is a consideration from time to time, but it was not a predominant consideration My view is that there is always going to be competition You cannot buy all your competition I would much rather concentrate, as we did, on looking for valuable companies—companies whose growth opportunities were still in front of them, where the synergy is, and where the merging or the molding of resources and management brings an opportunity to better exploit those In high-tech industries, elimination of competition is always a very short-term strategy.

Evaluate the Quality of Human Capital in the Acquisition

The third [consideration] was management In every case we were buying the human capital that would add to our own abilities both from a management point of view and from a technical point of view We were not looking to buy sick companies, but companies that needed a turnaround or modest repairing We were looking to help these companies and we were willing to add our help That's why the integration of Loral from the outside seemed so easy, was in fact easy! We were buying very considerable resources in people that joined us

Establish the Value of the Acquisition

> In every case, establishing the price [we were ready to pay for the acquisition] is the last part of the analysis. We first make a determination that this is a transaction that would be good for the future of the company; that it gives us values, or brings us skills that we do not have. In each case we made those decisions, those evaluations, before we ever looked at price Then we determined the value at which these assets, in Loral's structure, contribute to our forward growth In effect, we have been buying technologies that would be costly for us to develop internally Once we get a favorable analysis on those issues, then we talk about price. In every case the price is subordinate to the value of the business combination

Loral's Methodology

I asked about the specific methodology applied by Loral in its growth-by-acquisitions process Addressing my questions about how the principal players detect, analyze, and execute an acquisition opportunity, Bernard Schwartz stressed the following five points:

Rely on Your Own Evaluation

> The most important point, in my judgment, is to depend on your own operating assessments You have to develop your own strategy, your own technical capabilities and market capabilities, and not depend on outside sources The reason Loral was successful in every acquisition we made was that the team doing the assessment, doing the preliminary work, negotiating, was the same team that had the responsibility after the acquisition for integrating the newly acquired firm and for exploiting the operating requirements.

Keep the Evaluation Team Small, Highly Professional,
and Fully Responsible

Another point is the size of the team and the qualifications of its members Schwartz attaches great importance to using only operating managers on the small team that evaluates, decides to acquire, and implements acquisitions In that way, each member contributes his real-life experience and professional competence and remains fully accountable for the results In his words,

> In Loral, the team is a small team and is always the same. It is composed exclusively of operating people Although I have the reputation for making acquisitions, I am more interested in operations I am a CEO who is deeply engaged in the operations of our company In addition to myself, the team includes Frank Lanza, our chief operating officer; Mr. De Blasio, our chief financial officer; the senior vice president for daily support of the operations; the chief attorney; and our vice president for technology But we see it as an integration of disciplines. Our chief financial officer is as much an operator as is the technologist, as is the operating manager, and as our lawyer who is also much involved in operations This is the small team who goes into the analysis of potential acquisitions and we are the same team that is responsible for deriving the synergy of the

acquisition after the transaction has been completed. The only people on our team are operating people. I think this is a valuable way to approach this issue The team [members who have] daily responsibility for running the operations are the same who are also responsible for the acquisitions This is our basic strength

Use Investment Bankers Only for Raising Capital or for Introductions

A very interesting aspect of Loral's methodology for acquisitions, which we believe is appropriate for most high-technology acquisitions, is the way Loral handles the financial analysis of such transactions. In mergers and acquisitions in general, the widely accepted method for assessing the value of a potential acquisition is to ask for the help of investment bankers in making the analysis I asked Bernard Schwartz how Loral deals with the financial aspect of the acquisition analysis

> One cannot structure a successful transaction without financial acumen This is an area that I am very strong in, but our management team has, in addition to me, three very strong financial managers: the chief financial officer, the chief comptroller, and our treasurer
>
> Loral is well known for limiting the use of commercial and investment bankers in acquisition work We need them for certain kinds of things where they are experts: raising capital, for example That is their business, and we need them for that purpose. We may need them in terms of making introductions to management of companies that are not friendly. In terms of assessing the value or determining markets, however, or determining the value of the technology, we do not look to and we do not welcome the advice of investment bankers We are the experts We don't need them to give us that kind of advice

Digest an Acquisition before Making a New One

Loral's management was particularly careful to integrate each acquisition into Loral's structure and culture before taking on anything new The idea of absorbing organizations with distinctly different management cultures from that of Loral is of particular interest I asked Schwartz to comment on this Here is his answer:

> Different management cultures are always a problem, but it was never a determining issue in whether we should go forward with that decision The issue of merging the cultures was one of the tasks we handled after we decided to buy a company We have experience of buying small companies, large companies, divisions of very large companies with cultural characteristics much different from Loral's In this case, we were very careful to make sure that Loral's culture, our way of looking at things, prevailed after the acquisition It is not an easy task; it requires a lot of work, but we were successful in achieving our goal

Use the Right Timing

Most of Loral's acquisitions were made in the five years between 1990 and 1995 In this period, most companies engaged in defense-related high-technology business were looking for solutions to the problems created by drastic cuts in procurement by the United States and other governments Many defense contractors attempted to transform their technology for civilian use or to divest as much as possible from their military business Buying companies in the defense electronics sector in this period of time was much like swimming against the current. Referring to this phenomenon, Schwartz explained

> Swimming against the current actually made things easier for Loral We were one of the companies that recognized before others that the trend for consolidation would be so profound, so impactful to industry Therefore, when everybody was trying to leave the industry and to apply the technology to commercial applications, we concentrated in the defense area and therefore, we had an easier opportunity because we were one of the few buyers ahead of everybody else The early part of the cycle was very advantageous for us.

SUMMARY

Mergers and acquisitions have played and can play an important role in the development and the growth of a high-technology company High technology, more than any other business, generates opportunities for growth through acquisitions because of the large amount of start-ups created in this industrial sector Mergers and acquisitions are not unique to high technology, but the approaches appropriate for successful acquisitions in the high-technology industry differ significantly from those most often applied in general business.

In this chapter, we described the approach conceived by Bernard Schwartz and applied by him and a small team of competent managers in the spectacular growth of Loral Although Loral, before becoming part of Lockheed-Martin, was a high-technology company engaged specifically in defense electronics, we believe its experience to be relevant to many other high-technology enterprises It is certainly applicable to what we defined in chapter 2 as institutional high technology—companies engaged in high-technology projects for government agencies or for large private institutions.

Loral's strategy of growth by acquisitions was based on several interrelated elements: obtain leadership by using the synergy of the capabilities acquired with those already existing in Loral By doing so, become a more valuable and more important supplier to your customers Last, increase the value of the company to its shareholders

Loral achieved these strategic goals by using a particularly revealing approach for anyone interested in growing by acquisitions in high technology In its evaluations of acquisition opportunities, Loral focused on future business perspectives rather than on a company's past performance Loral's team carefully examined the business potential of the projects and the programs running in the company, and devoted time and attention to speak to the line managers of the potential acquisition. This approach gave Loral's management a much more reliable picture of the value of such acquisition for Loral and subsequently allowed Loral to establish a realistic price for the acquisition

The methodology for detecting, analyzing, negotiating, implementing, and finally integrating an acquisition into Loral's structure contributed much to Loral's success By relying on internal assessment made by a compact group of operating managers with hands-on experience in the business, Bernard Schwartz made sure that his team remained totally committed to making the reality better than their own assessments

I asked Bernard Schwartz to summarize his experience in mergers and acquisitions by giving some examples of transactions he considers a success as opposed to examples for which the results did not quite match the expectations His answer is probably the best witness of the effectiveness of the approach and the methodology applied by Loral:

> I am fortunate to say that I don't think we made any major mistakes, though some [acquisitions] had a longer-term benefit than others. When I say we did not make any mistakes, I mean that every acquisition we made fulfilled the promises we expected—but some far exceeded our expectations The acquisition of Ford Aerospace, for example, far exceeded what anybody had expected, though I must say that we internally understood the impact of a successful integration of Ford Aerospace with us, of what it would mean to Loral It elevated us in the scale of companies that were competing in this marketplace It made us a world-class player The size and the breadth of the technology was such that together with Loral's fundamental basic business, it created a new and much stronger entity It made us more important to the customer

For Further Reflection

1 What are the major differences between traditional industry and the high-technology industry that imply a different approach for mergers and acquisitions in high technology?

2 In your view, is Loral's approach applicable for most acquisitions in the high-technology sector, or is it appropriate mainly for companies engaged in military electronics? Substantiate your answer with supporting arguments

3 Bernard Schwartz emphasizes the importance of having only operating managers on his acquisitions evaluation team What are the advantages of this approach?

4 Loral's evaluation team used to spend considerable time talking to program managers and floor managers in the company evaluated What is the importance of this approach for results obtained by Loral prior to the acquisition and after the acquisition?

5. Compare the role investment bankers play in mergers and acquisitions in general with their role for Loral Why is it possible to use investment bankers in a much wider role in traditional industry?

6 Do the approach and the methods used by Loral in evaluating a potential acquisition help in integrating the organization into Loral's structure? If yes, in what way?

7 Why is acquiring companies a technique particularly appropriate for growth in high technology? What is the role of good timing and how important is it?

8 What are the major problems usually encountered in integrating a recent acquisition? Learning from Loral's case, what did Loral do to minimize these difficulties?

9 Explain the role of synergy in high-tech acquisitions and its relation to the value of the acquisition How did Loral establish the value and the price it was willing to pay for acquisitions?

10 How would you propose to modify—if at all—Loral's approach to mergers and acquisitions should your company deal with commercial high technology rather than institutional high technology?

References and Further Reading

Freior, Jerold. (1990) *Successful Corporate Acquisitions* Englewood Cliffs, NJ: Prentice Hall

Gaughan, P A (1994) *Readings in Mergers and Acquisitions* Cambridge, MA: Blackwell.

Greenwood, Justin (1995) *European Casebook on Business Alliances* London: Prentice Hall

Haspesbag, P C , and David Jemison (1991) *Mergers and Acquisitions* New York: The Free Press

Jenkinson, T , and Colin Mayer (1994) *Hostile Takeovers Defence, Attack and Corporate Governance* London: McGraw Hill

Krallinger, Joseph (1997) *Mergers and Acquisitions Managing the Transition* New York: McGraw-Hill.

Linch, R P (1993) *Business Alliances Guide The Hidden Competitive Weapon* New York: John Wiley.

Miller, B J (1994) *Mergers and Acquisitions* New York: John Wiley.

Rackham, N , L Friedman, and R. Ruff (1996) *Getting Partnering Right* New York: McGraw-Hill

Rock, M. L , R H Rock, and M Sikora (1994) *The Mergers and Acquisitions Handbook* New York: McGraw-Hill

CHAPTER

Organizing Strong Product Support

10

In previous chapters, we have mentioned the importance to a high-technology company of providing support for its products in order to ensure the business success of the company. In this chapter, we concentrate on a number of topics concerning the organization of strong product support Product support consists essentially of three elements operations support, logistic support, and after-sales service

A novel product often requires adequate support to make its operating features and capabilities obvious and easily accessible to the customer Therefore, we discuss first the different aspects of product operations support

Once the product is introduced and successfully operated by the customer, the issue of product logistic support becomes dominant The availability and the quality of logistic support may not only determine the customer's satisfaction with a high-technology product but may also determine the rank and reputation the entire company earns in the eyes of its present and potential customer base

A related but different issue from logistic support is after-sales service. The principal role of this service is to maintain constant touch with the customers and to promote future sales This view is lately replacing the concept of using after-sales service as a profit generator only and is becoming widely accepted by many high-technology companies

PRODUCT OPERATIONS SUPPORT

Depending on the complexity of the high-technology product, the company has to organize and emphasize various aspects of product operation support To introduce the product to the market successfully, the company may need to have product demonstrations It may have to organize special applications courses for more in-depth teaching and guidance so customers can make the best use of the product they are acquiring

Such instruction requires the preparation of highly professional instructors Last, the always important product user's manuals must be prepared with all great care and attention

Product Demonstrations

If a high-technology product is very innovative or complex, it may require effective demonstrations of its attractive features in addition to the normal advertising and publicity necessary for the market introduction of any product These demonstrations have to be adapted so that expectations of potential customers are targeted by the company

For products targeted to a highly professional customer base, such demonstrations are normally done at periodic conventions, which may take place several times a year in different countries Professional conventions are the most effective locations for demonstrating a novel product Here will be some of the most competent audiences, capable of judging, appreciating, and recommending the purchase of a new high-technology product Therefore, such demonstrations have to be carefully prepared to show convincingly and in a relatively short time all the most attractive features of the product Because those who attend a convention or a professional show normally want to see a large number of exhibits as well as hear important lectures, a presenter should plan on a demonstration of no more than 10 to 20 minutes at best.

One aspect that plays a determining role in the success of a product's demonstration is the quality of the personnel demonstrating the product The high-technology company should carefully choose some of its most competent and creative people for assignment to such conventions, where professional people can be expected to ask unanticipated, in-depth questions The company representative to the convention should be fully qualified and sufficiently imaginative to answer such questions convincingly

Another benefit of sending highly qualified people to professional demonstrations is their ability to sense the reactions of the customers correctly In this way they can bring back useful feedback to the company This feedback helps the company to improve its products and to effectively develop the future generations of similar products Unfortunately, reality shows that quite often the highly qualified people are too busy doing work in the company and the ones who are sent to the conventions are those who just happen to be available A good management, well aware of the importance of "selling" at these customer-scheduled opportunities, should try to avoid making such mistakes

The approach just described is appropriate for products addressing highly professional customers, but if the high-technology product is designed for a broader customer base, a slightly different strategy will be necessary For example, if the product is a personal computer or a software package, the number of possible demonstration points is so large that a company cannot send specialists to man every one of them Therefore, to demonstrate successfully the new, attractive features of the product while reaching as many potential customers as possible, an even more careful preparation is needed In addition to people trained as demonstrators, the use of audiovisual supports like video and multimedia becomes almost indispensable All these and other appropriate methods have to be specially and accurately designed for such demonstrations

Their task will be to draw the customers' attention to the product's features in a self-explanatory, simple, easy-to-understand, and effective way

Even though product demonstrations can determine the commercial success or failure of a high-technology product, such demonstrations are quite often prepared at the last minute Seldom is a high-technology product designed from the beginning with its performance demonstration in mind With a little care and advance planning, the product engineer should be able to design, develop, and prepare a set of effective demonstration aids without making an unreasonable investment This extra effort is likely to be justified in the critical period of the product's introduction to the market

Product Application Instructors

The effective demonstration of a sophisticated, high-technology product is just the first step necessary for its market success. Once the product is purchased, the satisfaction of customers depends very much on their ability to make best use of the product's features and capabilities This task can be greatly facilitated by competent, well-prepared application instructors These company personnel should be ready to assist the customer by offering guidance and advice on how to resolve problems and by answering questions concerning specific applications

Preparing a sufficient number of qualified instructors takes time and should normally be done simultaneously with the development of the product Although a good application instructor must not necessarily be a member of the development team, he or she should be thoroughly familiar with the embedded capabilities of the product The instructor should be able to grasp the needs of the customers quickly and be imaginative enough to point out effective solutions to their problems When unable to provide the right answer to a given question, the instructor should be an effective bridge between the customer and the expert in the company who can offer the answer

Application instructors often play a double role in providing support to the customer They conduct frontal teaching in product application courses and provide application support to customers, either on site or by communication lines The company should prepare, check, and qualify the performance of its instructors They should be trained through simulation of the situations they will encounter or in front of an audience of actual customers before they are sent to handle real problems at the customer's site

If the first customers of a new product are able quickly to use their acquisition easily and well, their experience will become a valuable asset for the promotion of further sales This ease of use will also greatly help the company to realize most of the market potential for the product Conversely, if customers are slow to learn how to use a product—even if it is great—and if they are not able to realize its potential to their best advantage, rumors are sure to spread and jeopardize the product's future, if not that of the entire company

Product User's Manuals

The good old product user's manual has not yet found a real substitute It remains the first and basic instruction tool This traditional manual, along with the more recent advent of embedded tutors, remains with the customer long after the introductory courses and demonstrations are over

Theoretically, those best qualified to write the user's manual would be the original designers or inventors of a product These people have the most knowledge of all the features and capabilities embedded in it Unfortunately, preparing a user's manual is not high in their priorities As described in chapter 2, the typical behavior of highly creative people will normally include avoidance of any work they consider routine or trivial In the eyes of such individuals, the real challenge is to innovate, to make a new product work, and not to describe how it works As a result, the important task of writing the instruction manual has to be assigned to others

The people assigned to write good and user friendly user's manuals should extract from the research and development people all the information necessary to describe the different modes of operation of the system or product They should also obtain clear indications of how to use all the features embedded in the product Then, based on a draft of the manual, the company should run realistic simulations with employees who have no previous knowledge of the system and can act as typical customers A good test would be to have them operate the product using just the manual as a guide

The user's manual will be the long-term reference guide for the customers It should have a good index to allow quick retrieval of specific information Unlike a novel, it does not have to be read entirely to satisfy A certain degree of repetition is not a disadvantage to a good manual Each topic should stand alone so the user can obtain a clear understanding of it without having to read the entire book

Product Application Courses and Tutors

Depending on the complexity of a high-technology product and on the number of functions and tasks the product can perform, a customer may require from the manufacturer a more elaborate course or even some period of formal training If the product is less complex or designed for the large public, a built-in tutor may be sufficient

For example, if the system is of the complexity of a new aircraft, a well-accepted procedure is for the customer's pilots to be formally trained and certified by the vendor's training school Sometimes, to be close to its customers, a high-technology company has to organize training centers in many different parts of the world In both cases, much of the customer's satisfaction depends on how well these courses are prepared, on the quality of the teaching devices, and, of course, on the competence and talent of the instructors. Management should always remember that the first impression a customer forms of a product and of the company providing this product is established during the initial training Therefore, as careful as management is to build performance and competitive capability in its products, it should also be careful to ensure first-rate application courses for its customers.

Perhaps the most successful example of built-in tutors are those embedded in a large number of high-quality computer software packages Examples are Microsoft's Word, Excel, and Access, 123 from Lotus and many others At the installation of the program, users are shown the basic features and capabilities of the software package They quickly become quite familiar with the basic applications Later, as they begin to make practical use of the software, they may return and review part of the tutor program or call up the embedded "help" function and obtain specific clues on how to solve a current problem

The built-in "help" function is another very useful feature along with the built-in tutor Built-in "tutors" and "helps" do not replace the product user's manuals or the frontal product application courses, but they have the advantage of instant availability to users at their moment of need Because it gives users quick access to information they need to solve their problems, the "help" function is an extremely attractive tool It has great potential to replace a substantial part of the written manuals one day

Because of these advantages, built-in tutors and help functions are becoming more widely accepted as useful tools for a variety of high-technology systems and equipment If a high-technology system or equipment has an embedded computer or microprocessor in it, there is an attractive possibility for incorporating a tutor and a help function as an integral part These functions can help a company gain an advantage over a competitor with similar products that lack such convenience With microprocessors, memory devices, liquid crystal displays, and associated computer components becoming more and more affordable, predictably in the near future we will see the competition in the high-technology market focus on products with embedded multimedia instructors There are already examples of such "intelligent" high-technology equipment in various types of electronic devices that help users control television sets, videocassette recorders, satellite receivers, and so on These instructors guide users any time they need help to make the equipment perform a complex function They also assist when the operator makes a faulty move, performs a wrong manipulation, or tries to execute a forbidden procedure

PRODUCT LOGISTIC SUPPORT

The purpose of product logistic support is to ensure that customers have the maximum availability of the product under fully operational conditions In the previous section, the focus was on adequate customer guidance and training, so customers could have the best use of all features of the product In this section, the emphasis is on keeping the high-technology product at full performance and on minimizing its down time

These goals can be achieved only if, in addition to a basically sound design and carefully monitored manufacturing process, the company provides sound product logistic support. The company must have adequate maintenance documentation, conveniently distributed repair stations, and a sufficient level of quickly available spare parts These, together with automatic test equipment (ATE), diagnostic systems (DS), and built-in test (BIT) features that monitor and warn the customer if some anomaly occurs during use, provide the basis of adequate logistic support

Maintenance Documentation

Depending on the complexity of the product and whether it was designed to be used by professionals or by the general public, the high-technology company has to prepare appropriate maintenance documentation to be used by the people responsible for periodic and breakdown maintenance of the product. If the customer is a professional organization, a company, or a government agency with its own maintenance personnel and facilities, the maintenance manuals must be written and illustrated accordingly They must enable the personnel, after appropriate training, to carry out all the periodic maintenance tasks as well as most of the trouble-shooting and occasional repairs It is beyond the scope of this book to detail what constitutes adequate maintenance documentation However, it must contain at least the following

- A functional description of the product
- The product's specifications
- Schematic diagrams, drawings, and assembly/disassembly instructions
- Trouble-shooting procedures
- List of test equipment jigs and fixtures necessary for trouble-shooting and final tuning of the product
- A full and comprehensive list of spare parts including part and vendor numbers

The documentation must provide all the information needed to secure successful maintenance of the product when performed on the customer's premises by reasonably well-trained maintenance personnel.

Documentation provided with products designed for the general public must target a "user level" of maintenance sophistication The general user is not supposed to perform any in-depth maintenance but just the minimum preventive actions necessary to avoid malfunctions Therefore, the high-technology company should include an appropriate maintenance section in the user's manual In addition, the company should provide a list of authorized repair stations To avoid expensive product liability claims, the company should clearly indicate and repeatedly emphasize in its manuals all possible warnings against dangerous and forbidden manipulations of the product

Repair Stations and On-Site Service

The commercial success of many high-technology products depends strongly on conveniently located, competent, and well-equipped service stations This is especially true for products ranging in price from $100,000 to $1,000,000 In this category, customers are most sensitive to the possibility of investing a substantial amount of money without having the guarantee of help from a nearby representative. Products below perhaps $1,000 in price are often looked on as commodities and sometimes even as "use and lose" items Products approaching or exceeding the $1,000,000 mark are often acquired by professional companies, large organizations, or government agencies that have their own maintenance facilities, making them independent of external help

Responding to customers' needs for fast and secure service, companies offering products in the first category mentioned have to be especially careful to establish the network of service simultaneously with the distribution or even before the beginning of the large-scale promotion of the high-technology product If the company fails to do so, it risks losing its reputation in this market segment Loss of reputation may be extremely expensive to repair, if repairable at all

Quality of service in the repair stations depends, first of all, on the quality and training of the technical personnel. Their ability to diagnose correctly and fix quickly just what needs to be fixed is highly appreciated by customers The technical staff must be equipped with all necessary test facilities, manuals, and spare parts For example, if the services provided to some expensive, unique, medical electronic equipment is slow, its down time may seriously hamper a doctor's ability to provide an effective treatment for patients

Customers tend to compare and exchange information on repair turnaround times and costs for similar repair services Their opinions are formed by which high-technology company provides the best support for its products They take this into account when making purchasing decisions in the future.

Another service much appreciated by many customers is the on-site maintenance provided by personnel of the repair station Any service or repair that can be done without having to dismantle and transport the product from its operational site is considered most advantageous by high-technology customers To provide efficient on-site service, the repair organization should devote some of its best people to it, taking into account that they will have to operate alone, and within the limitations of whatever test equipment they can take with them Such people often have to improvise and be creative in solving a problem without all the equipment and support available in the repair station In recent years, a number of factors have played an important and positive role in improving the quality of service available for high-technology products These factors are discussed in the next paragraphs

Built-In Test (BIT)

One of the first and most extensive uses of the built-in test (BIT) was its incorporation in the design and production of aircraft, both military and civilian Two main factors explain this occurrence First, aircraft can be considered high-technology systems with a high degree of complexity and sophistication Also, because airlines deal with people, distance, and time, avoiding down time is of critical importance to them

With the help of BIT, pilots of these expensive machines are able to maintain in-flight control of their system's performance Any malfunction detected by the BIT can either be handled on board or transmitted by the pilot to the closest repair station on the ground Often, such advanced notice allows the ground crew to select and prepare the necessary spare parts even before the plane lands Clearly, such procedures can significantly decrease the time the aircraft spends on the ground until it is fully repaired and declared operational

Recently, the popularity of BIT has grown because of its operational merits It has become a must in the specification list for many new, complex, high-technology systems, such as air traffic control systems, space communication systems, power stations, telephone exchanges, and others Built-in tests offer the advantage of having a constant, computerized surveillance of all important system parameters They also can provide a good first level of diagnostics, pointing out the unit most probably responsible for the anomaly The only logical reason for not having BIT in almost any high-technology product is the added cost and complexity it may entail.

If a high-technology company is requested to design and incorporate a BIT feature in some of its products, or if the company decides to do so on its own initiative, it should always be careful to avoid overdoing. To illustrate this point, assume that the BIT is requested to be so comprehensive that it becomes more complex than the system it is supposed to monitor The situation can be taken to the absurd by designing an additional BIT to monitor performance of the system's BIT The law of diminishing returns takes hold pretty quickly when a BIT is being designed Engineers need to remember that BIT will very seldom replace the more conventional repair station level of maintenance Usually, it is complementary to the repair facility and to be cost effective should be kept simple and not overambitious

Automatic Test Equipment (ATE)

One of the first customers for automatic test equipment (ATE) was the U.S Department of Defense It was soon followed by other U S agencies and their counterparts in countries with similar needs Beginning in the 1960s, as they introduced more and more sophisticated systems to their inventory, these customers had continued to have difficulty finding specialists who could maintain their systems and keep them fully operational. With the military forces in many countries, some of the maintenance tasks must be assigned to draftees Often these draftees become really proficient with the system only toward the end of their tour of duty. Consequently, a natural solution was for the military to request the supplier to provide automatic test equipment for the system and for its major subsystems as part of the delivery

The idea behind automatic test equipment is simple automate the test procedures of a complex system as much as possible By so doing, the customer gets two important advantages First, the level of technical personnel required to operate such test equipment is lower than for those running nonassisted, manual tests Second, the time needed to train ATE operators is much shorter than the time an individual needs to acquire sufficient experience to become an effective trouble-shooter

With the advances made in computer technology during the last two decades, most automatic test equipment is now computerized, and most of the tasks are done by specially developed software. The initial software is usually supplied by the company that designs and builds the product, but the user may subsequently have to modify and fine-tune the system to meet particular needs This modification requires frequent software updates in order for the ATE to accommodate the latest product's modifications To enable the customer to make such software modifications, one important consideration in the design of ATEs is the choice of the programming language It should be as user friendly as possible, easy to understand, and easy to apply by the customer's technicians who are not expected to have special education in computer programming.

As proof of the utility and importance of automatic test equipment, high-technology companies develop such equipment not only for government agencies and large corporations but also for themselves This equipment is seen more and more in the service and repair stations of high-technology companies They know it improves the service they provide and decreases the cost and turnaround time in their own repair stations

Diagnostic Systems

Recently there has been a development that draws from the theoretical work and the advances made in pattern recognition, artificial intelligence, and expert systems This is the introduction of diagnostic systems to some of the new ATEs and to other equipment in use in modern repair stations

The diagnostic systems take the advantages of automatic test equipment one important step further The ATE is able to perform the test procedure automatically, to print the test results, and to indicate whether a subunit is not performing adequately A technician is still needed to analyze the results and determine the cause for the malfunction Now, with the introduction of diagnostic systems, the goal is also to establish the cause of a default automatically Although most diagnostic systems have not yet attained this level, they are fast approaching it.

In the meantime, the diagnostic system is quite often capable of guiding the technician to the probable cause of a problem by using the preprogrammed experience of expert technicians and applying their logic to a given set of data In other cases, the diagnostic system is designed to be capable of "learning" from the experience accumulated during actual tests and trouble-shooting

Except for relatively simple situations, a truly comprehensive automatic diagnostic system is still in the future Even so, these systems are becoming very useful in the trouble-shooting of complex, high-technology systems To a large degree, diagnostic systems are a partial response to the anxiety expressed by some skeptics, fearful about the growing sophistication of high-technology systems These skeptics are afraid that high-tech systems will become so complex that they can't be maintained because of the lack of sufficiently trained personnel To the contrary, such advances as diagnostic systems are contributing to the maintenance of high-technology systems so substantially as to support even wider acceptance of complex high technology.

On-Line Maintenance

Significant progress has been made in providing on-line maintenance for widely computerized high-technology systems. On-line maintenance is the testing and diagnosis of a remotely located system by way of some sort of communication channel telephone, radio, or other With the advances in communication technology, a system installed thousands of miles away from a service station may be checked, analyzed, and diagnosed at that station This capability for on-line maintenance may allow the high-technology company to reduce significantly the number of fully equipped repair stations it must maintain to support its customers The company could then concentrate equipment and specialists in one or in a few maintenance centers from where the service would be delivered by remote communication

There is one caution for a company seeking to establish on-line maintenance On-line *diagnosis* may be made at long distance, but the spare parts and technician must be at hand to replace a defective subsystem or a faulty part Nevertheless, the professional level of the maintenance people and the investment in test equipment on site can be significantly reduced using the concept of on-line maintenance As more and more broadband communication channels come into use, capable of carrying high-speed data and video via fiber and satellites, and as the cost of using these channels becomes more affordable, we will probably see the on-line maintenance concept gaining wider acceptance This advance may require future high-technology products and systems to be designed from inception to be easily connected to remote stations Any added cost and complexity for this feature may be well justified

On May 20, 1996, the German high-tech company Siemens-Nixdorf published an

---

CASE 10.1

The Lufthansa Example

A multimedia maintenance system is changing the face of aircraft maintenance at Lufthansa German Airlines: BISAM—as the project is called—stands for Built-in Integrated Services for Aircraft Maintenance   The project is presently undergoing national field trials with 18 systems in various Lufthansa locations—initially shadowing conventional maintenance and repair operations And international links to the United States and Japan are already on the drawing board

   With BISAM, squawks can be reported while still airborne—either via automated monitoring system or by the crew Automatically encoded, they are transmitted to the BISAM database by satellite This allows the maintenance technicians at the destination airport to prepare for the job effectively, even before the aircraft lands, to obtain the required parts, and to request assistance from any specialist who may be needed To make the job even easier, BISAM also supplies the correct repair strategy along with each squawk—plus the latest data, since each operation is stored and analyzed.

   BISAM can even eliminate the need for on-site specialists: with the video-conferencing module in BISAM, worldwide communications and conference are possible from any workplace Multimedia remote diagnostics thus enable numerous squawks to be assessed and resolved in less time and at lower cost Lufthansa's workstations also allow high-definition images of even hairline cracks or minute corrosion to be sent directly to the expert's screen via Deutsche Telekom's high-speed ATM networks This is a method that will considerably simplify aircraft maintenance in the future

announcement in the *International Herald Tribune* (p 48) It provides a good illustration of how remote access maintenance is being applied in real life (see Case 10 1)

PRODUCT AFTER-SALES SERVICE

Product after-sales service and product logistic support are related subjects In logistic support, the emphasis is on how to prepare and organize an effective maintenance program for a high-technology product Here, we discuss the role of the after-sales service After-sales service encompasses product logistic support, product guarantee, and continuous contact with customers

The Role of After-Sales Service

More and more, companies are embracing the idea that the most important role of after-sales service is to promote future sales This end is achieved by keeping the customers happy and by presenting the company as being serious and responsible—a company that assists and follows its customers

To realize this concept, many high-technology companies place the after-sales service department directly under the vice president of marketing Because of the importance of after-sales service, its director should have at least some of the following tasks

1. Report to the management on customer satisfaction
2. Keep updated statistics on product reliability
3. Direct or survey the repair stations
4. Ensure the long-term availability of spare parts
5. Maintain constant contact with customers

Reporting to the management on customers' satisfaction with the company's products is an important task that must be formalized. The after-sales service organization must devise simple and reliable ways to measure this satisfaction Periodic meetings with customers or with their representatives, on-site interviews, and other appropriate means such as questionnaires should be used to collect enough data to produce a reliable sense of this satisfaction Customer satisfaction reports must be presented to management at predetermined periods Management must set aside time to discuss these reports and take corrective action if necessary

Keeping updated statistics on the real-life reliability of the company's products is another important function of the after-sales service arm The director will use these data as a quantitative way to draw the management's attention to potential or real problems They are also useful feedback for the designers of new products Usually, one of the high-technology performance measures is the mean time between failures, or MTBF. Any company strives to design its products to achieve the best MTBF rate possible During the design phase of the product, reliability engineers calculate and predict the mean time between failure based on accepted statistical models However, in practice, there is often a large discrepancy between the calculated MTBF rate and the one achieved in the field A reason for this phenomenon might be certain systematic failures that are not taken into account in the statistical models A well-organized after-sales service team can quickly detect these field failures, report them, and take corrective action before there is widespread customer disappointment with the product.

The after-sales service director, if not directly responsible for the company's repair stations, should at least be tasked to perform periodic surveys on their operations and on the satisfaction of the customers with the services they receive

If the repair stations report to the after-sales service director, the director's major drive should be to see that they offer efficient and prompt service, keeping in mind that the customers turning to these stations are in real need of help *The people in the repair stations must remember that a customer asking for service is a person who has voted confidence in the company by buying its products.* They should also understand that the company wants the customer not to regret his decision. This attitude is diametrically opposed to the one that assumes the customer has no choice but to pay any price for the work and spare parts needed to repair his product

If the repair stations are separate organizations, belonging sometimes to independent people who run these operations for business, the after-sales service director should conduct periodic surveys of the way his company's products are cared for by the repair station Here again, the company should devise methods for checking customer satisfaction Questionnaires, phone interviews, and many other methods could be used The important principle is to have reliable and sufficient feedback from actual customers

The customers of high-tech products expect, and rightly so, that their investment will keep its value long after expiration of the product's guarantee In many cases, especially for products in the sensitive price range described before, there is a formal requirement from the high-technology company to guarantee the availability of spare parts for a period of at least seven years from the date of purchase Unfortunately, it is not unusual for the original vendor of some product component to introduce a new model well before a reasonable support period expires Advent of the new model may interrupt manufacture of the earlier one With the nonstop pace of change in technology, such events are becoming the norm rather than the exception Therefore, someone in the high-technology company must be responsible for keeping constant track of parts availability When possible, more than one source of spare parts should be established

If an uninterrupted supply of some spare parts cannot be assured, the company must take appropriate action to develop equivalent subunits This may require using new parts, but if so, they must be adapted to fit the original subunit completely in form and function Although actual development of such equivalents is not necessarily the task of after-sales service, that department's duty is to make sure action is taken before a critical shortage of spare parts develops

The last of the five tasks of the after-sales service director—to maintain constant contact with the customers—is so important that it is discussed separately in the last section of the chapter

Product Guarantee and Product Liability

The purpose of the product guarantee is twofold First, it gives the customer confidence that the product has been professionally produced, using the best design and manufacturing techniques, and that if it fails, the company will provide a remedy Second, it protects the company against unreasonable claims from customers, especially with respect to "product liability" claims, as explained in this section

In its first role of the guarantee, creating customer confidence in the product, a company that is sure of the quality of its products can use the guarantee as a powerful sales promotion feature For high-quality products, a company may consider offering the customer an extended guarantee—perhaps three years instead of the standard 12 months This adds very little cost to the company but creates for the customer a feeling of strong confidence in the quality and reliability of the product This is especially important for a product with which the company is trying to penetrate a certain market, and even more so if the company has adopted a "market follower" strategy (see chapter 7)

The guarantee should include all parts and labor associated with repairing a defective product It should also assume responsibility for the quality of its vendors To clarify, a high-technology system might include some expensive purchased component—for example, a roentgen tube that is part of a medical system In this case, the company may want to exclude the component from the guarantee or transfer to the customer only the guarantee offered by the component's manufacturer Clearly, customers have very little control of such components and if alerted to such exceptions, their desire to purchase the system may diminish accordingly Worse, if they learn later that they have to pay to replace the tube while the system itself is still under the guarantee, customers may feel cheated and avoid doing any future business with the company News of an occurrence like this can spread quickly and cause significant and adverse effect to the company's reputation Therefore, the company should consider providing a full guarantee and price the product accordingly

The second purpose of the product guarantee—to protect the company from unreasonable claims from customers and from lawyers who make their living from pleading such claims—is not immediately obvious This is especially so to the less-experienced managers of high-technology start-ups and of young companies

In many countries, the law is such that if a company fails to provide a written guarantee with its products, the customer may sue the company and claim unlimited compensation Therefore, the company has a clear interest in limiting its liability to only specified conditions as written in the guarantee Of course, all lawyers are fully aware of this situation, when asked by the company to assist in formulating a written guarantee for a product, many tend to overprotect the company. The company management should be aware of this propensity and try to find the right middle path between the two extremes

The particular case of protecting the high-technology company from product liability claims requires further elaboration Apparently, in the United States, the law is especially severe toward companies whose products have caused physical damage and injuries to users There are many dreadful stories about companies that have been found liable in such cases and were ordered to pay huge amounts of compensation One example is the product liability lawsuit against a microwave oven manufacturer in the United States, described in Case 10 2

The list of lawsuits with severe consequences for high-technology companies, from aerospace to medical electronics, is extremely long The only logical conclusion must be for a company to take all precautions against the slightest possibility of being accused in similar circumstances

The best way for any company to protect itself from such claims is to be extremely careful in the design of the product It must consider all customers to be naïve and take all possible precautions to prevent misuse from happening This must be the moral and professional duty of any designer A company should know that it is liable for strong financial and other punishment in the case of neglect or truly faulty design However, in the United States, the law as it presently exists has been so abused that companies in the aerospace and other sectors find it necessary to invest significant amounts in buying product liability insurance—the cost of which, in one way or another, is obviously passed on to the customers

Seeing the negative effects of a too-severe product liability law on important branches of its industry, the European Union has passed a law that limits excessive and

---

CASE 10.2

A Product Liability Example

At the beginning of the massive market introduction of microwave ovens, a young woman was badly injured and burned all over her face as a result of an explosion in her new microwave oven Unaware, she had put in her oven a plate containing metal wires that caused an explosion The victim soon filed a lawsuit claiming product liability from the manufacturer

Despite the fact that the user's manual gave explicit instructions to avoid, and warned against, introducing any metallic objects into the microwave oven, the young woman was able to win the case with the help of a good lawyer The two major claims accepted by the court were negligence in the product's design and insufficient warning in the user's manual The company appealed the case to a superior court It introduced as evidence the user's manual instructions and claimed that, had the user followed the instructions, nothing would have happened The company also sought to reverse the negligence allegation, pointing out that thousands of users had been operating the same model with no accidents whatsoever

To the disappointment of the company, it was once again found guilty of negligence and was sentenced to pay the young woman extremely heavy damages. The higher court explained its decision by pointing out that warning the customer with simple instructions was not sufficient. The warnings should have been written in bold letters and several times throughout the manual so as to avoid any possibility that the user would overlook them Moreover, the court also accepted the plaintiff's claim that the product should have been so designed as to avoid accidents, even should the user make a reasonable mistake

---

disproportionate claims Although product liability is by no means restricted to high-technology products, its importance for the high-technology industry is more pronounced because of the inherent uncertainties associated with new products and new technologies

Keeping in Constant Touch with Customers

In most cases, the customers are the most important asset a company has Earlier, we have stressed the importance of maintaining contact with the people who have voted confidence in the company by buying its products However, many companies neglect to organize effectively in performing this important task.

A high-technology company may find many practical ways to stay in touch with its customers. It all depends on the nature of the company's products For a company specializing in large, high-technology systems, the number of its customers is relatively small and easily manageable However, despite strong contacts and interface with the customers before and immediately after the delivery of a large system, as the years pass, management has a natural tendency to devote most of their attention to new systems and new customers

Frequently, after a few years, contacts with the "old customers" are practically lost In the meantime, the customer may experience problems with the system Knowing that the period of the warranty has expired, this individual may turn to a repair station that is not totally qualified, to save money on the repair. After a while, the system degrades to the point that it needs to be replaced Then, the company learns that its customer is considering or has already purchased a competitor's system This situation could have been avoided had the management been more vigilant. Perhaps the company could have been better organized, with someone like the after-sales service director having the formal responsibility of maintaining constant touch with all customers

If the company operates in the general high-technology market and its products are sold to a very large number of customers, the method of keeping in touch with customers will be different from the previous case Here, some simple statistical methods that are used to probe public opinion can be extremely useful Almost any high-technology company requests its customers to fill in and mail back a card attached to their product guarantee If correctly designed, this card can be very helpful in determining a statistically meaningful stratified random sample of a very large population This will allow the sample to be polled and eliminate the need to call and interview an excessive number of people With good sample information, a good statistician should have no difficulty establishing reliable conclusions about customers' satisfaction with the product

The methods for keeping track of a company's reputation with its customers and the way the customers appreciate or criticize its products may vary, but two principles are always valid. First, the company's management should be aware of the importance of staying connected to customers Second, they should appoint a specific person to be responsible for ensuring that this connection is maintained The second point must be not just a slogan but a useful and practical reality

---

SUMMARY

The purpose of this chapter was to focus the attention of the managers of a high-technology company on the importance of product support This subject is often treated as being of secondary importance In some companies, the management pays only lip service to maintaining strong product support and does little to ensure that it happens

Given the critical importance of this topic, we first devoted attention to the product operation support. We dealt with organizing successful product demonstrations for both novel professional high-technology products and products addressing a broader customer base Then the subject of preparing product applications instructors was described The success and acceptance of a highly sophisticated product may depend on the quality and competence of the people who instruct customers in making the best use of the new product's novel features

Next, we discussed the basic tool supporting the operation of most high-technology products the product user's manual The problems associated with writing effective user's manuals were examined and suggestions for overcoming some of the difficulties were made

To further enhance product operation and customers' ability to take full advantage of all product features, the subject of providing application courses and using built-in tutors was covered With the introduction of computer technology into many sophisticated high-technology systems, it is increasingly possible to build a tutor into the system to provide help to the user at any given moment

Next, product logistic support was examined and discussed First, the product maintenance documentation was described An outline was given for what such documentation should contain Then, we discussed the need for repair stations and on-site service for the support of high-technology products. The factors playing a key role in the successful organization and operation of such services were outlined and discussed Then, we examined modern methods for building maintenance capability into the high-tech product itself For one such method, the built-in test (BIT), its obvious advantages were outlined. Some possible drawbacks were identified, and ways to avoid them were recommended.

The role of automatic test equipment (ATE) was described as part of the maintenance apparatus Approaches for successful design of this equipment were proposed Then, we examined the utility of another recent development: diagnostic systems These may be part of an automatic test equipment system or an independent element in a well-equipped repair station The overview of all essential parts of product logistic support was completed with an examination of the trend toward use of on-line maintenance This type of maintenance is made possible by the recent advances in high-speed data and video communication technology

We concluded the chapter with a discussion of product after-sales service Although related to product logistic support, this is a separate subject that deserves special management attention The primary role of after-sales service is to promote future sales, so we described the most important tasks of the after-sales service department Each task was discussed and specific recommendations were given for the most important management considerations In the same framework, we discussed the role of the product guarantee

Emphasis was placed on the importance of the guarantee, not only to create confidence in the product but also to limit company liability against unreasonable claims by customers The subject of product liability was discussed at length because of the extremely serious consequences a company may suffer from failure to address this issue professionally Finally, we treated the importance for a company of maintaining constant communication with its customers Practical suggestions for how to perform this task were described Ideas were offered for both the company dealing with large, high-technology systems and the company addressing the general high-technology market

By treating the broad subject of product support seriously, the management of a high-technology company may contribute more to the company business success than by many other activities The importance of the subject is beyond any discussion However, product support is still handled today by many companies only as a side issue The material in this chapter should help them avoid this mistake.

For Further Reflection

1 What are the basic reasons that make product support more important for high-technology than for low-technology products?

2 Describe factors that are important in the success of a novel product demonstration when the product is addressing a professional market Do the same for products addressing the general high-technology market

3. Outline the role of product application instructors, of product user's manuals, and of product application courses and tutors What are some critical points that management must take into account when preparing instructors, manuals, and courses?

4 What is the role of product logistic support? How do maintenance manuals differ for products designed for the general public and products designed for professionals?

5 What are the advantages of a built-in test (BIT) and what pitfalls should one avoid when designing BIT in high-technology products?

6 Outline the role of automatic test equipment and of diagnostic systems Explain the potential of on-line maintenance by describing a scenario where such maintenance is most appropriate

7. What is the difference between logistical support and after-sales service? What are the most important tasks of the latter? How should a high-technology company organize for effective after-sales service?

8 Describe and explain the two major purposes of the product guarantee

9 What is product liability and what should a company do to protect itself from unreasonable claims?

10 Outline and describe some appropriate ways for a company to stay in touch with its customers, both companies dealing with large, high-technology systems and companies selling to the general high-technology market

References and Further Reading

Carlisle, John A , and Parker, Robert C (1989) *Beyond Negotiating Redeeming the Customer-Supplier Relationship* New York: John Wiley

Hauser, John R (1993) "How Puritan-Bennett Used the House of Quality," Working Paper 67 Cambridge, MA: Sloan School of Management
> The author asserts that managers don't need any more vague advice about paying better attention to customers In this article, practical, step-by-step methods are described In 1990, a medical equipment manufacturer needed to redesign one of its products to beat an aggressive competitor It used a method called the "House of Quality," which relates market research information directly to product design, thereby helping the company focus effectively on the most important product benefits The new design revolutionized the product and was a phenomenal success This paper makes a good complementary reading to the text in this chapter

Hauser, John R , Duncan I. Simester, and Birger Wernerfelt (1994) "Customer Satisfaction Incentives," Working Paper 76 Cambridge, MA: Sloan School of Management
> This working paper deals with methods for enhancing customer satisfaction Customer satisfaction incentive schemes are increasingly common in a variety of industries The authors offer explanations as to how and when using incentives for employees on customer satisfaction is profitable and offer several recommendations for improving on current practice

Faced with employee groups (including managers) who may have shorter time horizons than the firm, such systems enable a firm to use customer reaction to monitor implicitly how employees allocate effort between the short and long terms These systems can be used to encourage employees to make trade-offs that are in the best interests of the firm

Jones, J V (1995) *Integrated Logistic Support Handbook* New York: McGraw-Hill

Military Handbook, MIL-HDBK 63038 "Technical Manual Writing Handbook."

Pecht, Michael (1995) *Product Reliability, Maintainability and Supportability Handbook* New York: CRC Press

Ushakov, Igor (ed) (1994) *Handbook of Reliability Engineering* New York: John Wiley and Sons

CHAPTER

How to Keep Ahead of Competition and Perpetuate Success

The purpose of this chapter is to summarize the most important topics treated throughout the book and show how theory can be applied to perpetuate success. We begin by examining the principal factors that often cause a high-technology company to decline, then discuss ways an alert management should act to fight these factors successfully

If for any reason a high-technology company finds itself in jeopardy, the immediate question is what should be done to save it We examine the lessons learned from high-technology companies that have made a successful comeback through traumatic restructuring From this analysis, we learn the strategies that can be used to pull a company back from crisis

Finally, a high-technology company, like any association, society, or fellowship, must have its common code, rules, and standards to behave in a coherent and effective way These rules govern the decisions made by all levels of management and shape the company culture Much of the material treated in previous chapters describes in some detail the recommended principles a competent management should follow in all business aspects of the high-technology company In this chapter, we summarize these rules as ten "commandments " These are the basic rules that should be observed by a high-technology manager to continuously achieve above-average results

THE SEEDS OF DECLINE

In our discussion of the critical factors for success (chapter 2), we mentioned some of the reasons that high-technology companies fail to adapt to the changing business environment. We noted that as a high-technology company develops and grows from a "start-up" to a mature and diversified company, it needs to change its organizational structure, this process is often accompanied by painful personnel shifting, which is always difficult to manage

The seeds of decline are inevitably sown with the very success of the high-technology company We reexamine below the most frequent reasons for apparently strong and healthy companies to decay and either pass through critical restructuring periods or worse, fade away and disappear Analyzing a number of typical real-life cases, we find three common factors that can be generalized to explain why a high-technology company will decline management shortsightedness, resistance to change, and success blindness Although these factors often work in combination, it is important to examine each of them separately

Management Myopia

Managers of high-tech companies are usually highly intelligent and talented people; they are accustomed to the analysis of complex situations, and they have innovative ideas, with a good understanding of novel products and technologies Even so, time after time we witness situations in which companies behave as if "tomorrow will be just like today " Especially when "today is a beautiful day," there is a natural tendency to change nothing and hope it all lasts as long as possible The problem is that if one does not prepare his house for winter in summer, the roof may collapse An illustration is the story of Wang Word Processing Systems (Case 11 1 on page 240)

Myopic management and the inability of a high-technology company to predict the future correctly have been only partial reasons for the decline and sometimes total disappearance of one-time successful companies. There is another, related but slightly different cause for decline: resistance to change We examine it next

Resistance to Change

Resistance to change is by no means a phenomenon specifically reserved to high technology Examples of this phenomenon abound in a vast variety of socioeconomic fields However, in other fields, the pace of change is relatively slow compared to the pace in high technology. To the general resistance to change, one must add the high-technology specifics, as explained in chapter 2 There we saw the frequent refusal of high-technology management to adjust organizational structures to changing company needs or even to introduce modifications to existing products We noted that such behavior risks freezing innovation and discouraging entrepreneurial initiative This mind-set is addressed in Case 11.2 on page 241

The quotations in Case 11 2, in our view, provide an accurate assessment of the problems created by the resistance to change factor in the high-technology industry For more systematic and detailed analysis of these factors and the methods to fight their negative effects, refer again to chapter 2 and to some of the literature recommended at the end of that chapter

Success Blindness

Many good high-technology companies attained success in a relatively short period of time There are many examples of "garage operations" becoming multimillion dollar companies in two to three years or less Achieving success in such a short time has often created a strong feeling of superiority and self-confidence among the managers of

---

CASE 11.1

The Decline of Wang

Only a few may remember today that Wang was a big name in the 1980s The company was one of the first to sense the potential in office automation and more particularly in word processing In the late 1970s, Wang's computers and software were widely accepted as a standard for word processing in the industrialized nations Wang made its success by designing a family of special purpose computers, specifically optimized for the tasks of word processing These machines treated text much faster and more efficiently than the general purpose mainframe computers then available At that time, personal computers (PCs) were not yet as popular and flexible as they became by the end of the 1980s The technology offered by Wang was by far the best answer to the need for computer-assisted word processing This brought Wang in a very few years to the position of a world leader in word processing

Unfortunately for Wang, the advances made in microprocessors and in compact memory devices soon allowed the building and marketing of a new generation of general purpose personal computers known as PCs. One of the first application software packages offered to PC customers was for word processing The possibility of replacing the typewriter with a much more flexible and powerful machine was one of the driving factors that made PCs so popular in a very short time.

In the mid-1980s, Wang was still claiming that PC word processing was no threat to its interests in the much more demanding professional market—namely, large and medium-size corporations These accounted for a major percentage of its customer base At that time, if Wang's management had seen the future more realistically, the company could have used its financial strength to become a full competitor in the PC market, or could have capitalized on its word processing software experience and adapt it for use in PCs Instead, Wang chose to keep its special purpose hardware and software as inadequate weapons in the losing battle against the new intruders By the end of the 1980s, the technology offered by Wang was largely obsolescent and the company sank into oblivion

---

these companies. They begin to believe that "everything we touch is a success," or "we know better," or "don't teach us how to do business "

The phenomenon is not difficult to understand Remember that the initial accomplishment of the company, in most cases, is a direct result of someone's successful bet on a risky product or technology This helps to explain how managers develop their mind-set Being master forecasters with proven achievements naturally creates a sense of self-confidence, self-reliance, and unwavering belief in their own judgment

Self-confidence in moderation is not a negative quality for a manager. However, exaggerated self-confidence has often led to disastrous results One of the most frequent manifestations of too much self-confidence, or success blindness leading to catas-

---

CASE 11.2

Resistance to Change

Following are excerpts from an interview with George Taucher, a professor at the International Institute for Management Development (IMD) in Lausanne, Switzerland, that appeared in the *International Herald Tribune,* December 15, 1994

> Success creates a strong tendency to resist change and continue with tried-and-true methods even when that success begins to falter The resistance to change in corporate structures runs very deep IBM is often cited as an example. Top managers knew that change was on the way, but it was not possible for them to act decisively until there was an intellectual acceptance within IBM that change was needed (p 14)

To the question of what companies can do to avoid this trap, Taucher replied:

> Let me answer by way of an example. The highly successful German engineering plastics and pharmaceuticals group, Hoechst, has strong corporate structures going back more than 100 years The company recognized that it was necessary to move to a decentralized unit system, but much of the staff resisted and the then-chairman was against the change as well. He has since retired, and a new structure is now rapidly being put into place In five to ten years' time, Hoechst will be a loose federation with a small holding company at the top (p 14).
>
> This sort of structure encourages the spirit of entrepreneurship by allowing the individual members of the group to run with their own projects and compete for markets This idea is very difficult for management of large centralized groups to accept. Administrative logic points the opposite way, suggesting that synergy and savings are obtained by organizing common services and procedures for the whole group These can be calculated mathematically, whereas you cannot easily calculate the value of entrepreneurship to a company (p 14)

Another useful example of a positive approach is the way Japanese companies address the same issue Asked what European businesses can learn from the Japanese practice, Taucher replied

> An important factor favoring change in Japan is that managers as a whole are not in love with their existing products the way Western companies sometimes are Thus they do not hesitate to kill the cash cow early on and devote the necessary resources to new technologies Moreover, the Japanese system of loose conglomerates seems to avoid the success-to-failure syndrome by combining the advantage of size with the benefits of small, dedicated organizations (p. 16)

trophic results, has been the stretching of the company's resources to the breaking point Encouraged by initial success, management begins to invest in larger production capacity, in lavish office buildings, and in other symbols of success Usually, most of this investment is financed by loans made by banks and other financial institutions that have bought the success story of the company and have voted confidence in its future

As long as the cash flow into the company follows the projected forecasts, everything is fine If, however, for whatever reason—reduced customer demand, a regional or world crisis, a shortage of supply—the cash flow falls significantly below the forecast, the company can no longer meet its short-term financial obligations without borrowing more money at less attractive terms This situation can quickly degenerate into a vicious circle of borrowing new money to meet existing obligations If the crisis persists for a sufficiently long time, the moment inevitably arrives when no bank, person, or institution will advance any additional credit to the company on any terms

The number of good and otherwise healthy companies that have gone bankrupt because of cash flow problems is so large that the financial adviser of any company is bound to warn his management of the danger However, success blindness has contributed many times, especially in the high-technology industry, to managers' refusal to heed such warnings

Success blindness may manifest itself in a large variety of problem areas other than those relating to cash flow Investing in increasingly risky ventures, ignoring troublesome signals, and taking short-cuts are just a few examples of different demonstrations of the same phenomenon However, cash-flow insolvency is the most frequent and the most dangerous result of success blindness Therefore, any responsible management should be specially careful to avoid falling into this trap

EXTERNAL THREATS

We have discussed some of the most important internal reasons for decline Now we examine two external factors that have caused problems to many high-technology companies a declining market and increased competition

A Sharp Drop in Market Demand

If the demand for the products of a high-technology company tumbles all of a sudden, for reasons beyond the control of the company's management, this company is thrust into a very profound crisis that is extremely difficult to resolve For example, after the disintegration of the Soviet bloc, the defense budget in most Western countries was slashed by significant amounts The reduction in defense procurement money designated for new equipment was proportionally even larger This was because most of the reduced defense budget had to be dedicated to the inflexible needs of payroll, fuel, maintenance of the existing forces, and so on The drop in procurement sent shock waves through the high-technology industry engaged in aerospace, defense electronics, naval systems, and other military applications

Another example is the crisis that hit the airframe manufacturers during and immediately after the Gulf War The problems began with a sharp decline in passenger travel—a direct result of the war This caused losses for many airlines Then, deregulation and the desire to compete aggressively for every remaining potential passenger triggered a price war among airlines This further increased the losses, driving some of the weaker companies into insolvency One of the fist steps taken by many airline companies to save cash was to cancel previously firm orders and purchase options for new aircraft This, in turn, created one of the worst crises experienced in the aircraft manu-facturing sector Not only were thousands of employees in the companies affected di-rectly, but the impact flowed out to all the companies' subcontractors

A dramatic example of the almost total loss of an entire market occurred in East-ern Europe after the fall of communism Industry there, under the rules of the planned economy, had received periodic orders from government institutions When the system collapsed, all of a sudden no one was there to place orders or to pay for them Almost overnight, hundreds of companies in all these countries and millions of employees found themselves in a desperate situation with no one demanding their services

These examples are real The reasons for an external impact on demand might vary, but management must be alert and watchful Managers need to be prepared with adequate contingency plans to accommodate sudden, sharp drops in market demand Later in this chapter we examine methods for accomplishing this

Stiff, Aggressive Competition

Throughout this book, we have treated competition as a positive and healthy factor in the life of any high-technology company Therefore, competition in its usual sense should not alarm a competent firm However, aggressive and sometimes unfair compe-tition may cause serious problems and even destroy a company Being able to identify the causes of the problem is important

A high-tech company may suffer from strong competition for internal reasons, such as obsolescence of its product lines, technological inferiority, or similar problems we have discussed earlier Sometimes, however, the problems are beyond the control of the company's management

One example of unfair competition is the unauthorized production in China of audio compact discs (CDs) and CD-ROMs for distribution on the world markets at prices no legitimate company can meet The Chinese companies are able to offer their products at these prices by refusing to pay for the right to reproduce the discs, in abso-lute disregard of intellectual property rights According to U S complaints, some 29 CD factories there turned out 75 million pirated discs in 1994, despite the copyright law passed in China in 1991

FIGHTING BACK

"Prevenir vaut mieux que guerir" says an old French proverb, meaning "better prevent than heal " However, if for one or another reason a high-technology company finds it-self in a critical business situation where its survival is at stake, the company can learn from the example of other businesses that have successfully endured such trauma

Exactly as for a living person, the first and probably most important step in any recovery process is to diagnose accurately the causes of the crisis Most often, there is more than one reason for the company to be in bad shape Company management must create a list, in descending order of importance, of all the problems the company faces They should then divide the causes into two categories internal problems and external problems Although the managers in charge of a recovery operation will generally have to deal with more than one problem at a time, we have analyzed each one separately to be able to describe the appropriate responses methodically and completely

Recovery from Internally Created Problems

We have seen the problems created by management shortsightedness and resistance to change Here we examine some of the approaches taken by companies that have been successfully pulled out of such situations One such company is Hewlett-Packard. In an article published in the *New York Times* and reprinted by the *International Herald Tribune* (p. 13) in January 1995, Lawrence M Fisher describes the approach taken by Hewlett-Packard to fight internal resistance to change (see Case 11 3)

Another illustration worth learning from is the case of Digital Equipment In the 1970s and the 1980s, Digital Equipment was one of the world leaders in the market of mini- and midicomputers With PCs becoming more and more powerful and especially with the ability to connect PCs to networks, Digital saw its market share drop progressively but did little to adapt to the change By the mid-1990s, the company had suffered several financial losses that forced it into a painful restructuring period The resolution of the management of Digital to pull the company out of the crisis, as expressed in their pledge made public throughout the media, is an example of determination worth quoting (see Case 11 4 on page 247)

Recovery from External Problems

In chapter 2, in the discussion of market uncertainties, we used my personal experience as an example of how to handle a sharp drop in market demand The same example is applicable here We analyze in more detail all the essential measures we had to take to recover from that blow At that time, I was the managing director of a mid-size company designing, developing, and producing high-technology electronic products with annual sales of some $200 million The company had won contracts to design and develop three major subsystems of a large aerospace project At the end of the development phase, the company expected to receive production contracts amounting to at least $500 million The project was canceled for reasons totally beyond the control of our company.

The day after cancellation of the project, we had a full-blown crisis on our hands In chapter 2, we described some ways to avoid such situations—as much as possible—and suggested how to prepare contingencies when a company accepts the risk of having most of its eggs in a single basket. When the crisis struck, the following list of emergency measures was established and applied by the top management of the company

1. Inform the company's staff
2. Establish tight cash-flow control
3. Launch an aggressive marketing campaign
4. Restructure the company's personnel

The first step was to inform all levels of management and explain the situation to all the company's 2,500 employees

---

The PC Turnaround at Hewlett-Packard

For the first decade of the personal-computer revolution, U.S.-based Hewlett-Packard Co had the dubious distinction of being the most prestigious manufacturer consigned to that great wedge of market-share charts dubbed "other " Today, however, Hewlett-Packard is one of the world's fastest-growing personal computer companies, ranked ninth in worldwide sales and third in sales of PC-based servers (larger machines used on networks), according to International Data Corp , a market-research firm in Framingham, Massachusetts

Because of new product lines, more aggressive marketing and sharp price reductions, Hewlett-Packard's PC revenue has grown impressively, to $2 5 billion last year from $1 4 billion in 1993 and $670 million in 1992, according to International Data And unlike International Business Machines Corp or Digital Equipment Corp , both of which concede they lose money on PCs, Hewlett-Packard makes a profit on its personal computer business

"Hewlett-Packard has had significant growth for two reasons: They have done a better job, and some of the other majors have done a poorer job," said Seymour Merrin, a PC-industry consultant based in Mountain View, California

How Hewlett-Packard, said to have been founded in a garage in Palo Alto, California, nearly missed the greatest market opportunity of the last 10 years is a lesson in the mixed blessings of a strong corporate culture And how the company worked to alter its direction and latch on to that opportunity reflects a transformation not only in its own culture but in the direction of the industry itself.

As more computing tasks move from large machines to small ones, a company that wants to be a market leader in computers simply has to be a strong force in PCs Until recently, such a calling was foreign to Hewlett-Packard While the company succeeded in other commodity-like businesses with low profit margins, dominating the printer market and doing well with calculators, it proved to be a self-defeating snob when it came to PCs

After all, the company built its computer business selling the best test measurement equipment—made by engineers for engineers—with high quality at a high price Not surprisingly, that elitist approach fell flat when the company ventured half-heartedly into the populist and price-sensitive PC market

"It was as if they thought PCs were a crummy business, where people kill each other for a nickel," said Doug Van Dorsten, an analyst with the brokerage firm Hambrecht & Quist "They noodled around at the $300 million to $400 million level for years, which for a company their size was just stupid "

Re-engineering had yet to enter the corporate vocabulary when Hewlett-Packard's executives recognized the errors of their ways and set out in the early 90's to reinvent their PC business The turnaround owed much to their willingness to examine and change nearly all their established practices

But as successful as the turnaround has been, it remains a work in progress Hewlett-Packard still lacks an entry in the fast-growing home computer market and is racing to make up for lost time in that segment

In retrospect, the company's earlier underperformance in PCs is hardly mysterious. Hewlett-Packard's personal computers were robust and reliable, but they were priced 25 percent higher than comparable models from IBM and Compaq Computer Corp —and at that time, those companies were losing market share to second-tier clone machines from vendors like Dell Computer Corp. and Gateway 2000 Inc that were priced 25 percent lower yet

Moreover, most of Hewlett-Packard's PC sales were through its direct sales force when the bulk of the industry was selling through stores and mail order

Today, of course, the architects of the turnaround at Hewlett-Packard are quick to concede their mistakes "The product had been wrongly positioned, in the wrong channels and at the wrong price points," said Richard C Watts, vice president and general manager of Hewlett-Packard's personal-information products group The PC "was a convenient terminal on which we could make a few more bucks—big mistake," he said "It took us a long time to figure out some fairly fundamental rules of the game "

Enumerating those rules was the easy part, said Mr Watts, who succeeded Robert J Frankenberg, now chief executive of Novell Inc., as head of the division last year Rule No 1, said Mr. Watts, was that prices had to come down Rule No 2 was that the company had to convince dealers that Hewlett-Packard was a serious contender And No 3, perhaps the hardest, was that the company had to find a way to differentiate its products from what was increasingly thought of as a commodity The difficulty, of course, lay in the execution

Many of the PCs that Hewlett-Packard sold before 1992 were purchased by companies that had adopted its large computer systems In those mini-computer and small mainframe-class machines, Hewlett-Packard was a technology leader Some loyal users of those machines might be persuaded to pay a premium for Hewlett-Packard's PCs, but they could hardly generate the sales necessary [for Hewlett-Packard] to be a leading participant in the PC business

Still, leaving its home turf for the rough and tumble of the broader PC market required a small rebellion within the company "I was under pressure from some H-P managers to go into highly differentiated niches, but when you do that, there is not much volume," said Jacques Clay, general manager of Hewlett-Packard's personal computer division, which is based in Grenoble, France "So the first thing I did was to take us back into the price-sensitive broader market "

Basing the desktop business in France reflected both Hewlett-Packard's historic strength in the European market and its belief that its growth would be increasingly global

The Information Campaign

When a company is hit by a disaster, the first duty of management, immediately after assessing the damage, is to give its personnel a full and accurate account of the situation Team spirit and morale of the company's staff are major assets and most of the employees in a high-technology company are intelligent people Therefore, the best approach is to tell them the truth and outline a realistic plan for recovery

---

CASE 11.4

The Digital Equipment Pledge: Whatever It Takes

Good morning Want to be here tomorrow? Here's a little something we learned Success is not the result of spontaneous combustion You must set yourself on fire

> If your competition does 50 push-ups, you do 51 If they go the extra mile, you go the extra 10 If they are fast, be faster If they are smart, be brilliant If they have the bigger hammer, you have the sharper nail
>
> Don't solve problems, anticipate them Don't promise results, get them Treat every challenge as an opportunity in work clothes Know that well done is better than well said That it is not just the hours you put in, but what you put into the hours
>
> Let others dream of worthy accomplishments That's okay You stay awake and do them Believe you can't be beat and you won't be beat; that there is plenty of room at the top But not enough to sit down ·

It's easy to put these words down on paper At Digital, we're putting them into practice Whatever it takes. Not fancy words Just real ones Mission-critical marching orders for everyone From our president to the person who turns the lights off very late at night

Today, Digital is working as never before to be the company you rely on to implement networked platforms and applications in heterogeneous environments

Today, we are working hard to do it quicker and more cost-effectively than anyone else. Simply put, today we are working to make ourselves indispensable to our customers And you will begin to see tangible examples of that effort every day at Digital

Whatever it takes does not mean that we will compete unfairly or bend the rules, that ethics and integrity will be sacrificed on the altar of profits It does mean that we will go to the nth degree to win your business. And keep your business It means we will play tough But fair

We intend to go as far as guts and talent and vision will take us And share the benefits with you along the way.

Source: Digital (1994, December 6) "Whatever it Takes " *International Herald Tribune*, p 5

In our case, the information campaign covered the entire company's personnel After having debated the situation in the company's management board and after having reached a consensus on the necessary action, the entire management staff of the company was invited to an enlarged management meeting At this meeting, we gave a full account of the direct and consequential damages the cancellation of the major project had caused the company We went into detail explaining how it affected us in the short term and what immediate actions were necessary We described possible scenarios for the mid- and long-term future of the company Ample time was devoted for questions, remarks, and suggestions We saw quickly that people were ready to suffer and make big sacrifices as long as they understood the necessity and sensed that the management had a plan and a policy with a fighting chance of success

Next, a series of meetings was organized with the entire company's personnel Within a week, in department after department, no employee was left without a chance to ask questions or express views directly to management, up to and including the managing director himself These meetings were an excellent opportunity to explain the emergency measures and mobilize as much support as possible for actions and unpopular procedures that in normal circumstances would have generated strong negative reactions I am strongly convinced that without the personal presence of the chief executive officer and the demonstrated commitment by all management levels to execute the recovery plan the program could not have been effectively applied and most probably would have failed

Establishing Tight Cash-Flow Control

Many good companies have gone bankrupt because of cash insolvency In our case, the threat was more mid term The company had sufficient cash to face its immediate obligations, but the projected income lost from the canceled project was sure to hurt us badly and even jeopardize the company's financial position

We decided, therefore, to stop any activities requesting cash outlays unless this activity was absolutely necessary to generate short- and mid-term income. The only exceptions to this strict rule were a few cases of promises and commitments made to customers before the crisis In each case, we checked with customers to see how critical for them would be postponement of an activity that would bring us income only in the long term. In many cases, customers consented to delay these activities In other cases, we had to respect those the customer judged to be critical to maintain our reputation for being a reliable company

To help us decide whether an activity should be continued or stopped, we divided all activities into two general categories activities covered by firm orders of stable and reliable customers, and activities not having such a guaranteed source of income Activities of the first category were automatically authorized to continue Those of the second were examined in greater detail. Activities such as internally funded long-term research and development, capital investment, subcontracting, and purchasing of any parts and materials not necessary for projects in the first category were automatically stopped As usual, there were also activities that fell into the gray area between these two categories These were examined case by case

Because we had defined the criteria for stopping or continuing an activity, we avoided any discussions about the "importance" of the activities This allowed us to cool some highly emotional issues, typical in the high-technology environment where people strongly identify with their work and support the importance of their activities passionately To such people, we consistently explained that nobody doubted the importance of their work but that the real issue was securing the cash necessary for survival of the company It is here that we reaped the benefits of having involved all company personnel through the information campaign

A more difficult issue was what to do with personnel whose activities were to be stopped Clearly, if one does not or cannot dismiss these people and they continue to be on the payroll, just stopping their activities is no solution We examine this matter later in the chapter.

Parallel with these measures, we gave instructions to accelerate the collection of all accounts receivable by the company and arrange, to the extent possible, longer terms of payments with vendors and suppliers Our company had an excellent credit record from long years of dealing with banks and financial institutions, so we did not have special problems keeping our credit lines open However, a blow like the one we had to absorb can make banks and creditors quite nervous Therefore, we extended our information campaign to include meetings with managers of such institutions It is always better to explain the situation and describe the recovery plan in person than risk having rumors proliferate and damage the company's image

Aggressive Marketing Campaign

We could stop the "bleeding" of cash from the company, but this did not replace the projected income lost from the interrupted project Therefore, we urgently needed to substitute new orders for the lost workload We had prepared, well in advance, some contingency planning in case this specific project was canceled Now we had to launch an aggressive campaign to market these alternative projects to potential customers worldwide To this end, we mobilized the best marketing and the technical people available in the company. Good and competent people who had been working on projects and activities that were no longer funded by a customer were also attached to the marketing teams They helped fortify the effort and accelerate the preparation of brochures, surveys of potential customers, preparation of proposals, and other tasks

In addition to the main drive to promote substitute projects necessary for the long-term prosperity of the company, a parallel marketing effort was organized This was to sell the idle capacity in the manufacturing departments and in some of the laboratories created by the cancellation of the major project Even with all the restructuring of personnel, we would still have a large number of employees idle or working on tasks not fully funded by a customer As long as we retained these employees on the company payroll, we had a strong interest in accepting short-term orders from customers to put this underused capacity to work at almost any price Even if an order for short-term work covered only a fraction of the accounting cost of such employees, it was better to accept the order than to absorb the full cost of unused personnel and facilities This policy initially was not accepted without resistance by some people in our accounting department, but after evaluation of the alternatives, everybody became convinced that it was the logical course to take We sent some of our professionals, temporarily idle, to potential customers with instructions to bring more work at the best price they could obtain All these activities required the investment of substantial monetary and human resources, but the marketing campaign received priority for the funding needed

Restructuring Personnel

One of the most painful tasks management must face in times of crisis is dismissing some of the good employees who for many years faithfully served the company and contributed to its success. This method for cutting expenses should be used only as a last resort If, and only if, the long-term survival of the company—hence the securing of continuous employment for the majority of the company's staff—justifies such measures, then management has the moral right and duty to resort to cutting personnel If such measures are taken just for the sake of improving the year's balance sheet or as the only remedy for an accumulation of problems, the management risks becoming discredited in the eyes of its own employees It risks destroying the morale, the team spirit, and everything else that makes a high-technology company good and viable in the long term

One of the important issues management must consider before deciding to cut personnel is the nature of the work shortage. If the drop in market demand for certain types of skill is long term or permanent, there are only two possible ways to handle the situation In the first case, the company can train and transfer employees from an expertise no longer needed to disciplines for which there is a present or future demand In the second case, the company must release such personnel As difficult and painful as this decision might be, there is clearly no way a company can continue to employ people with skills for which there are no longer customers In this instance, the duty of the management is to dismiss these people, making every effort to compensate them by arranging for early retirement or other appropriate remuneration as applicable

In our case, the sharp drop of workload resulting from the cancellation of our central project did not come as a total surprise Therefore, to prepare for the possibility of such a blow, we purposely stopped hiring people more than a year before the event As a result, a significant shortage of personnel developed in the company, and almost every other project, except for the central project, became understaffed It was not easy to resist the pressure of the affected project managers who tried to get more people, but we realized that we might need to fire hundreds of people if the biggest project in the company was interrupted As it turned out, the first step of restructuring was relatively easy The moment the project was canceled, we were able to transfer some of the best people to projects desperately hungry for additional staff

The next relatively easy step was to assign people to tasks we would have otherwise subcontracted By stopping subcontracting to outside vendors, we were able to absorb about 10 percent of the people previously dedicated to the lost customer and employ them on tasks for which we otherwise would have paid subcontractors We did so even though accounting showed us that in most cases the cost of doing the work in the company was significantly higher than the cost of subcontracting Here again, reason prevailed Because we had decided to retain the people concerned on our payroll, doing the work in house was much cheaper than spending additional money for outside contractors This action helped offset their salaries, but more important, precluded demoralizing idleness for them in the short term

Not only did we move people from the canceled program to other projects but, according to the criteria described above, we sought to reassign every person in the company who was performing a task or an activity not attributable to a paying customer.

The most difficult part of the restructuring began only after we had used all our internal flexibility After moving people from projects and tasks with no customer to activities that could generate income, we still found ourselves with a couple of hundred people who could not be reassigned to work funded by some customer These employees were divided roughly into three categories

1. High-quality, experienced people whose skills would be difficult to replace at the moment contracts for new projects were signed
2. People with skills that might be needed again as the workload increased, but who we could eventually hire when needed and quickly train to reach the level of experience necessary
3. People with skills unlikely to contribute to any future business the company hoped to win

The first category—highly qualified and experienced employees—we decided to keep at almost any cost Losing such people would have been a long-term penalty to the company This, coupled with the danger that such people would join the competition, could have caused irreparable damage to the company Therefore, we assigned as many of these people as we could to the marketing effort described above. Then we reviewed the internal research and development effort, stopped as part of the emergency measures This time we took into account both the future market needs and the skills of the highly qualified people whom we wanted to employ meaningfully As a result, a new or rather modified internal research and development (IRD) program was established

From the second category, the best 10 percent of truly talented people were assigned to company-funded activities We had the unpleasant duty of releasing all the remaining employees of this category and the entire group in the third category. Even so, we tried to help as much as we could For the employees approaching the right age, we arranged for early retirement, for the others, we helped them find alternative employment outside the company Throughout my professional career, looking into the eyes of people who had to be dismissed was the worst of all experiences I can remember. The only reward was to see the company emerge after a year or so of intensive fighting for survival—healthy, restored, and vigorous again

THE TEN COMMANDMENTS

This section summarizes the management principles that in my experience have played the most important and decisive role in the successful management of high technology Although these ten rules are certainly not divine laws, all my professional experience strongly supports their strict application Readers are free to gamble and breach these commandments at their own risk The ten commandments for a competent high-technology manager are these.

1. Strive for total company excellence
2. Keep people highly motivated
3. Cherish your people and your customers
4. Respect your innovators so that your company's days may be long
5. Risk, but do not gamble
6. Trim your company regularly
7. Don't build yourself monuments
8. Build your company's competitive muscle
9. Foresee and prevent rather than solve problems
10. Be tough but fair in competing

Throughout the book, application of these principles was included in the context of each chapter Here, however, we review the principles from a more general perspective. References to the material in the chapters will be made wherever appropriate

Strive for Total Company Excellence

While discussing the management competence factor (see chapter 2), we explained that a person cannot expect to perform successfully as a high-technology manager without setting high and ambitious standards of achievement for all the activities of the company This includes choosing the best people and the best equipment for every job Obviously, this means the best engineers and scientists, but it also means the best marketers, best working environment, most modern tools, and so on

In chapter 5, we discussed the importance and contribution that the total quality management (TQM) approach brings in building the success of the high-technology company Total quality management is another manifestation of the vital drive for excellence, for constant and continuous improvement of quality.

Our first commandment calls for an undivided, straight to the top drive to achieve and beat the state of the art in all aspects of the company's activities With the approach of the millennium, we see a market that is increasingly global The world will continue to become smaller and more competitive Unless the management strives to keep a company world class in every respect, surviving, let alone prospering will be more and more difficult For more details and concrete steps of how to achieve or at least approach the desired degree of excellence, refer to the cross-referenced chapters and the corresponding references and further readings

Keep People Highly Motivated

Motivation is the most powerful force behind any individual or group achievement Highly motivated people can overcome the most dreadful obstacles and prevail against forces many times stronger than they are Motivating people is one of the first duties of any manager In chapter 3, we examined some practical approaches for achieving a high level of motivation in the company We stressed the motivation of young researchers, researchers in their mid-careers, and senior researchers

Motivation played an important role in our discussion of the relative advantages and disadvantages of different organizational structures (see chapter 5) In chapter 5, we discussed the role of performance evaluation criteria for generating the right motivations in individuals and organizations

Here, we emphasize again the importance of measuring performance People who know exactly how their performance is going to be measured and evaluated are strongly motivated to achieve at least the level of performance they are expected to reach This is the secret of the management by objectives (MBO) technique We outline briefly the essence of this technique, as it yields truly positive results and was not described in the previous chapters

Management by objectives consists of defining the personal objectives of every manager in the organization The best approach is to ask all managers to write a list of personal objectives which, if achieved, will make them proud of their achievements

The list should contain no more than 10 clearly and, if possible, quantitatively defined objectives. Then, each manager and his or her superior discuss the objectives As a result, the list may be modified to reflect the agreement between the manager and the superior After agreement that the list contains indeed the most significant goals and contributions the manager can make to promote success of the company, a schedule to make periodic progress reviews is established These periodic reviews are usually scheduled twice a year in advance Unlike the goal-setting meeting between each manager and his or her boss, which is usually held privately, the reviews have a stronger motivating effect if they are conducted in a larger forum—the president with all the vice presidents, each vice president with his or her group's managers, and so on

Management by objectives can help a company achieve much better coordination of expectations for each of the organization's key players It is an excellent technique by which to channel the energy of all managers in the direction that makes a real contribution to the company's objectives

Cherish Your People and Your Customers

The two major assets a high-technology company has are its people and its customers Nothing has a stronger impact on the success of the company than the morale of its employees and the satisfaction of its customers with the company's products.

To develop and keep a high esprit de corps among employees, company management has to have genuine concern for the well-being of all its people In chapter 2, we discussed the role and the importance of team spirit and suggested how a competent manager should proceed to develop this bond among employees In chapter 3, we looked at the impact of high management involvement on morale of the key personnel of a high-technology company

To promote and keep a high level of customer satisfaction for its products and services, a high-technology company, in addition to offering high-quality products, must make a consistent and continuous effort to build and maintain a first-class reputation In chapter 3, we described the "listen-to-the-customer" method as a way to develop and offer to the market certain products that answer local customers' needs In chapter 7, we debated the issue of establishing an image and reputation Then, in chapter 8, we devoted a paragraph to serving the customer's needs best Finally, most of chapter 10 was dedicated to providing strong product support and after-sales service

A competent manager should always remember that a customer is someone who has voted, or is about to vote, confidence in the company's products The customer should never be disappointed

Respect Your Innovators That Your Company's Days May Be Long

One of the serious dangers a high-technology company faces is the gradual extinction of the innovative spirit that characterized its beginning as a start-up and that often helped create the company's reputation A high-technology company without innovative products is virtually doomed to decay and eventually to disappear In chapter 3, we explained the paradoxical need to stimulate innovation in a company whose major business is innovation The factors working against encouraging inventors and innovators were explained

Further in chapter 3, a detailed discussion on creating a culture of innovation and entrepreneurship in a mature high-technology company was provided Seven of the most successfully applied methods were illustrated with examples In chapter 5, we discussed the continuous innovation process adopted by a number of high-technology companies, following the successful application of this method in Japanese industry

The positive attitude toward inventors and innovators in a high-technology company must come from the highest level of management, through the channels, and down to every employee. Not all innovative initiatives are truly fruitful Separating those that are worth implementing from those that are not requires management attention and time However, the investment of effort in keeping the innovative spirit in the company is well worthwhile

Risk but Do Not Gamble

Nothing great is ever achieved in high technology without certain risks Risk-aversive people should stay away from managing high-technology companies, but high technology is no place for gamblers, either One of the duties of a competent high-technology manager is to inquire, get information, analyze, and reduce the amount of uncertainty that naturally exists when one deals with innovation In chapter 2, we dealt with the problems created by the innovation uncertainty factor We distinguished between market uncertainties, technological uncertainties, and supply uncertainties, and discussed methods to reduce each one

In finding ways to minimize the research and development cycle, we devoted special attention to methods for reducing uncertainties and innovation risks in R&D organizations (see chapter 4) Then, in chapter 7, we concentrated on another risk-reduction activity that has often decided the outcome of a high-technology competition: namely, the intelligence collecting activity Legal methods for collecting intelligence data and ways to evaluate analyses and to act on the results were described and illustrated with examples

The difference between a risk-accepting person and a gambler is tremendous The first makes great effort to evaluate, quantify, and reduce risk so that in the long run, the benefits of accepting the risks largely compensate for the relatively few events that go against the risk taker Even the most competent manager is bound to fail from time to time when taking a risk If, however, in the large majority of cases, this person's assessments are right, the rewards will allow the company to continue taking calculated risks

The gambler, on the other hand, has unwavering faith in his own judgment Thus, he is ready to take uncalculated risks Unlike the risk-accepting person who will never take a risk that could ruin the entire company, the gambler is ready to play "Russian Roulette" with the company's fate These people can be extremely dangerous as managers of high-technology companies because they frequently need to make balanced decisions in an environment rich in uncertainties, and by nature, they prefer to rush headlong into commitments without assessing them

Trim Your Company Regularly

Even the fairest garden, planted on the most fertile soil and enjoying the loving care of its owner, needs periodic trimming and pruning to avoid decline and degeneration So does a high-technology company if it wants to stay on top of technology, keep its competitive edge, and enjoy a world-class reputation

Trimming the company is a difficult but necessary task of the successful high-technology manager It is a most important task It encompasses a large variety of activities in many sectors of the company's life. Any sector, left to itself, tends to grow beyond control, get fat and thick, and clog the efficient flow of work and information If allowed, it will block the company's ability to respond quickly and effectively to changing needs of the dynamic high-technology business

Trimming begins at the top. Top management should avoid letting its staff functions grow beyond what is absolutely necessary to ensure a reasonable level of control and coordination of the operating units It should function without interfering in everyday decisions made by these units A small staff of high-level professionals who are respected by the managers of the operating units and who can guide and advise them can add great value to the company. A lean and professional staff will always contribute more than a large group of clerks and bureaucrats busily trying to prove their indispensability

Trimming should continue through all levels of the organization Factors that encourage development of overstaffed departments are temporary workloads that necessitate hiring new personnel, perpetuation of existing situations by inertia, and resistance of managers to reduce the number of people reporting to them for fear of losing status and importance in the organization Paradoxically, when a section is overstaffed, work flows more slowly through it People feel uncomfortable if, for lack of work, they need to stay idle. Therefore, work that could be done in a few days tends to linger for weeks in such departments

A good rule of thumb is to maintain a significant (120 percent to 150 percent) overload of work in every department. An old saying attributed to Napoleon—"If you want something done quickly and efficiently, give it to the busiest person"—holds well in industrial organizations Many jobs in the high-technology industry require a specialist to be done correctly. Hence, the company must keep on its payroll a minimum number of such specialists. These people can handle a large number of similar tasks simultaneously when the workload is high If the workload drops, they tend to devote an unnecessarily long time to performing a simple task As many experienced high-technology managers have noted, a high-technology company makes substantial profit when the workload is significantly higher than the presumed company capacity, whereas the company becomes nonprofitable if the workload just reaches or falls below capacity.

Trimming excess manpower is just one aspect of the overall trimming effort needed A competent manager should periodically cut expenses in almost every field of company activities To illustrate, most high-technology companies order a large variety of scientific, business, and other publications and periodicals Spending on such publications is not the heaviest burden for the company, and some of these publications are indeed indispensable for keeping the scientific and commercial staff up to date Yet, as time passes, the company goes on paying for material that is obsolete or not as important as when originally ordered. It helps, therefore, to cut perhaps 50 percent of the budget allocated to such literature and see what happens Usually, the people who really need their publications will strongly protest and defend their case Many others won't even notice the change The management should, of course, consent to satisfy the demands of the first group and increase the allocation as necessary In the process, however, all the unnecessary periodicals will be pruned out This action will also set a good example for the company, showing that nothing is sacred when it comes to savings, not even professional literature

The same principle of cutting expenses "until it hurts" can both refresh the organization and save significant resources in all aspects of the company's activities It is easier to correct an excessive cut by listening to the protests that follow it than to search out all those unnecessary expenses that accumulate and that nobody complains about Trimming the company keeps it lean, clean, dynamic, and better prepared to fight in the competitive business of high technology

Don't Build Yourself Monuments

One of the leading indicators of decay and decadence in an apparently successful company is the investment made by the company in luxury buildings, opulent company headquarters, lavish company cars, and other extravagance All such sumptuous investments do little or nothing to help the company invent better products, stay ahead of the curve in technology, or compete better in the marketplace

A good manager can distinguish between investments made in luxury and investments made to provide a modern, neat, and attractive work environment for all employees of the company. A high-tech company that strives to get the best people for every job must give them the quality of work environment they deserve without indulging in any excessive luxury One key is whether the motivation to make an improvement is to enhance the working environment or to make a display of status

The problem with luxury in a high-technology company is not limited to the direct, unnecessary expenses it requires The bigger problem is the bad example a luxury-seeking manager can set for the entire company staff Soon, people start paying more attention to status symbols than to real achievement Some of the most important motivating forces start working in the wrong direction Therefore, the more successful a company is, the more its management should avoid the temptation to start monument building

Build Your Company's Competitive Muscle

Building competitive muscle has been discussed in many sections of this book It is a duty of the high-technology manager equally as important as discouraging monument building In chapter 2, we emphasized the need to invest in the best available process technology so that good people with good processing tools can compete on an equal basis with anyone in any other company

Periodically, the company's staff need to be trained, sent to refresher courses, and educated in subjects important to company success High-tech companies paying special attention to this subject may require every manager to complete a relevant cycle of courses as part of a well-established career development program. Courses ranging from review of technologies to the art of negotiating techniques are sometime prerequisites for promotion to a position with higher responsibility

In chapter 4, we saw the need to invest in simulation and modeling tools and techniques to shorten the research and development cycle. In chapter 5, we showed how investments made in computer-aided design and manufacturing (CAD-CAM) can smooth the transition from research and development to production In the same chapter, we noted how managers can make best use of the optimized production technology (OPT) and just-in-time (JIT) methods, which have proven themselves in the mass production lines as well as in the research and development environment of a high-technology company The importance of opening the company's bottlenecks was shown through an examination of theory and some illustrative examples.

In chapter 6, we explained the need to invest in information systems that help reduce the queuing penalty in a multiproduct high-technology company. Finally, in chapters 7 and 8, we looked at building a strong marketing organization, capable of providing adequate real-time intelligence and global representation In chapter 9, we discussed the issue of investing in acquisitions. Finally, in chapter 10 we explained the benefits of a strong product support

All these investments contribute significantly to the company's competitive advantage in the high-technology market They are priority investments that are the best guarantees for the continuous success of the company

Foresee and Prevent Rather Than Solve Problems

The old saying is right. "An ounce of prevention is worth a pound of cure " Despite the wide acceptance of the wisdom expressed in this proverb, many high-technology managers devote most of their time to fire fighting Once fire breaks out in the company, it naturally becomes the number one priority and managers are then expected to dedicate all their time and attention to solving the urgent problems that have ignited the blaze. Although there is no practical way to avoid all emergencies arising in a fast-moving company, experience shows that a great many of them could have been avoided through foresight Often there are steps an alert manager can take to defuse the problems ahead of time

The big advantage of preventing problems is the gain in management time As a rule, preventing a problem takes only a fraction of the time a manager must spend solving a full-blown problem Most emergencies result from not taking appropriate management action in time, or, again quoting Napoleon, "There is nothing urgent; there are only people who are late " A competent manager should consciously devote time to anticipating problems and take the necessary action before a problem grows to dimensions requiring much more effort to be solved

In chapter 4, we described, as an example, the action taken by my company to recover from a crisis resulting from the cancellation of a major project We also mentioned that long before the cancellation, we took a number of steps in anticipation of the possibility of such an event Without these steps, our recovery would have been many times more difficult, and perhaps not possible at all

Be Tough but Fair in Competing

Throughout this text we have emphasized the competitive character of the business environment typical of high technology Consequently, we devoted ample attention to how to "brush," "comb," and prepare the company to be successful in such competitions Two entire chapters were dedicated to methods and techniques (chapters 7 and 8) that can help a company prevail in local and global competitions

In high-technology competitions, the company must play tough and play smart, but stay fair and honest Even in real war, a civilized combat force must maintain a high level of moral behavior if its goal is to achieve a long-lasting victory In business, a company must be honest with customers, care for the interests of partners, and be respectful toward competitors

In chapter 8, we noted the growing need for industrial cooperation and for joint ventures between companies that may often compete and cooperate at the same time The only way such cooperation can last and bring the expected long-term benefits is for the partners to treat each other's interests as their own A frequent mistake is for one partner to take advantage of a temporary weakness of the other partner This is certain to ruin the spirit of mutual trust and cooperation and eventually to break the joint venture A competent management, interested in the long-term success of its business, should know how to discern and abort such initiatives taken by its staff, as tempting as the circumstances might be Partners should be faithful to each other and honor their obligation, not only to the letter but, most important and in all circumstances, to the spirit of the agreement

An equally important behavioral rule is that a company must respect its competitors Never should a manager use, or allow his colleagues to use, defamation and slander Time after time, I have witnessed such methods being used by competitors In most if not in all such cases after some initial successes, these tactics failed miserably We were able to gain points by playing fair In this respect, the spirit of the biblical rule applied to our case would mean "Never do to your competitor what you would not have done to you "

Holding to high moral values in business without being naïve is the best policy for any high-tech manager Such an attitude makes his company a reliable supplier, a faithful partner, and, therefore, a good company with which to do business

---

SUMMARY

Most of the subjects treated in this book dealt with various management issues that distinguish the high-technology company from any other business Understanding and mastering these issues is an important prerequisite for successful management of high technology. In this chapter, the emphasis was on how to keep a good high-technology company competitive and ensure its continuous success

First, we examined the internal reasons that most frequently cause a good high-technology company to decline Then, we explored some of the usual external threats that may adversely affect the prosperity, if not jeopardize the future, of a high-tech company Many high-technology companies were not able to recover after suffering from some of these problems. Those that fought back successfully and were able to restructure and adapt their business to the changing environment have shown the way Their example was outlined as a positive lesson for high-technology managers facing similar situations.

Finally, we endeavored to extract the essence of the rules of high-technology management We condensed them into the Ten Commandments given in the last section of this chapter These rules are not meant to replace the in-depth study of the high-technology enterprise, but they put in a nutshell most of the important lessons learned in 25 years of applied high-technology management, lessons reflected throughout this book

For Further Reflection

1 Explain the mechanism that "sows the seeds of decline" in a successful high-technology company Illustrate by examples from your professional experience or from cases described and discussed in the literature

2 What can be done by the management of a high-technology company to minimize the impact of external factors that can jeopardize the future or the existence of the company? Give some typical examples.

3 List and discuss the most important methods used by high-technology companies to recover successfully from critical downturns and dangerous business crisis situations

4 Discuss each of the "Ten Commandments" for the successful high-technology manager Give examples from your personal experience that support or contradict the behavior recommended by these "commandments."

References and Further Reading

Afuah, Allan N , and James M Utterback (1995) "Dynamic Competitive Strategies: A Technological Evolution Perspective," Working Paper 137 Cambridge, MA: Sloan School of Management
> This paper stresses the importance of establishing a dynamic process of product innovation in high-technology companies The authors assert that as technology evolves, so do industry characteristics and critical success factors Technological evolution influences the kinds of products (niche, differentiated, or low cost) offered over time Firms that do not have the capabilities to offer appropriate products may be forced to exit They propose a dynamic model based on a technological evolution perspective that suggests a link between the product-market position and the resource-based views of competitive advantage

Ashkenis, Ron, Dave Ulrich, Todd Jick, and Steve Kerr (1995) *The Boundaryless Organization* San Francisco: Jossey-Bass
> These authors were part of the brain trust that helped dissolve boundaries at General Electric They offer ideas for loosening boundaries vertically (between hierarchical levels), horizontally (between departments), externally (between companies), and geographically (between companies and those in far-flung divisions) A groundbreaker theoretically, the book offers a multitude of practical ideas

Carr, D K , and Henry J Johansson (1995). *Best Practices in Reengineering* New York: McGraw-Hill
> At the beginning of the 1990s, many company executives were exploring the advantages of reengineering their operations In this book the authors balance the picture and warn that many managers who expected big gains from reengineering projects have been disappointed Carr and Johansson, of Coopers & Lybrand Consulting, studied companies to see what worked and what didn't The book covers the sixteen "best practices" in detail—including the all-important answer to the question: What process should we reengineer?

Collins, J C , and Jerry I. Porras (1995) *Built to Last* New York: HarperBusiness
  Most companies don't last more than a few decades This book dissects those that have—
  like General Electric, 3M, Ford, Motorola, and Merck—to reveal the secrets of their
  longevity This book makes a good complementary reading on the material exposed in this
  chapter

Dawling, W F , and L R Sayles (1978) *How Managers Motivate* 2nd ed. New York:
  McGraw-Hill

Fisher, Lawrence M (1995, January 15) *International Herald Tribune*, p 13

Frankel, Ernst (1993) *In Pursuit of Technological Excellence. Engineering Leadership,
  Technological Change and Economic Development* New York: Praeger

Grove, A S (1983) *High Output Management.* New York: Random House

Hammer, Michael (1993) *Reengineering the Corporation A Manifesto for Business Revolution* New York: HarperBusiness

Lawer, E E (1986) *High Involvement Management* San Francisco: Jossey-Bass

Markides, Constantinos C (1996) *Diversification, Refocusing, and Economic Performance*
  Cambridge, MA: MIT Press
  This book examines the results of various diversification strategies Starting immediately
  after World War II, many companies diversified widely, primarily in areas unrelated to
  their core businesses In the 1980s, however, as corporate acquisitions and hostile takeovers
  ran rampant, this trend toward diversification and conglomeration began to reverse The
  author claims that today there is ample evidence that corporate managers are responding
  in significant numbers to takeover threats by shedding unlucrative divisions and subsidiaries and concentrating on boosting the core product lines that have been their company's bread and butter

Mills, D Quinn, and G Bruce Friesen (1996) *Broken Promises An Unconventional View
  of What Went Wrong at IBM* Cambridge, MA: Harvard Business School Press
  In this book D Quinn Mills and G. Bruce Friesen analyze the last crisis that IBM went
  through The authors argue that what went wrong was that IBM went back on two unwrit-
  ten commitments it had made over the years to customers and employees: singleness and
  loyalty IBM had convinced customers that only IBM could supply all their computing
  needs by renting them the equipment and by providing on-site maintenance and support
  For employees, IBM offered lifelong job security The shift in IBM's policy from rental to
  sales in the early 1980s made it just another computer company competing on price As a
  consequence of the massive reorganization and layoffs that followed, the close link that employees had with their customers was damaged The authors claim that this link might have
  kept IBM better tuned into market changes.

O'Toole, James (1995) *Leading Change* San Francisco: Jossey-Bass
  James O'Toole asserts in his book that the only way to gain the commitment and loyalty of
  your staff is through leadership based on integrity, honesty, and respect That means letting
  your people participate in decisions and giving them freedom to achieve results their own
  way

Robert, Michel (1995) *Product Innovation Strategy* New York: McGraw-Hill.
  A consultant, Robert studied two kinds of companies: those that can bring new products to
  market successfully, and those that can't The results of this study can be found in his
  book—how to find ideas and opportunities, how to pick out ideas with the potential for success, how to analyze the risks of developing a product, and how to create a master plan for
  launching it If you fail to create new and innovative products, says Robert, your company
  will fade away

Strebel, Paul (1993) *Breakpoints. How Managers Exploit Radical Business Change* Cambridge, MA: Harvard Business School Press

> This book is a good complementary reading on the issues discussed in this chapter Concentrating on recovery from external problems, Paul Strebel claims that many excellent companies have fallen from grace, not because they ignored their customers or lacked superior management skills but because business conditions shifted beneath them The author examines factors that have brought companies close to breakpoints and shows that breakpoints may be as enterprising as Drexel Burnham Lambert's promotion of the junk bond market—or as dramatic as its collapse In an environment of fluctuating markets, proliferating technologies, and changing political frontiers, the management challenge is no longer to manage only growth Now managers must cope with breakpoints or sudden shifts in the rules of the game

Taucher, George (1994) "Avoiding the Rags-to-Riches Syndrome " *The International Herald Tribune,* December 15, pp. 14-16

Utterback, James M. (1994). *Mastering the Dynamics of Innovation How Companies Can Seize Opportunities in the Face of Technological Change* Cambridge, MA: Harvard Business School Press

> In his book, Utterback confirms and emphasizes the need to encourage innovation in order to remain competitive He asserts that existing organizations must consistently abandon past success and embrace innovation—even when it undermines their traditional strengths The book draws on the rich history of innovation by inventors and entrepreneurs—ranging from the birth of typewriters to the emergence of personal computers, gas lamps to fluorescent lighting, George Eastman's amateur photography to electronic imaging—to develop a practical model for how innovation enters an industry, how mainstream firms typically respond, and how, over time, new and old players wrestle for dominance He sets forth a strategy to do so and identifies the responsibilities of managers to lead and focus that effort

Wright, P , Mark J Kroll, and John Parnell (1995) *Strategic Management Concepts and Cases* Upper Saddle River, NJ: Prentice Hall

> This publication is a good source of case studies applicable to the subjects treated in this text Among others, there are cases dealing with external environmental opportunities and threats, the internal environment: the firm's resources, organizational mission, and goals, and others

CHAPTER

A Case Study

12

In an article published in *Business Week* on July 22, 1996, Gary McWilliams gives an interesting account of the business situation facing the CEO and management in a leading high-technology industry The case described is typical, therefore of particular interest for analysis and study

The reader is invited to examine the text and its appendix carefully, answer the questions at the end of this section, and propose a well-structured alternative strategy for the management of Compaq

Compaq at the Crossroads *

It was a close one Faced with a sudden and totally unanticipated slow-down in sales, on Mar 1, Compaq Computer Corp. Chief Executive Eckhard Pfeiffer was forced to warn analysts that the computer maker was unlikely to hit expected revenue and earnings for the quarter ending Mar 31 The news sent Compaq's stock plummeting 18%, to 41%, in one day After the announcement, Pfeiffer jumped into high gear He ordered incentives for dealers and cut prices 20% to lift demand It worked: Revenues for the March quarter jumped 42% The stock quickly recovered most of its loss

Pulling off such a save would be cause for celebration at most companies But inside the $14 8 billion PC giant, it was soul-searching time The cost of hitting Pfeiffer's growth target was a four-point drop in gross profit margin to 20 3%, its lowest ever and far short of the company's 23% to 24% goal That exposed a troubling truth For more

*Reprinted from July 22, 1996 issue of *Business Week* by special permission, copyright © 1996 by the Mc-Graw-Hill Companies, Inc

than two years, Compaq has been running twice as fast only to stay in place—shipments and revenue have been hitting new highs, making it the world's top PC maker But profits have barely budged.

It was time for a better formula. So on Apr 15, Compaq drafted 20 managers from around the world for what became known as the "Crossroads" meeting In a conference center at the company's Houston headquarters, Vice-President for Corporate Development Kenneth E Kurtzman assembled five teams to tear apart Compaq's businesses and assess each unit's strategy and that of key rivals Three weeks later the teams presented Pfeiffer with some sobering recommendations. Each business unit must be first or second in its market within three years—or Compaq should consider getting out of that line Also, the company should no longer use profits from high-margin businesses to carry marginally profitable ones—each unit must show a return on investment

FAST TRACK

Fine But Pfeiffer had his own requirement that would make achieving these goals a bit more complicated whatever happened, he insisted that the company remain on the superfast growth track that he laid out three years ago Pfeiffer wants Compaq to keep growing at 20% to 25% a year so that in 2000 it will be a $40 billion behemoth and the No 3 computer maker in the world, just behind IBM and Fujitsu Ltd

Now, executives at Compaq have a new formula To hit Pfeiffer's top-line targets, the company will move aggressively into all sorts of new product areas that will make it a full-line information technology company capable of competing across the board with companies such as IBM and Hewlett-Packard Co On July 2, Pfeiffer announced a sweeping restructuring that created nine new divisions alongside the core desktop, laptop, and home-PC businesses The new units will focus on fast-growing areas such as Internet products and services, small business systems, and engineering workstations. Pfeiffer also elevated a fledgling $100 million networking equipment business to a full division

By year-end, Compaq will produce everything from computers for toddlers to mainframe-class servers able to run global financial networks. There will be powerful engineering work stations and lightning-quick network switches, too Meanwhile, the company is stepping up its role as a venture capitalist, investing in companies with promising new products and technologies that can help the divisions compete especially on the Internet

VIRTUALIZING

The second part of the formula for producing profits along with growth will involve wider use of outsourcing and partnership deals. That's because the new financial yardstick—return on assets—will force the divisions to slash investment in assets such as plant, inventory, and overhead wherever possible If the $3 billion home-PC business can cut its asset base, for instance, it can still deliver a 20% annual return to the company—even though price competition in home PCs will likely keep operating margins at around 2%

To get there, Compaq has already started "virtualizing" parts of its business After cutting $57 off the cost of each home PC last year by building the chassis at its plant in Shenzhen, China, the company went a step further in cutting the cost of business desktop PCs: Instead of investing millions to expand the Shenzhen plant, Gregory E Petsch, senior vice-president for operations, persuaded a Taiwanese supplier to build a new factory adjacent to Compaq's to build the mechanicals for the business models The best part of the deal· The Taiwanese supplier owns the inventory until it arrives at Compaq's door in Houston "This is the right way to do it," says Sanford C Bernstein & Co computer analyst Vadim D Zlotnikov

By 1999, Pfeiffer expects each division to achieve best-in-class return on assets PCs will have to better Gateway 2000 Inc 's 21% return on assets, the networking business must beat 3Com Corp 's 18% return, and workstations will have to top Sun Microsystems Inc 's 14% return

If the Crossroads plan is successful, Pfeiffer will have created the blueprint for the computer company of the next century: a giant with the nimbleness of a consumer-electronics maker and the all-encompassing service and support capabilities of big computer companies such as HP and IBM "We're at a turning point in our company's history," says Pfeiffer.

The new plan will also involve a new regime After living through the four-year growth sprint that took Compaq from $4 1 billion in sales in 1991 to $14 8 billion last year, Chief Financial Officer Daryl J White resigned on May 29, citing "burnout " A month later, Systems Div chief Gary Stimac, a key player in moving Compaq into its leading 40% share in PC servers, quit "It would take another multiyear commitment in time and energy," says Stimac "I had to evaluate my personal life " Meanwhile, industry reports have Senior Vice-President for North America Ross Cooley resigning by yearend Cooley, however, declined to comment

For a few years, Pfeiffer has been assembling a new team of operations-savvy executives The new CFO, Earl L Mason, worked at Inland Steel Industries Inc and Digital Equipment Corp Michael J Winkler, general manager of the PC Products Group, came to Compaq after a long career at Xerox and Toshiba America Information Systems. Consumer Group General Manager Michael D Heil worked at Los Angeles Cellular Telephone Co and Sony Corp of America Chief strategist Robert W Stearns joined from McKinsey & Co

BIG IRON

One of the biggest jobs falls to John T Rose, general manager of the enterprise computing group Rose, a former DEC executive who joined three years ago, is responsible for pushing Compaq into "big iron" territory With Intel Corp 's new Pentium Pro chip and Microsoft Corp 's industrial-strength Windows NT, Compaq figures it finally can build the servers and workstations that can take on even the biggest computing jobs The first such products are hitting the market now

Compaq, already the top supplier of PC servers used in smaller networks, sees itself as the standard-bearer for the low-priced "Wintel" (Intel-based computers using Microsoft Windows software) technology as it sweeps into the last bastion of the mainframe and minicomputer And some important customers agree While IBM and HP are also promising powerful new Pentium Pro-based machines, buyers question whether those companies will push the technology as aggressively as Compaq, since the new setups can compete with their older, more profitable proprietary machines

That's why Smith-Kline Beecham PLC chose Compaq over IBM and HP to supply the drugmaker's servers "The big difference with these guys is they're intent on pulling this off," says Lou Valente, vice-president for North American information resources "I don't see that intensity coming from other companies," he says

To compete in the big-iron business profitably, Compaq is counting on a series of relationships with other companies that can supply the kind of hand-holding that companies such as IBM are famous for Instead of investing in legions of field technicians and programmers—and building up costly assets—the computer maker will use the resources of systems integrator Andersen Consulting and software maker SAP, among others These companies have the personnel to install and maintain systems the way IBM or HP do So Compaq gets to play in the big-iron market without incurring the costs of running its own services or software businesses Using these partners, Compaq is already delivering packages of networks, servers, and services to big customers including General Motors, British Telecommunications, First Interstate Bancorp, and Deutsche Bundespost

Compaq, however, may not be able to play through their intermediaries forever "The real solution is to create your own capability It takes longer and is more painful but ultimately, it is more successful," says Graham Kemp, president of G2 Research Inc

Small and medium-size companies are also a key market for server technology To reach them, Compaq will rely on its existing network of resellers But it will give them new tools, including "blueprints" for installing and managing networks that can be applied in cookie-cutter fashion "Our goal is to create a Compaq standard" for network and systems tasks, says Cooley

KID STUFF

The powerful new Intel/Windows NT technology also provides Compaq with a chance to crack a small but lucrative new market: engineering workstations While only about 900,000 workstations will be sold this year vs. about 60 million PCs, profit margins are nearly twice as high. Sun, HP, Silicon Graphics, and others sold $13 3 billion worth of such machines last year and sales should expand at a 10% annual rate through the decade, says market researchers Dataquest/Gartner Group

Meanwhile, Pfeiffer continues to push into fast-growing consumer markets On July 15, the company will trot out an all-new line of home PCs. But the company has more than PCs in mind And, again, Pfeiffer is counting on alliances to cut costs and provide expertise that Compaq can't duplicate For example, the company is working with Mattel Inc 's Fisher-Price Inc to produce PC add-ons for small children And a deal with Thomson Consumer Electronics Inc is aimed at new hybrid computer/consumer-electronics products

Pfeiffer also sees other opportunities for PC technology in the home One of the biggest, he says, will be "home automation"—using computers to control air-conditioning, heating, and security systems Pfeiffer has already pumped funds into startup Intellon Corp., which is developing chips for controlling everything from stereos to refrigerators from a PC

The challenge in the consumer business, says Pfeiffer, is not finding new products and technologies to pursue but narrowing the focus to a manageable number Even a $15 billion giant such as Compaq could get distracted by taking on too much, he warns "We see lots of opportunity. This field is growing so fast, there is a major challenge in reallocating our resources," says Pfeiffer

One place he's not shy about placing resources, however, is in cyberspace Despite a late start in the Internet, Compaq is looking to pick up speed by developing relationships with Internet software and service companies On July 7, for example, it became the exclusive supplier of servers to Internet service company U S. Web Corp

Compaq also has been aggressively making investments in Internet start-ups It paid $6 million in January for 7% of Raptor Systems Inc , a developer of security software for the Internet Compaq is also a limited partner in Safeguard Scientifics' $40 million Internet Capital Group fund and in funds run by Kiciner Perkins Caufield & Byers, including one that backs startups using Sun's Java

STRUGGLE

Pfeiffer's No. 1 objective on the Net is to make Compaq servers synonymous with so-called intranets These networks use Internet technology within a corporation for things such as e-mail, employee communications, and electronic purchasing Since February, Compaq has shipped Netscape's Commerce Server and Microsoft's Internet Information Server programs with all its server computers. "Compaq is ahead of everyone else in that space right now," says Forrester Research Inc analyst Jon Oltsik

The explosive growth of the Net will create unprecedented demand for servers and, perhaps, unprecedented competition Compaq started early in PC servers and holds a commanding 40% market share, which has translated into healthy profit margins Now, companies such as Dell Computer Corp are hoping to make this a high-volume, commodity business—similar to desktop PCs "Compaq is definitely going to lose some share," says HP Marketing Manager James P McDonnell "The question is how fast and how much "

Indeed, Wall Street worries that price pressure and market-share erosion in servers could hurt Compaq's earnings Its stock has been trading recently at around $46—well below its 52-week high of $56 75 On July 17, analysts expect Compaq to report earnings for the June quarter about flat with last year's $246 million

Between the new competitive challenges and the new growth/profit formula, Pfeiffer certainly has taken on a huge job But the 33-year computer-industry veteran is known for his tenacity Once a goal has been set, he's not likely to fall short. Says Mentor Graphics Corp Chief Executive Walden C Rhines, a former colleague of Pfeiffer's at Texas Instruments Inc : "I never ever saw Eckhard miss a forecast He'd sell the electricity out of the building before he'd miss a forecast " Pfeiffer will need all the juice in Houston to power Compaq through this next growth spurt

For Further Reflection

1. Was Compaq ready for the slowdown in sales during the first quarter of 1996? Is such an event totally unexpected? In your opinion, what should a company like Compaq do to absorb the impact of such events with minimum damage to the company?

2. The article says, "After the announcement, Pfeiffer jumped into high gear " Why, in your opinion, did the CEO of Compaq not do so earlier? Comment on Mr Pfeiffer's goal-setting approach

3 From the facts and data presented, give your opinion on the management style of Mr Pfeiffer, as reflected in the article. What aspects of this style do you like and approve, and what are attitudes that you would criticize?

4 Comment on the method and the approach taken by the management of Compaq in establishing the new strategy for the company What do you find appropriate, what is lacking, and what would you modify?

5 What are the major points in the "new formula" proposed by the executives at Compaq? In your view, are they adequately addressing the major problem that caused the announcement made by Mr Pfeiffer on March 1, 1996?

6 From the published material, and from your personal knowledge, make a comparative analysis of the major strengths and weaknesses of Compaq versus its competitors How does the new strategy propose to address the drawbacks of the company, and how does it strengthen its advantages?

7 In Mr Pfeiffer's words. "The challenge in the consumer business is not finding new products and technologies to pursue but narrowing the focus to a manageable number " Referring to McWilliams's article, does Compaq's policy support this point of view?

8 Assuming that you were assigned the task of consulting with Compaq on their efforts to prepare the company for the challenges of the twenty-first century, prepare a comprehensive proposal, addressing all important issues, including the following

a Innovation. How should the company prepare a competitive edge using innovation as a marketing weapon?

b Reengineering· How should the company be reengineered to increase profitability, reduce cost, and shorten cycle times?

c Market Strategy Propose a market strategy based on your own analysis of the strengths and weaknesses of the company

d Product Support Should the company use external resources, as mentioned in the article, or create its own capability, as suggested by the president of G2 Research Inc ?

e Mergers and Acquisitions Should the company make more aggressive moves in this area to gain time and capture strategic positions?

f Contingency Planning How should the company prepare for negative developments? Enumerate the most probable/dangerous ones.

APPENDIX 12A

Excerpts from Compaq's 1996 Annual Report

Following is a selection of data extracted from Compaq's 1996 annual report The sole purpose for providing this data is to add to the discussion of the case study on Compaq Efforts were made to ensure the exactness of the information provided, but given that the excerpts lack the completeness of the original report, the data should not be used for any purpose other than the one stated above

REPORT OF MANAGEMENT

Responsibility for the integrity and objectivity of the financial information presented in this Annual Report rests with Compaq management The accompanying financial statements have been prepared in conformity with generally accepted accounting principles, applying certain estimates and judgments as required

Compaq maintains an effective internal control structure It consists, in part, of organizational arrangements with clearly defined lines of responsibility and delegation of authority, with comprehensive systems and control procedures. We believe this structure provides reasonable assurance that transactions are executed in accordance

Four-Year Financial Summary (Year end December 31, in millions)

	1996	*1995*	*1994*	*1993*
Sales	18,109	14,755	10,866	7,191
Cost of Sales	13,913	11,367	8,139	5,493
	4,196	*3,388*	*2,727*	*1,698*
Selling and G&A expenses	1,912	1,594	1,235	837
R&D Cost	407	270	226	169
Purchased In-process technology[1]		241		
Other Income and expense, net	1	95	94	76
	2,320	*2,200*	*1,555*	*1,082*
Income before provision for income taxes	1,876	1,188	1,172	616
Provision for income taxes[2]	563	399	305	154
Net Income	*$1,313*	*$789*	*$867*	*$462*
Earnings per share[3]	$4 66	$2 87	$3 21	$1 78
FINANCIAL POSITION				
Current assets	9,169	6,527	5,158	3,291
Total assets	10,526	7,818	6,166	4,084
Current liabilities	3,852	2,680	2,013	1,244
Long-term debt	300	300	300	73
Stockholders' equity	6,114	4,614	3,674	2,654
OTHER INFORMATION				
Income before taxes as a % of Sales	10 4	9 7	10 8	8 6
Effective tax rate[2]	30	28	26	25
Net income as a percentage of sales	7 2	7	8	6 4
Net income as a % of average total assets	14 3	14 7	16 9	12 8
Net income as a % of average stockholders' equity	24 4	24 9	27 4	19 8
Current ratio	2 4	2 4	2 6	2 6
Working capital	5,317	3,847	3,145	2,047
Number of employees	18,863	17,055	14,372	10,541

[1] Represents a $241 million ($ 87 per share) non-recurring, non-tax deductible charge for purchased in-process technology in connection with acquisitions in 1995

[2] The Company's effective tax rate in 1996, 1995, 1994 and 1993 reflects the Company's decision to reinvest indefinitely a portion of the undistributed earnings of its Singapore manufacturing subsidiary

[3] All share and per share data have been adjusted to reflect the company's three-for-one and two-for-one stock splits in 1994 and 1990, respectively

with management authorization and generally accepted accounting principles. An important element of the control environment is an ongoing internal audit program

To assure the effective administration of internal control, we carefully select and train our employees, develop and disseminate written policies and procedures, provide appropriate communication channels and foster an environment conducive to the effective functioning of controls We believe that it is essential for Compaq to conduct its business affairs in accordance with the highest ethical standards, as set forth in Compaq's Codes of Conduct These guidelines, translated into numerous languages, are distributed to employees throughout the world, and reemphasized through internal programs to assure that they are understood and followed.

Price Waterhouse LLP, independent accountants, is retained to audit Compaq's financial statements Its accompanying report is based on an audit conducted in accordance with generally accepted auditing standards, including a review of the internal control structure and tests of accounting procedures and records

The Audit Committee of the Board of Directors is composed solely of outside directors and is responsible for recommending to the Board the independent accounting firm to be retained for the coming year. The Audit Committee meets periodically and privately with the independent accountants, with our internal auditors, as well as with Compaq management, to review accounting, auditing, internal control structure and financial reporting matters

MANAGEMENT'S DISCUSSION AND ANALYSIS OF FINANCIAL CONDITION AND RESULTS OF OPERATIONS

The following discussion should be read in conjunction with the consolidated financial statements

Results of Operations

The following table presents, as a percentage of sales, selected consolidated financial data for each of the three years in the period ended December 31

	1996	*1995*	*1994*
Sales	100 0%	100 0%	100 0%
Cost of sales	76 8	77 0	74 9
Gross margin	23 2	23 0	25 1
Selling, general and administrative expense	10.6	10 8	11 4
Research and development costs	2 2	1.8	2 1
Purchased in-process technology[1]		1.6	
Other income and expense, net		0 7	0 8
	12 8	14 9	14 3
Income before provision for income taxes	10 4%	8 1%	10 8%

[1] Represents impact of a $241 million ($.87 per share) non-recurring, non-tax deductible charge for purchased in-process technology in connection with acquisitions in 1995

Sales

Sales for 1996 increased approximately $3 4 billion or 23% over the prior year as compared with an increase of $3 9 billion or 36% in 1995 from 1994 North American sales, which include Canada, increased 33% during 1996, compared with an increase of 33% in 1995 from 1994 International sales, excluding Canada, represented 47% of total sales in 1996 as compared with 51% in 1995 and 50% in 1994 European sales increased 12% during 1996 compared to an increase of 40% in 1995 from 1994 Other international sales, excluding Canada, increased 17% during 1996, compared with an increase of 37% in 1995 from 1994 We believe that the lower rates of growth in Europe were related to lower market growth in this region Certain other international markets also experienced adverse market conditions The Japanese market in particular experienced a very aggressive pricing environment throughout 1996

The personal computer industry is highly competitive and marked by frequent product introductions, continual improvement in product price/performance characteristics and a large number of competitors Approximately 76% of Compaq's CPU sales in 1996 were derived from products introduced in 1996 These new products have been designed to allow us to achieve low product costs while maintaining the quality and reliability for which our products have been known, thereby increasing our ability to compete on price and value

The significant increase in sales in 1996 stemmed primarily from an increase in the number of units sold and an increase in sales of options associated with CPU products In 1996 Compaq's worldwide unit sales increased 22% while they increased 20% in 1995 The 1996 increase included a 25% expansion in unit sales of commercial CPU products, an 11% increase for consumer CPU products and a 33% increase for enterprise CPU products According to third-party estimates, worldwide unit sales of personal computers increased approximately 16% to 18% in 1996 in contrast to a 25% to 26% increase in 1995 Competition continues to have a significant impact on prices of our products, especially those aimed at the consumer market, and additional pricing actions may occur as we attempt to maintain our competitive mix of price/performance characteristics. We attempt to mitigate the effect of any pricing actions through implementation of design-to-cost goals, the aggressive pursuit of reduced component costs, manufacturing efficiencies and control of operating expenses

Index